ANDREAS BOECKH/ HARALD BARRIOS

Resistance to Globalization
A Comparison of Three World Regions.

1. Introduction

Over the past decade, the term "globalization" has been at the center of a variety of debates and discourses which try to come to terms with a diverse but nevertheless related set of issues such as the changing structure of the world economy and its consequence for national and international governance and governability, the rise of a global civil society, and the question of cultural hegemony, intercultural communication and universal values. Some of the theoretical discussions and the issues they are dealing with are older than globalization and the globalization debate itself, e.g., those on imperialism and dependence (Wallerstein 1979), on the possibilities and limits of cooperation in international politics (Keohane/ Nye 1977), or on the limits of national regulation and social policies in a capitalistic economy (Scharpf et al. 1976, Schmitter/ Lehmbruch 1979).

The scientific take-off of new paradigms tends to be associated with an inflationary use of its central terms. Quite obviously this is also the case in the globalization debate. The frequency with which the term "globalization" is being used is inversely related to the precision of the term which almost has been beaten to death by overuse. However, despite the fuzziness of the term and different meanings which are associated with it, there is considerable evidence that the phenomenon exists (see below).

When we look at the scope of the globalization processes and their effects on national policy options and regulation abilities, we can basically distinguish three positions. Dominating the early phase of the debate (and still very much alive) we find a strong globalization hypothesis presenting sweeping assumptions about wide-ranging effects of globalization everywhere in the world (Robertson 1992, Narr/ Schubert 1994, Waters 1995). According to this position, globalization is changing the structure of the international system as well as the parameters of the daily lives of people all over the world, introducing universal standards of economic behavior and limiting, if not destroying the ability of the nation-state to maintain national standards in all fields related to the economy such as economic regulation, fiscal and social policies etc. (Lisbon Group 1995). The strong globalization hypothesis was (and still is) shared by authors originating from very distinct theoretical schools and political camps. We find it in a neoliberal context in which globalization is hailed as the beginning of a new age of global prosperity (Maxeiner/ Miersch 1997), breaking down national and international barriers to growth. It is also shared by authors who come from an intellectual tradition which is very skeptical about the benefits of capitalism for mankind, be it global or not (Forrester 1996, Altvater/ Mahnkopf 1996, Hardt/ Negri 2000). In the eyes of many demonstrators, globalization stands for the ultimate hegemony of capital, the gradual elimination of social and environmental standards in the interest of capital accumulation, and for the loss of cultural diversity and autonomy (Grefe et al. 2002).

In political science, the early debate focused on the assumption that globalization implies a drastic reduction of the regulating capacity of the nation state with regard to its classical functions in the field of economic and social policies, raising the issue of governability and political legitimacy. Supporters of a strong globalization hypothesis were criticized on two accounts: That their concepts were lacking precision, and that they had little empirical foundation (Beisheim/ Walter 1997). Globalization skeptics (representing the second of the three positions briefly presented here) maintain that not much has changed with regard to state capacities, and that shrinking margins for state activities are mainly the result of domestic conditions or endogenous factors (Hirst/ Thompson 1996, Meyer-Stamer 1997, Rodrik 1997). The implications of these contrasting points of view are substantial, as they lead to quite different global scenarios: While those who see an imminent demise of the nation-state perceive a tendency toward a world without public governance dominated by transnational corporations (Touraine 2001), their challengers observe the emergence of a neo-mercantilist rivalry between powerful capitalist states striving for competitiveness at the expense of others (Porter 1990).

The backdrop of this dispute is the more general controversy whether the ongoing process of global transformation is leading to more uniformity across nations and world regions, both culturally as well as with regard to previously divergent political economies. While the latter view of a world of "capitalistic rivalry" (Hart 1992) is consistent with the assumption that different types of capitalism, e.g. the American, the German or the Japanese variant, will persist at least for some time (Berger/ Dore 1995), the contenders of the end of the nation-state thesis predict a worldwide convergence toward the same type of economic and political rules and the same pattern of state functions (Castells 1998).

As the debate continued, empirical studies were carried out to try and test some of the main assumptions of the strong globalization hypothesis (Esping-Andersen 1996, Beisheim et al. 1997, Walter et al. 1997). Some of the results of this research ultimately lead toward a third position which casts doubts both on the strong and the weak globalization hypothesis. On the basis of comparative diachronic and synchronic analyses, this third group presents a highly differentiated picture of the world-wide process of globalization (Frieden/ Rogowski 1996, Held et al. 1999). As it turns out, globalization works quite differently in different regions of the world, showing various patterns of change and adjustment in both directions: adjustment to the requirements of a globalized world and adjustment of the globalization impulses to regional, national, and even sub-national patterns of economics and politics.

Empirical findings confirm that the path dependency in the development of different regions also continues in the era of globalization. While it is undeniable that the world market increasingly becomes the reference point for national economic policies, it is also undeniable that different world regions deal with this situation in different ways which reflect their distinct traditions and policy patterns.

It is this third position of the debate with which our conference was concerned. We have brought together three world regions which have very distinct traditions in dealing with their external environment, and which have been integrated into the world market to different degrees. In spite of its state-centered traditions, Latin America never has been completely outside the world market and has always to some degree followed market rules, if we leave Cuba aside for a moment. The situation is different for the rentier states in the Middle East, and different again for the countries in Eastern Europe which had to manage a very demanding transition from socialism to some sort of capitalism. In sum, plenty of empirical evidence seems to exist which contradicts the assumption of fast homogenization across different types of economies and political systems.

On the other hand, it would be certainly exaggerated to contend that not much has happened so far. Especially in the financial realm the lowering of transaction costs as well as sweeping policy changes in a number of countries resulted in an extraordinarily high mobility of private capital (Strange 1994, James 1996). Rapid shifts of portfolio investment have created new opportunities for emerging markets, hand in hand with new risks and constraints. How does this dynamic of change influence the different models of capitalism in different world regions? Have the deeper structures of political organization, legal systems, and traditions of political culture been affected? To what extent can we observe homogenizing trends? To what degree can regional, national and local traditions and patterns resist the demands originating from globalization, or even transform them to their own needs? Or are we already dealing with some kind of anti-global backlash, emphasizing regional and national idiosyncrasies.

The focus on "resistance to globalization" of this conference does not represent a normative choice in the sense that globalization pressures ought to be resisted. It is an attempt to contribute to the empirical research on what globalization means in different world regions. "Resistance" here has a double meaning: It can signify active, intentional resistance to tendencies which are rejected on political or moral grounds by presenting alternative discourses and concepts founded in specific cultural and national traditions, even if these traditions sometimes are modern constructs and not at all "traditional" and autochthonous. It can also mean resilience with regard to globalization pressures in the sense that traditional patterns of development and politics are resistant to change and transform the impulses originating from globalization processes in a way that their results are very different when compared across regions and are not conducive to globalization.

By choosing "resistance to globalization" as a focus, the conference also was trying to avoid the functionalist bias which characterizes much of the research on globalization (Leborgne 1997, Jessop 1997). Often it is assumed that the reduced capacity of the nation state with regard to its classical functions is compensated for by transnational and/ or sub-national institutions (Böhret/ Wewer 1993, Rosenau/ Czempiel 1995, Messner/ Nuscheler 1996). It is also assumed that – even allowing for regional differences – the specific sub-national, national and transnational arrangements are in some way compatible with the basic logic of capitalism, and produce some sort of multi-facetted globalization (as opposed to the uniformity hypothesis). However, one has to be aware of the possibility that the local, sub-national, national, and regional patterns of politics and development which cannot be subsumed under a purely capitalistic logic of competition and market rules will coexist with globalized structures for quite a while without yielding very much ground and in ways which may turn out to be a serious barrier to further globalization. It is precisely this kind of questions, the articles in this volume are dealing with.

There may be an analogy to the debate about regime transition and consolidation of democracies. At the beginning of the "third wave of democratization" (Huntington 1991), it was often assumed that at the end of this transformation process one would find liberal democracies with high standards of freedom and accountability. Meanwhile a whole literature on "democracy with adjectives" (O`Donnell 1994, Merkel 1999) presents ample evidence that the results of regime transitions more often than not are "low intensity democracies" with embedded authoritarian characteristics which are not in transition to something better, but which are here to stay, the possibility of regression not excluded. The same may happen with globalization: The result may not be a new and functioning division of labor between sub-national, national and transnational structures, and a creative coexistence of national or regional traditions on the one hand and global rules and requirements on the other. Furthermore, both visions, the globalized world with global prosperity or the globalized world under the undisputed hegemony of capital, may be far too dramatic: One cannot exclude the possibility that at the periphery of world capitalism we may find a situation in which globalization pressures already have rendered traditional development and political patterns dysfunctional, and in which, at the same time, the remnants of these patterns prevent a functioning capitalism from taking hold. In a way, much of the globalization literature (mostly unknowingly) shared the Marxian assumption that modern capitalism will break down all barriers and transform the whole world according to its needs. By looking at our evidence which will be presented in the following paragraphs, a little skepticism would be in order.

In this volume various levels and sources of "resistance to globalization" (in the double meaning of active resistance and resilience) are investigated by political scientists, economists and geographers doing research on the Middle East, Russia and Latin America. On the ideological level, they range from the bold assertion of a competing universalism by the Islamic regime in Iran (Fürtig in this volume) to the defensive invocation of (real or invented) traditional values and morality and complaints about their loss (Hegasy and Lübben on Egypt, Makarychev on Russia). On the political level, we find everything from rational decisions of rentier regimes to defend the political economy of their power against economic liberalization (Beck) and the rise of civil societies associated with globalization to bad governance and "worst political practices" (Ledeneva, Shastitko on Russia) and the use of federal structures for predatory purposes by rent-seeking coalitions on the sub-national level (Faust on Brazil).[1] In Russia, the sheer size of the country is a very effective barrier against an even spread of globalization impulses which results in considerable cleavages between different regions with regard to the degree of their exposure to globalization (Zubarevich). In Venezuela, after 70 years of rent-fueled development, the politics of plenty (Karl 1997) with its specific patterns of rent dependent political legitimacy and clientelistic rent distribution seem well ingrained and hard to transform even long after the rent itself has turned into a development barrier and the times of affluence are over (Boeckh).

If we want to assess the effects the different sources of resistance to globalization have on the globalization process itself, we have to look at the results of the different studies in more detail. On the ideological level, the very concept of globalization as the establishment of universal standards of capitalistic rationality and liberal individualism has been challenged explicitly by the radical-political Islam and in particular by the Iranian leadership (Fürtig). We are dealing with competing claims of universalism, which in the words of a former Deputy Foreign Minister of the country is presented as a conflict between "the world of arrogance i.e. the materialistic West and the world of Islam". Globalization in the Western sense is nothing but the attempt of the Western countries, particularly the United States, to force their norms and concepts on the rest of the world, establishing their cultural, political and military superiority and destroying any sense of self in the countries which do not belong to their cultural sphere. In this respect, the Iranian discourse has quite a bit in common with the complaints about Western dominance and cultural colonialism of Egyptian intel-

---

[1] Of course, there is no neat separation of political and ideological spheres. As these articles show, ideological discourses can be used and are used for political purposes, and collective political experiences breed certain ideologies.

lectuals (Hegasy, Lübben) and some Russian authors and politicians (Makarychev).[2] They also invoke the "true" Egyptian, Islamic or Russian values and call for the rejection of foreign (alien) concepts and norms, overlooking the fact that they present an element of choice for people in formerly fairly closed societies (Hegasy). In Egypt, different government agencies tried for a while to serve different audiences with specific discourses: an Islamic discourse to neutralize the Islamic opposition, and a modern and secular discourse for the benefit of Egyptian intellectuals and the international community. Only after this threatened the ideological unity and hegemony of the governing elites, a new discourse on morality was created to form some sort of national unity on moral grounds and to immunize the country against demands for human rights originating from the international civil society (Lübben). In this case, the instrumental character of discourses becomes particularly evident.

Both in the Arab world as with some Russian elites, the anti-globalization discourse seems to be rather defensive. Their own societies are seen as victims of globalization, the interpretation of the globalization process often comes close to conspiracy theories, and it confuses globalization with Americanization (Hegasy, Lübben, Makarychev). The similarities with anti-imperialistic tendencies and the dependency debate of the 1970s in Latin America are striking. The defensive posture, the self-image as a victim did not and does not present a way out of the situation of inferiority, but it did and does provide a convenient explanation of the causes of inferiority which puts the blame on the external forces, thus avoiding a frank and open discussion of internal and home-made deficiencies. The Iranian leadership, however, does not have this problem. In the Iranian version of the "Clash of Civilizations" there is no question about its outcome: The demise of the West is a foregone conclusion (Fürtig).

Often the defensive reaction against globalization implies the return to those (imagined or real) traditional values which are at least partially responsible for the backwardness of the respective societies, a tendency which is likely to prevent a successful response to globalization pressures and may cement the parochialism of these societies. The Iranian confidence (over-confidence), even though tempered by pragmatic considerations in the foreign policy of the regime (Fürtig), that their version of Islam will determine the future course of globalization, leaves the defensive posture in other countries far behind. Nevertheless, it may not be much more than one of the compensatory ideologies which seem to pop up in societies after they have been through humiliating experiences. What previously was considered the cause of backwardness and inferiority now is declared to be the core element of one's identity and superiority. More than once, societies have claimed a supposed cultural and moral superiority after

---

[2] and some Western European critics of globalization, for that matter.

humiliating defeats. The Anti-Yankeeism of the South of the United States after the Civil War and its criticism of the mindless materialism of the North had quite a bit in common with the "Arielismo" in South America at the turn of the 19th to the 20th century (Rodó 1994) after Latin American societies as compared with the United States had fallen hopelessly behind in economic and military terms (Boeckh 1999). The same is true with the German anti-democratic and elitist critique of the United States after WW I, claiming the superiority of the German "culture" over the superficiality and shallowness of Western "civiliza-tion" and decrying the mediocrity of mass education and culture. Compensatory ideologies provide emotional comfort at a certain level of intellectual sophistica-tion. They do not present viable strategies to overcome the deficits which have caused the respective nations to fall behind. On the contrary, they tend to block a productive response to external pressures and therefore constitute a case of pathological learning. Nevertheless, they can contribute both to the political stabilization of regimes in countries which are still at the margin of globalization and to the political legitimacy of anti-globalization elites. This is particularly the case if these countries control strategic resources like oil which makes it easier to fend off globalization demands (see below).

But can anti-globalization ideologies and discourses bring about reversal of globalization processes already under way? Looking at Russia, the article of Makarychev informs us that the defensive, or as he calls it, alarmist tendency toward globalization processes in Russia is only one of several positions in the fairly fragmented political discourse of this country. It also seems to be losing ground. But the author also states that globalization in Russia is not yet consid-ered to be beyond the point of no return and might be politically reversed. The extremely unequal distribution of globalization gains (both in social and regional terms – see the article by Zubarevich) puts any society under stress and poses problems for those political elites who want to keep their country on the track of globalization. If the results of the globalization process fall short of expectations for a long period of time, the discourse of anti-globalization elites gains credibil-ity and a political reversal may take place. In Latin America, for instance, the results of economic liberalization vary from disappointing to disastrous. In the fall of 2002, a reversal of the general orientation toward liberalization and glob-alization can no longer be excluded.

Another finding from the studies presented in this volume seems to be the important role the political interest of elites play in fostering or slowing down the spread of globalization. Quite obviously they constitute a very effective filter for globalization impulses. The most obvious cases of politically motivated resistance are the countries in the Middle East, which rank very low on all globalization indices, and where "resistance to globalization is, to a high degree, the result of decisions of authoritarian regimes that try to resist globalization to preserve their authoritarian rule" (Beck). To explain resistance to globalization as the result of a rational choice of political elites not only deviates from the result of a rational choice of political elites not only deviates from the culturalist explanations which abound in this region, it also points toward the political economy of power in rentier states. Using the concept of "subjective rational choice" of elites in rentier states, the author is able to explain both the resistance to globalization and the significant intra-regional variance with regard to this resistance: Different regimes have liberalized their economies to various degrees. In reversal of an often quoted phrase, one is tempted to say "Its politics, stupid", even though this would be as simplistic as the original phrase. As Beck shows, the crisis of petrolism did force changes upon the rentier states. Political resistance can slow this process down, it can keep the liberalization tendencies at a level which seems to be manageable for the authoritarian elites, but it cannot avoid the process altogether when the economic foundations of rentier states have crumbled. Here we seem to have a situation in which globalization pressures seriously have undermined the old patterns of power and politics without really replacing it. In these cases the resistance of political elites and old development coalitions prevent the new model from taking hold. The mediocre results of reforms and liberalization attempts can be explained (although not exclusively) by political factors.

In Venezuela, the relationship between oil rent, politics and the prevalent development pattern was different from the one in the Middle East: Since 1958, the oil rent has helped to stabilize democracy and not authoritarian regimes. The rent-dependent development was supported by a broad democratic consensus, and the political pattern of clientelistic rent distribution was widely accepted. In Venezuela the crisis of the rent dependent development destroyed the democratic consensus of the country. Venezuela is not a case with which one could demonstrate that failed expectations with regard to the results of liberalization and globalization can lead to policy reversals. Except for one short-lived attempt which was politically botched up, the country never seriously tried to liberalize and to follow the rules of a globalized world. The reason is quite simple: Both the needs of political elites to produce political legitimacy by means of clientelistic transfers and the corresponding expectations of the population across all social sectors would make such a move politically very costly (Boeckh). The question raised in the article by Shastitko on how to compensate the losers in the globalization process does not even arise in Venezuela: In a society in which every politically relevant social group for generations has been dependent on rent transfers with regard to its material well-being, almost everybody will be a loser. It is hard to imagine that it will be possible to find a democratic consensus for a globalization strategy. The present government of Hugo Chávez is moving in the exact opposite direction even though the corresponding politics of populist distribution obviously is economically not sustainable.

The study by Jörg Faust presents an interesting "intermediate" case of resistance to globalization in which political elites at different levels of government are divided on the issue of globalization and the distribution of its costs. While on the national level various governments tried to translate globalization pressures into market and political reforms, the federal structure and generally fragmented nature of the Brazilian state made it possible for sub-national elites to "shift costs of economic adjustment onto the federal government". More than once, this brought the federal government to the brink of financial disaster. Only then could the effects of the "predatory federalism" be curbed or reversed. This raised the adjustment costs for the Federal government considerably. In spite of the progress which has been made after the crisis of 1999 to bring fiscal policies at the sub-national level into line with the necessities of adjustment policies at the national level, the battle is not yet over. Fundamental policy reversals cannot be excluded.

"Informal rules" (see the article by Alena V. Ledeneva) and "administrative barriers" (see the article by Andrei Shastitko) are not exclusively Russian phenomena. Everyone familiar with Latin America and the Middle East can point to similar patterns of working around the rules and rent extortion in their regions. They do not constitute acts of intentional resistance to globalization, but they increase the resilience of the respective societies with respect to globalization processes and they can put the breaks on capitalistic development by raising the transaction costs. They are systemic problems of transition societies (Zubarevich) or even more than that: Ledeneva sees Russia "in the grip of path dependency" pointing out that in Soviet times "the planned economy was not really a planned economy .... and was actually run with the help of .... informal arrangements operating according to unwritten rules, and the market economy today is not really a market economy". Both authors agree that there are no quick fixes for these problems. Top down reforms tend to fail (Ledeneva) and the administrative bodies have developed a great ingenuity in outfoxing all attempts to take away their sources of rent extortion (Shastitko). This type of resilience to globalization is hard to tackle because of its subterranean nature. Political conflicts over globalization can be solved one way or another by the outcome of power struggles between competing elites. Solving the problems analyzed by Ledeneva and Shastitko requires different approaches and takes more time. Both authors see some hope in collective learning experiences of those who participate in the game but are harmed by it, in positive demonstration effects, in the compensation of the losers when sources of rent extortion are taken away, and in outside pressure.

What can the conclusions be from the insights offered by the articles in this volume? Resistance to globalization has been analyzed at the level of ideologies and discourses, at the political level and with regard to administrative "worst practices". Almost all the authors are inclined to assume that these aspects of resistance can slow down but not permanently block the process of globalization. At the same time, they often describe situations in which old patterns of political control and the old rules of closed economies and societies no longer work and the new ones are not yet in place. The question remains if they ever will, and how long such an impasse can last. Can an imperfect transition be the final result of change the same way as democratic transitions in many countries ended up being something that was neither fish nor fowl? Since we all are standing on the shoulders of Marx and Comte, we are inclined to see social development as a irreversible process following some programmatic idea of progress. In the long run, the economic necessities of a globalized word may lead to the establishment of market rules, and finally defeat the pockets of resistance. But "in the long run we are all dead" (Keynes) and unable to confirm or disprove our predictions. In the short run, the process of globalization may well be slowed down or even reversed.

References

Altvater, Elmar/ Mahnkopf, Birgit 1996 : Grenzen der Globalisierung, Münster.

Beisheim, Marianne et al. 1997: Globalisierung – Rhetorik oder Realität? Zum Stand der Denationalisierung in der G-7 und der Bundesrepublik. In: Fricke, Werner (ed.): Jahrbuch Arbeit und Technik, Bonn, pp. 96-180.

Beisheim, Marianne./ Walter, Gregor 1997: Globalisierung – "Kinderkrankheiten" eines Konzeptes. In: ZIB 4 (1), pp. 153-180.

Berger, Suzanne/ Dore, Ronald (ed.) 1995: Convergence or Diversity? National Models of Production in a Global Economy, New York.

Boeckh, Andreas 1999: Wie man Unpassendes passend macht: Das Elend des Fortschritts in Lateinamerika. In: Thiel, Reinold E. (ed.): Neue Ansätze zur Entwicklungstheorie, Bonn, pp. 82-95.

Böhret, Carl/ Wewer, Göttrik (ed.) 1993: Regieren im 21. Jahrhundert. Zwischen Globalisierung und Regionalisierung, Opladen.

Castells, Manuel 1998: The End of the Millennium, Oxford.

Esping-Andersen, Gøsta (ed.) 1996: Welfare States in Transition, London.

Forrester, Vivianne 1996: L'horreur économique, Paris.

Frieden, Jeffry/ Rogowski, Ronald 1996: The Impact of the International Economy on National Policies: An Analytical Overview. In: Keohane, R. O./ Milner, H. V. (ed.): Internationalization and Domestic Politics, Cambridge.

Grefe, Christiane et al. 2002: Attac. Was wollen die Globalisierungsgegner? Berlin.

Hardt, Michael/ Negri, Antonio 2000: Empire, Cambridge.

Hart, J. A. 1992: Rival Capitalists: International Competitiveness in the United States, Japan, and Western Europe, Ithaca.

Held, David et al. 1999: Global Transformations. Politics, Economics and Culture, Stanford.

Hirsch, Joachim 1995: Der nationale Wettbewerbsstaat, Berlin.

Hirst, Paul/ Thompson, Grahame 1996: Globalization in Question. The International Economy and the Possibilities of Governance, Cambridge.

Huntington, Samuel P. 1991: The Third Wave - Democratization in the Late Twentieth Century, London.

James, Harold 1996: International Monetary Cooperation since Bretton Woods, Washington D.C.

Jessop, Bob 1997: Die Zukunft des Nationalstaates: Erosion oder Reorganisation? In: Becker, Steffen et al. (ed.): Jenseits der Nationalökonomie? Weltwirtschaft und Nationalstaat zwischen Globalisierung und Regionalisierung, Hamburg, pp. 50-95.

Karl, Terry Lynn 1997: The Paradox of Plenty. Oil-booms and Petro-States, Berkley etc.

Keohane, Robert O./ Nye, Joseph 1977: Power and Interdependence, Boston.

Leborgne, D. 1997: Von der Reorganisation der Arbeit zur regionalen Partnerschaft. In: Becker, Steffen et al. (ed.): Jenseits der Nationalökonomie? Weltwirtschaft und Nationalstaat zwischen Globalisierung und Regionalisierung, Hamburg, pp. 123-151.

Lisbon Group 1995: The Limits of Competition, Cambridge.

Maxeiner, Dirk/ Miersch, Michael 2001: Das Mephisto-Prinzip. Warum es besser ist, nicht gut zu sein, Frankfurt/M.

Merkel, Wolfgang 1999: Defekte Demokratien. In: Merkel, Wolfgang/ Busch, Andreas (eds.): Demokratie in Ost und West. Festschrift für Klaus von Beyme, Frankfurt/ M., pp. 288-306.

Messner, Dirk/ Nuscheler, Franz 1996: Global Governance. Organisationselemente und Säulen einer Weltordnungspolitik. In: Dies. (ed.): Weltkonferenzen und Weltberichte, Bonn, pp. 12-36.

Meyer-Stamer, Jörg 1997: Globalisierung, Standortkonkurrenz und Entwicklungspolitik. In: Internationale Politik und Gesellschaft 4, pp. 378-388.

Narr, Wolf-Dieter, Schubert, Alexander 1994: Weltökonomie. Die Misere der Politik, Frankfurt/M.

O'Donnell, Guillermo 1994: Delegative Democracy. In: Journal of Democracy 5: 1, pp. 55-69.

Porter, Michael 1990: The Competitive Advantage of Nations, London.

Robertson, Roland 1992: Globalization: Social Theory and Global Culture, London.

Rodó, José Enrique 1994: Ariel, Mainz (first published in 1900).

Rodrik, Dani 1997: Has Globalization Gone Too Far?, Washington D.C.

Rosenau, James N./ Czempiel, Ernst-Otto (eds.) 1995: Governance without Government, New York.

Scharpf, Fritz W. et al. 1976: Politikverflechtung, Kronberg.

Schmitter, Philippe/ Lehmbruch, Gerhard (eds.) 1979: Trends Towards Corporatist Intermediation, Beverly Hills.

Strange, Susan 1994: The Structure of Finance in the World System. In: Sakamoto, Yosshikazu (ed.): Global Transformation. Challenges to the State System, Tokio/ New York/ Paris, pp. 228-249.

Touraine, Alain 2001: Globalisierung. In: Loch, Dietmar/ Heitmeyer, Wilhelm (eds.): Schattenseiten der Globalisierung, Frankfurt/ M., pp. 41-64.

Wallerstein, Immanuel 1979: The Capitalist World Economy, Cambridge.

Walter, Gregor et al. 1997: Globalization Processes in the OECD World, Bremen.

Waters, Malcolm 1995: Globalization, London/ New York.

Zürn, Michael 1998: Regieren jenseits des Nationalstaats, Frankfurt/M.

2

MARTIN BECK

Resistance to Globalization and limited Liberalization in the Middle East

1. Introduction[1]

As a result of Stephen Krasner's (1994: 13) sarcastic remark referring to analysis on globalization, that "academic reflections about international political economy are beginning to sound more and more like American political campaigns", it has become common to start any analysis on globalization by critically discussing the vagueness of the concept. Since there are different competing ideas on globalization, it is indeed a necessity to clarify the term. Yet, even more intriguing from the perspective of a researcher working on the Middle East is the fact that the Middle East is fairly neglected by general research done on globalization. However, researchers are not to blame for this oversight. Rather, this neglect seems to be appropriate if one is interested in positivistic research on globalization. Compared to other world regions, the process of globalization has yet to encompass the Middle East.

This article intends to prove that the degree in which the Middle East participates in globalization is indeed very low. In order to do so, three indicators of globalization (the spread of internet hosts, the growth of exports and the development of Foreign Direct Investment) will be examined in more detail (chapter 2). Additionally, an explanation of this finding will be offered (chapter 3). Unlike other studies that focus on cultural elements of the Middle East, this analysis focuses on rational actions of the Middle Eastern ruling elites. In other words, the basic thesis of this article is that the Middle Eastern resistance to globalization is, to a high degree, the result of decisions of authoritarian regimes that try to restrict participation in globalization in order to preserve their authoritarian rule.

Within the general trend of resistance to globalization in the Middle East a significant intra-regional variance can be observed. Thus, the article also aims to contribute to an explanation of the fact that in some countries the resistance to globalization is less marked than in others (chapter 4). Finally, a conclusion will be presented (chapter 5).

---

[1] This article, which is based on research funded by the Volkswagen Foundation, is a revised and updated English version of Beck (2001). I want to thank Muna Shikaki for thoroughly editing the first version of the manuscript.

2.The Middle East as a Region Resistant to Globalization

Although the term "globalization" is rather vague, scholars would hardly deny that increasing interdependencies crossing the boundaries of nation states are core elements of globalization. Thus, globalization can be defined as "social de-nationalization" (Beisheim/ Dreher/ Walter/ Zangl/ Zürn 1999: 19).[2] In examining phenomena of social denationalization, most scholars focus on aspects of communication, trade, and economics. Therefore, the spread of Internet hosts, the growth of exports, and the development of Foreign Direct Investment (FDI) are major indicators of globalization. Consequently, I shall examine how these indicators have developed in recent years in the Middle East in comparison with other world regions.

There are good reasons to extend the definition of the term "globalization" i.e. social de-nationalization, to other fields, especially security and culture (Beisheim/ Dreher/ Walter/ Zangl/ Zürn 1999: 19, 31-2, 39-42). As far as these fields are concerned, it can be argued that the Middle East is participating — or is forced to participate, respectively - in globalization. The Middle East is one of those world regions that are actively trying to preserve their own cultural heritages against the challenges of an allegedly uniform Western culture dominated by American values. Moreover, Islamist groups, especially Bin Laden's terrorist network, are without any doubt major threats in the newly emerging global security system.

This paper will be confined to the core issues of globalization. The simple reason behind this is that the main aspects generally referred to with the term "globalization" are expanding boundary-crossing activities in communication, trade, and economics. Since the Middle East is rarely examined by research on globalization, the primary aim of this article is to connect the Middle East to the mainstream research on globalization, rather than to apply an extended concept of globalization to the Middle East, the latter being an important, yet secondary aim.

2.1 Communication: Spread of Internet Hosts

The data presented in Table 1 (see Table 1 at the end of this text) clearly indicate that the Middle Eastern participation in cross-national communication, as provided by the World Wide Web, is fairly low.[3] The only major exception is a country with traditional strong ties to the West, i.e. Israel. Globally, in 1999 approximately 7,500 Internet hosts serviced one Million people. Yet, in the Middle East there were only 25 Internet hosts per 1 Million people- much less than in Latin America with nearly 1,000 Internet hosts. There is only one world

---

[2] This and all following non-English quotations have been translated into English by the author.
[3] In order to make possible some further impressionistic comparisons, data of some Muslim and non-Muslim developing countries are also presented.

region- extremely poor South Asia- that is connected to the Internet to a lesser degree than the Middle East. Even Sub-Saharan Africa surpasses by far the Middle East in this respect.[4]

2.1 International Trade: Value of Merchandise Exports (1983 and 1998 in Millions of US-Dollars)

The development of Middle Eastern merchandise exports between 1983 and 1998 clearly contrasts with worldwide trends (see Table 2 at the end of this text).

Whereas *all* other world regions witnessed a relatively high increase in their value of merchandise exports, the Middle East faced a severe decrease of its exports in the same period. A comparison with South Korea indicates the significance of recent trade development in the Middle East. In 1983, the value of Middle Eastern merchandise exports exceeded that of South Korea's by almost 500%. Only 15 years later did the value of merchandise exports of South Korea exceed the exports of the whole region of the Middle East and North Africa.

2.3 Economics: Foreign Direct Investment

A look at the development of FDI in the last decade of the 20th century clearly demonstrates that the Middle East is a special case (see Table 3 at the end of this text).

Although the Middle East almost came close to the worldwide trend of doubling FDI in the period between 1990 and 1997, it can be demonstrated that the Middle East countries only managed to do so because the 1990 level was extremely low. For example, by 1990 the FDI of Mexico had already matched all FDI of the Middle East. Only seven years later, Mexico's FDI was twice that as of the entire Middle East.

2.4 Conclusion of the Quantitative Analysis

The data illustrates that compared to most other world regions, the Middle East is highly resistant to globalization in the fields of communication, trade, and economics. This result holds true even if there are few doubts that an examination of additional factors might yield different results. In other words, it may be the case that some of the indicators exaggerate the actual trends. For instance, several people can use one single Internet host; at the same time it is plausible to assume that the relation of Internet hosts located in Internet cafés to private Internet hosts is fairly high in the Middle East, especially in comparison to industrialized countries. Moreover, there are significant intra-regional variances in the Middle East which will be examined in chapter 4 of this paper. The general finding is that Middle Eastern resistance to globalization is overwhelming.

---

[4] This is primarily due to the comparably high number of the Internet hosts in South Africa.

3. Middle East Resistance to Globalization: Attempting a Rational Explanation

3.1 Oil and Petrolism

The thesis presented above corresponds with findings of research conducted by specialists on the Middle East regarding the socio-economic development of the region. Obviously, the "oil factor" is of special importance (see Table 4 at the end of this text). Thus, researchers with very different theoretical perspectives— like Samir Amin (1982: 48) and Alan Richards and John Waterbury (1996: 69-70), respectively—agree on the fact that the Middle East, as a result of the oil revolution in the early 1970s, has become a world region highly integrated in the international economic system. Beginning in the early 1980s, this trend was clearly reversed by steadily shrinking oil prices. With regard to the 1980s, Gil Feiler (1991, 1993) demonstrates the stagnation of the regional labor migration system that was developed in the 1970s as a result of the oil bonanza in the Middle East (Ibrahim 1982: Chap. 3; Pawelka 1985: 284-305).

Impressed by regional developments that had been caused by the oil price increases of the 1970's, a group of researchers attempted to thoroughly analyze these empirical developments on the basis of the classic economic concept of rent theory.[5] By adapting this concept to the Middle East, the term "petrolism" was coined by Bahgat Korany (1986). Based on the rent income of oil-exporting countries, petrolism is a system that deeply shapes the entire Middle East. Basically, there are two channels through which a significant part of the oil income is funneled into the socio-economic systems of the poorer non-oil-exporting countries of the Arab Middle East: The ruling elites of the Gulf countries decided to transfer part of their external income in the form of political rents towards governments with no or low oil income, especially in the Mashriq. By doing so, the Gulf States aimed at strengthening conservative elite segments in countries whose radical elites had challenged the traditional monarchies in the 1950's and 1960's. In an indirect way, i.e. by private actors, petrodollars were transferred to the poorer non-oil exporting countries. Since the Gulf monarchies enjoyed high income but shortage of labor, they decided to "import" Arab labor from the poor but more developed countries, especially from the Mashriq. These migrant workers kept their family ties and transferred a good deal of their income to their families back home.

Petrolism reached its peak in the 1970's when oil prices were rising, and in turn, increasing the economic rents received by the oil-exporting countries. The influx of petrodollars enabled the political elites to avoid painful socio-economic reforms and made possible the existence of a socio-economic system characterized

---

[5] A rent is an income that does not originate from investment or labor.

by what has been called "underdevelopment de luxe" by Peter Pawelka (1993: 161). As a result of petrolism, the Middle East witnessed numerous phenomena of globalization in the 1970's. The degree to which the Middle East was connected to the world economy was based, first, on oil-exports, and, second, on so-called petrodollar recycling. Since the productive sectors of the gulf economies were confined to the oil sector, the Gulf States had to import a huge range of commodities, comprising agrarian goods, luxury durable consumer goods, key-ready industrial plants and sophisticated arms systems.

In the 1980's, the system of petrolism witnessed a crisis that continues till this day. The main reason for this crisis were decreasing oil prices, accompanied by a severe drop of the value of traded goods, and—with a certain time delay—a decrease of political-rent payments and boundary-crossing transfers of labor migrants. Thus, in the 1980's, the globalization push of the Middle East had already been replaced by a trend of "re-nationalization" at a time when other world regions had started experiencing phenomena of globalization which are of major interest in the recent debate.

Despite these findings a further examination of the questions posed above is still necessary: The resistance to globalization of the Middle East still requires some explanations since this outcome cannot be explained solely by economic factors. Rather, some political aspects have to be taken into consideration. Why did the Gulf States not use the petrodollars in order to promote self-sustainable growth? Although the new-industrializing countries in East Asia could not rely on a huge capital influx, they managed to promote industrial growth. Moreover, economic factors hardly contribute to the fact that the Middle East is connected to the World Wide Web only to a degree comparable to the least-developed and poorest regions on the globe.

In addition, the intra-regional variance has to be explained.

3.2 The Concept of Subjective Rationalism

The variant of rational-choice theory used in this paper is based on the premise that, first, actors know about their goals and, second, that they are able to choose among the perceived alternatives the one that best suits their interests (Elster 1986, March 1986, Zürn 1992: 78-91). This variant of rational-choice theory does not refer to rationality of goals but of means, for example it is *not* assumed that the goals of the actors are rational or the result of rational analysis, respectively. Rather, a much more modest assumption is made, that the actors choose the best of all perceived means in order to attain their goals.

The concept is "subjective" insofar as it is *not* assumed that the actors are perfect rationalists. To be more precise, the actors may even be rational if they do not choose the best alternative from an objective point of view. In other words, it is only required that they choose the best of the alternatives as perceived by the actors. Moreover, it is not assumed that actors are perfectly informed about the consequences of their actions. Yet, the beliefs that are the basis of the actors' decisions must be coherent and in accordance with the evidence available to them (Zürn 1992: 97).

3.3 Globalization as a Threat

Since the concept of subjective rationalism covers, in principle, an indefinite amount of potential goals, these goals must be determined exogenously. In order to avoid the problem of tautology, the goals must be discovered *independently* of the behavior of the actors. In principle, this is possible either by using hermeneutic approaches (like critically examining historical sources or drawing mental maps) or by deducing them from proven theories. The difficulties in applying the first approach are enormous since political systems in the Middle East are highly sealed off. Yet, the concept of petrolism, based on rent theory, enables the researcher to determine the preferences of the actors in a relatively reliable manner, thereby answering the question regarding the way the elites of the Middle East should rationally react to the challenges of globalization.

In the 1970's, the political elites of the Middle East were released from one - if not the major - problem that leaders of developing countries normally face establishing a stable regime. As a result of the massive infusion of petrodollars, most of the political elites of the Middle East no longer suffered from a severe lack of material means. Since a rent income is generated as the result of natural advantages and organizational skills, contrary to profit seekers rent seekers are not forced to reinvest a big share of their earnings in order to generate a future income.[6] As a result the tendency of Middle Eastern regimes not to consider economic development as a primary task was reinforced. Thus, the available material resources were primarily "invested" in politics. To be more concrete, politics were chosen that combined "stick and carrot". The mixing ratio varied in different countries and periods. The "carrot" was realized by establishing complex systems of patronage, thus privileging various social groups to a different degree. Virtually all the social groups were incorporated in the rent-seeking system -according to their relevance – for the maintenance of the political order. The upper classes benefited from subsidies for entrepreneurs, the middle classes from career opportunities in the public sector; even the rural marginalized groups benefited from the system, albeit to a much lesser degree, from subsidized bread prices.

The "stick", i.e. repression, was always used when autonomous groups of society attempted to challenge the power monopoly of the ruling elite. With the major exception of Iraq, most regimes of the Middle East preferred to promote the

---

[6] For the rent-seeking concept, see the contributions in Buchanan/ Tollison/ Tullock (1980).

dissolution of civil society in a gentle way. However, all regimes used the stick as their *ultima ratio*. As a result, compared to most world regions, civil society is very weak in the political systems of the modern Middle East. To summarize, petrolism strengthened the state, thereby cementing the authoritarian structures in the Middle East.

From the perspective of a political elite socialized by the system of petrolism, there is no genuine attraction in participating in "opportunities" offered by trends of globalization in the 1980's and 1990's. In order to benefit from international trade dynamics, export-led growth has to be promoted. However, in the long run, this implies the creation of a private sector independent of state subsidies, which is not in the interest of a political elite concerned about potential centers of counter-power. Moreover, the securing of FDI requires the drastic containment of rent-seeking circles, since their existence directs social activities towards political as opposed to economic efforts. However, containment of the rent-seeking system would endanger the political stability of the existing regimes. Finally, free access to the Internet with vast opportunities to obtain all kinds of information would highly complicate the political control of society and social organizations. In short, participating in globalization requires a policy of *far-reaching economic liberalization* that political elites of the Middle East are hesitant, if not reluctant to implement because of the *political implications*.

Thus, when the preferences of Middle Eastern political elites- whether to promote structural change in order to participate in the benefits of globalization or not- are built upon the theoretical basis of petrolism, the conclusion should be clear: the political elites of the Middle East do not share a genuine interest in participating in globalization. This result is confirmed indirectly by general research on globalization. As has been stated by Marianne Beisheim, Sabine Dreher, Gregor Walter, Bernhard Zangl and Michael Zürn (1998: 165), "social denationalization" results in "political de-nationalization", i.e. a growing relevance of political institutions beyond the national central state. For instance, the state will no longer be capable to implement efficient social and economic policies with instruments confined to the national level. Yet, as Zürn puts it referring to Oran Young, effective and efficient governing does not require a strong nation state. One can conclude from this fact that "de-nationalization (...) is not a nightmare" (Zürn 1998: 165). However, as far as the Middle East is concerned, one should add that this assertion applies to most people but not to the ruling elites.

4. Resistance to Globalization and Intra-Regional Variance

The conclusion that the Middle East is a world region highly resistant to globalization has been based on an inter-regional perspective. When the perspective is re-directed towards the region itself and focuses on single states of the Middle East, new questions arise. Why was the increase of FDI in Syria and Egypt very modest, whereas Tunisia managed to quadruple its FDI? Moreover, how are we to explain that Jordan's merchandise export were increasing by over 300% between 1983 and 1998 but those of Iran and Saudi Arabia were drastically shrinking in the same period? Why is the Internet much more widespread in Egypt than in Saudi Arabia or Syria?

In comparison to some fast-growing developing countries, the increase of FDI and merchandise exports in Tunisia and Jordan, respectively, may not be outstanding. Furthermore, the spread of Internet hosts for instance in Bolivia and South Africa exceeded those in Egypt by more than 100% and 1000%, respectively. Nevertheless, the data presented in tables 1 to 3 indicate significant intra-regional differences in the Middle East. It seems as though some Middle Eastern countries made much more rigorous efforts in order to liberalize their systems than others. Yet, different reactions of Middle Eastern elites to the chances of globalization do not contradict the results of the analysis presented above. Rather, as will be shown in the following sub-chapter, the concept of subjective rationalism can also contribute to an explanation of the different degrees to which Middle Eastern countries participate in globalization.

4.1 Search for a Rational Explanation of Intra-Regional Variance

The readiness of Middle Eastern political elites to respond to globalization seems to be determined by the "rent influx" factor. Scaling the states of the Middle East according to different indicators of rent policy, the result is that the seriousness to which liberalization attempts, especially in the fields of economics, are pursued by the elites correlates with the degree to which the countries suffer from the crisis of petrolism (Beck/ Schlumberger 1999). In Table 4, the magnitude of rent income is presented for several countries on the basis of four indicators, which give us some idea about the crisis of petrolism.

As the previous table indicates, the higher the magnitude of rent income and its disposability for the state bureaucracy under petrolism the lesser the pressure to take measures of liberalization. Thus, it is plausible that countries like Saudi Arabia or Libya refrained from implementing far-reaching measures of liberalization in the course of the 1980's and 1990's, whereas Egypt and Jordan had to meet the challenge of shrinking income from abroad by "opening" their economies to a much higher degree. A middle-range position was taken by Syria whose elite (contrary to the Jordanian monarchy) managed to avoid an acute rent crisis by extending the oil sector and limiting the downfall of its income from political rents by joining the alliance against Iraq in the Second Gulf War.

There are some cases that can only be explained if intervening variables are taken into consideration, such as the Kuwaiti attempts to promote economic development. However, in principle this thesis that the degree to which political elites of the Middle East pursue strategies of liberalization depends on rental income and the crisis of petrolism is confirmed.

At the same time, it should be highlighted that the rent concept does *not* claim to *fully* explain the intra-regional variance. In particular, the rent concept does not contribute to an explanation of why the Internet is more widespread in Jordan, and especially in Kuwait, than it is in Saudi Arabia and Syria. Yet, as far as this fact is concerned, *another rational* explanation, i.e. one beyond the rent concept, seems to be available. The systems of the Middle East have developed various kinds of authoritarian regimes that curtail rights of freedom to a different degree. Regimes with a higher degree of liberty are less concerned about the political implications of the spread of the Internet. Furthermore, the Kuwaiti figure can be also partially traced back to the fairly high material means available to the regime.

The plausibility of the analysis presented above is based on some presuppositions that require some further analysis. Decisions by political elites to implement far-reaching measures of liberalization are *not* the result of pure economic crisis phenomena. Rather, these decisions are also the result of political deliberations. However, if this assertion holds true, the question arises why some regimes, such as Egypt, pursue economic policies that "undermine their political basis and, in the long run, threaten to destroy it" (Albrecht/ Pawelka/ Schlumberger 1997: 56). Indeed, it seems as if the decision of the Egyptian elite to pursue even a limited strategy of liberalization could endanger the stability of the authoritarian regime in the long run. Thus, the question that should be answered is whether such behavior is compatible with the concept of subjective rationalism.

In other words, is it not a declaration of bankruptcy for the concept of rationalism - and so for the rent theory in the form presented here - if petrolistic political elites apply policies that, in the long run, may result in political suicide? As will be shown, the concept of subjective rationalism can easily be defended against this attack. Two approaches are available. George Tsebelis (1990: Chap. 5) puts forward a concept according to which a certain behavior is often falsely qualified as irrational since it has not been taken into consideration that a certain "move" in a "game" is a move in another game at the same time. In order to apply this concept to the case examined here, one should investigate whether the stability of the regime depends to such a high degree on external support, that it becomes rational for the political elite to act in a responsive way to this pressure - e.g. by liberalizing the political system - even though this may endanger the stability of the authoritarian rule in the long run. Thus, according to this perspective, it would be rational for authoritarian political elite to liberalize the political system if the withdrawal of political support by the dominant forces of the international system posed an immediate threat to the stability of the political system.

In this case, the political elite would act rationally if it ignored the possible long-term consequences of its behavior.

Such a scenario cannot be excluded. However, with some possible exceptions,[7] one should not overestimate the ability and the willingness of the dominant powers of the international system to overthrow regimes even of relatively weak developing countries if there is no internal support for doing so. Even in cases where the United States of America were willing to actively destabilize regimes in the Middle East, especially in Libya and Iran as well as in war-torn Iraq, this interest could not prevail over the ability of the ruling elites to preserve the existing regimes.

A more promising answer to the question raised above can be formulated through an approach developed by Adam Przeworski (1991: 54-5) who examines processes of political liberalization in Eastern Europe and Latin America. This approach is also fruitful for the examination of economic (and political) liberalization processes in the Middle East. The basic assumption of Przeworski is that authoritarian regimes do not fear the loss of support of the population, but the emergence of centers of counter-power, for example, the development of autonomous social organizations. As has been analyzed above, authoritarian regimes tend to neutralize centers of counter-power either by co-optation or by repression. Yet, if this holds true, why then there are regimes in the Middle East that pursue *any* politics of liberalization? In other words, does a political elite, whose primary goal is to preserve its power position, act irrational by "opening" the political system, thereby making possible a transformation of the regime towards a democracy in the long run?

Przeworski shows that *in crisis situations* even rational actors who agree upon their goals (in this case: survival of the authoritarian regime) may have different assessments on how the common goal should be best achieved. Thus, inside an authoritarian political elite some reform-oriented opposition to the ruling hardliners may arise. According to this perspective, the goal of the reformers is *not* to promote basic changes of the authoritarian system. On the contrary, hardliners and reforms agree on stabilizing the authoritarian regime. However, they disagree on whether the most effective strategy to do so is to fight actual or potential challenges to the regime by repression or by "gently" integrating opposition movements into the system. The reformers can always argue that if a liberalization process should lead to undesired side effects, such as the development of "radical" movements not willing to cooperate with the existing regime, the liberalization process can be stopped again.

---

[7] The case of the PLO during and after the Second Gulf War is such an exception (Beck 2002: Chap. 2).

Paradoxically, even if the calculation of the authoritarian reformers seems to hold true in the short run, this *may* result in long-term developments which are detrimental to the interests of the authoritarian elite. Under certain circumstances, limited liberalization efforts may result in long-term changes that are difficult to control for the ruling elite. Thus, it is possible that - contrary to the intentions of the reform-oriented segment inside the authoritarian regime - a liberalization process may finally result in the transformation into a democracy. In other words, in our complex world even highly rational actors lack the means necessary to be perfectly informed about all long-term consequences of their actions. Therefore, even if a liberalization process leads to a result that is not intended, it should not be concluded from this that the reformers acted irrationally. To change the perspective, even if a liberalization process finally results in a democratic transition, this does not prove the thesis that the reformers of the authoritarian elite intended to democratize the political system.

What conclusions can be drawn from Przeworski's analysis on *political liberalization* for the problem of *economic liberalization* posed above? The members of an authoritarian regime may not only disagree on political, but also on economic issues. It is assumed that all members of the authoritarian elite prefer an economy based on rent income and rent -seeking circles to a market-oriented system whose dynamics are hardly to control. Yet, in a crisis situation - a precondition that has been clearly fulfilled in the Middle East since the 1980s - elite members have good reasons to assume that limited liberalization may be the best way to manage the economic crisis, thereby stabilizing the authoritarian regime. Continuing the path chosen in the 1970s could shrink the financial means available to the ruling elite to a degree that could endanger the material basis of the existing regime.

4.2 Is Limited Liberalization a Rational Strategy to Manage the Crisis of Petrolism?

A perfectly liberal economy is characterized by free allocation of all resources and the absence of factors constraining competition. Thus, all measures strengthening the role of the market in the economy can be labeled as liberalization (Murphy/ Niblock 1993: xiii). Therefore, the assessment of whether a policy is to be attributed as liberalization is not a phenomenon independent of place and time (Penrose 1993: 3). This hint is not only important in order to understand that a measure correctly labeled as liberal today can be illiberal tomorrow. Rather, from a rationalist point of view, the insight of Penrose also implies that actors promoting economic liberalization are not necessarily in favor of a perfectly liberal system. In other words, members of a political elite who promote programs of economic liberalization may be protagonists of only a limited liberalization aimed at preserving main features of a basically illiberal system. Similar to the case of political liberalization as analyzed by Przeworski, supporters of economic liberalization are not necessarily followers of a market economy.

Concerning the question of what kind of *economic* path should be chosen, the internal segmentation of authoritarian regimes is not only proven empirically but also reflected theoretically. Hartmut Elsenhans (1981: 231-44) presents an additional motive of reform-oriented segments to promote economic liberalization. If these segments succeed in convincing the top elite of the regime, they at the same time advance their position within the elite. Thus, according to Elsenhans, the reformers are not only in favor of liberalizing the system because they believe that this is the best strategy to stabilize the political system. Rather, they also do so since they benefit personally from a new policy approach. Thereby, Elsenhans shares Prezeworski's assumption that all segments, including the reformers, are unified by the interest to preserve the authoritarian structure of the system.

After these introductory theoretical remarks, it is time to prove the high likelihood that contemporary Middle Eastern state bureaucracies are segmented along the question of whether a liberalization policy should be pursued or not; such a scenario does not contradict the assumptions of the concept of subjective rationalism. In order to make this plausible, it may help to take a brief look at one major aspect of the academic debate on liberalization policies of Middle Eastern rentier systems. Do academic researchers believe that economic liberalization will solve, or at least mitigate, the issue of social injustice and, in particular, the problem of unemployment in the Middle East?

On the basis of a concept indebted to economic liberalism, Erich Weede (1997: 53, 59) agrees with this. According to this author, rentier systems are always more harmful to social justice than market systems, and they create fewer jobs than market economies. Pawelka (1993: 132-3, 153-4; 1997: 7) contradicts this assertion by claiming that liberalization is not a suitable strategy in order to solve the problem of unemployment. Giacomo Luciani holds an intermediate position. According to him, structural adjustment in the Middle East can be realized without adding to social injustice; yet, whether such a strategy is suited to solve the problem of unemployment is hard to judge by theoretical means.

This article does not intend to contribute to this academic debate. Furthermore, there are few reasons to believe that political elites of the Middle East base their decisions on academic insights. Rather, by briefly presenting this debate it should be made plausible that rational actors inside a political elite may very well disagree on the effects of liberalization policies if even established experts on rent theory are far from having reached any consensus on the impact of liberalization policies on rentier systems in crisis.

Thus, a political elite of a rentier system exposed to a crisis may be attracted by the opportunities of globalization. Taking into consideration the data presented in tables 1 to 3, it is obvious that some regimes of the Middle East indeed tried to participate in globalization - to a limited degree of course. It is hardly possible to make any serious prognosises whether these elites are able to control the impacts of liberalization in the long run.

Since the 1980's, World Bank and International Monetary Fund have promoted export-led growth instead of import-substituting industrialization (Penrose 1993: 5-6). If such a policy is pursued, this will increase merchandise exports, thereby contributing to social de-nationalization. From the perspective of state bureaucracies of the Middle East such a strategy implies major dangers since it requires a cut of subsidies for inefficient companies. Thus, the state elite has to deal with resistance from the private sector as well as from middle and lower classes suffering from unemployment which is hardly avoidable in the short run. At the same time, such a strategy also provides some chances for the elite since highly inefficient and costly rent-seeking circles are curtailed.

Attracting FDI is among the major benefits offered by trends of globalization. FDI helps to compensate for the shrinking material resources available in the rentier system. Although some resistance from Islamic groups is to be expected, the political implications of attracting FDI seem to be limited in the short run. The reason behind this is that foreign capital is satisfied if rule of law is guaranteed. Unlike the national bourgeoisie, foreign capital does not demand political participation.

Therefore, it is not surprising that passing liberal laws of investment were among the first measures of liberalization that had been implemented in the Middle East in the 1970's. However, in most cases, these measures proved insufficient in attracting large amounts of foreign capital since bureaucratic barriers of the rent-seeking system were not abolished. Only few countries of the Middle East, such as Morocco, have so far managed to overcome the international capital's resistance invest in the Middle East. Only the future can show whether other countries will manage to follow and whether Morocco will be able to control the dynamics provoked by foreign investment in the long run.

Participation in the process of communicational globalization may offer most chances as well as dangers from the perspective of authoritarian regimes. On the one hand, intensively relying on the Internet, thereby using the opportunities of decreasing transaction and information costs, comes close to a necessary precondition for a successful economic liberalization process. On the other hand, it seems to be extremely complicated to control access and use of the Internet; the Internet is used to acquire and spread information that may endanger the stability of the authoritarian regimes. This may help to explain why, with only one major exception - namely Kuwait - Middle Eastern resistance to globalization is especially marked regarding this indicator.

5. Conclusion

Compared to other world regions, the Middle East stands out for its resistance to trends of globalization which have been noticeable in the international system since the 1980's. At that time and despite the clear inter-regional particularity of the Middle East, a significant intra-regional variance could be observed.

The concept of subjective rationalism can contribute to an explanation of both phenomena: the Middle Eastern resistance to globalization, and the intra-regional variance. In the Middle East, the decision on how to meet the challenges of globalization are primarily made by authoritarian state bureaucracies that had managed to build up strong state apparatuses vis-à-vis their societies in the 1970's at the latest. These regimes do not have a genuine interest in economic or political development. Rather, their behavior is driven by the preference to maintain their privileged power positions.

Since globalization means social de-nationalization, the Middle Eastern elites lack any vested interest in getting involved in globalization, i.e. social de-nationalization, in the fields of communication, trade, and economics. The simple reason behind this is that processes stimulated by participating in globalization reduce the ability of the authoritarian regimes to preserve their privileged power positions vis-à-vis their societies.

However, since the rent-based system of petrolism has been undergoing a severe crisis since the 1980's, *limited* participation in globalization is especially attractive for those regimes that suffer most from this crisis, such as the Middle Eastern countries with no or little oil reserves that were not capable of managing the crisis of the system by improving their rent policies. In this perspective, elites that take policies of economic or political liberalization are not in favor of transition to market economies or democracies, respectively. Rather, the intention is to stabilize the authoritarian regimes by partially taking advantage of opportunities made available by globalization. However, since the impacts of liberalization policies are very complex and difficult to control in the long run even for rational actors, it is an open question whether the plan of authoritarian reforms works out. Yet, due to the very restricted participation in globalization, most of the regimes in the Middle East are far away from having unintentionally laid the foundations of a transition towards market economies and democracies.

Tables

Table 1: Internet Hosts per 10,000 people (January 1999)

Country/World Region	Number
Algeria	0.01
Egypt	0.31
Iran	0.04
Israel	161.96
Jordan	0.80
Kuwait	32.80
Lebanon	5.56
Morocco	0.20
Saudi Arabia	0.15
Syria	0.00
Tunisia	0.07
Yemen	0.01
World	75.22
Middle East and North Africa[8]	0.25
Low-Income Countries[9]	0.17
Middle-Income Countries[10]	10.15
Low-Income and Middle-Income Countries	3.08
East Asia and Pacific	1.66
Latin America and Caribbean Islands	9.64
Middle East and North Africa	0.25
South Asia	0.14
Sub-Saharan Africa	2.39
Bolivia	0.78
Brazil	12.88
Indonesia	0.75
Kyrgyz Republic	4.04
South Africa	34.67
Tajikistan	0.12

Source: World Bank (2000: 266-7).

---

[8] The Region „Middle East and North Africa", as defined by the World Bank (2000: 290-1), includes Algeria, Bahrain, Egypt, Iran, Iraq, Israel, Jordan, Kuwait, Lebanon, Libya, Malta, Morocco, Oman, Qatar, Saudi Arabia, Syria, Tunisia, United Arab Emirates, West Bank and Gaza, and Yemen. The figure presented includes low-income and middle-income countries, i.e. all countries mentioned above excluding Israel, Kuwait, Malta, Qatar, and the Un. Arab Emirates.
[9] Yemen is the only Middle Eastern country listed as a low-income country by the World Bank (2000: 290-1).
[10] According to the World Bank list (2000: 290-1), Israel, Kuwait, Malta, Qatar, and United Arab Emirates are high-income countries of the Middle East. With the only exception of Yemen (see footnote 5), all other Middle Eastern countries mentioned in footnote 4 are listed as middle-income countries.

Table 2: Merchandise Exports (1983 and 1998 in Millions of US-Dollars)

Country/World Region	1983	1998 [11]
Algeria	12,480	9,380
Egypt	3,215	*3,908* [12]
Iran	19,950	13,150
Israel	5,108	23,282
Jordan	580	1,750
Kuwait	11,504	9,700
Lebanon	691	716
Morocco	2,006	7,295
Saudi Arabia	45,861	38,800
Syria	1,923	*3.916*
Tunisia	1,850	5,746
Yemen	701	*2,481*
World	1,757,216	5,414,844
Middle East and North Africa	118,705	103,782
Low-Income Countries	88,785	334,896
Middle-Income Countries	410,520	953,662
Low-Income and Middle-Income Countries	493,984	1,288,084
East Asia and Pacific	97,271	537,234
Latin America and Caribbean Islands	99,355	270,876
South Asia	14,868	50,743
Sub-Saharan Africa	49,231	*84,706*
Brazil	21,899	50,992
Indonesia	21,152	48,840
Pakistan	3,077	8,370
South Africa	18,508	26,322
South Korea	24,446	133,223

Source: World Bank (2000: 268-9).

---

[11] These figures are based on preliminary estimates made in 1999 (World Bank 2000: 269).
[12] These and the following italics in tables indicate data for years other than those specified. The closest available year is presented instead.

Table 3: Foreign Direct Investment (1990 and 1997 in Millions of US-Dollars)

Country/World Region	1990	1997
Algeria	0	7
Egypt	734	891
Iran	-362	50
Israel	101	2,706
Jordan	38	22
Kuwait	Not available	20
Lebanon	6	150
Morocco	165	1,200
Saudi Arabia	1,864	*-1.129*
Syria	71	80
Tunisia	76	316
Yemen	-131	-138
World	192,662	400,394
Middle East and North Africa	2,711	5,240
Low-Income Countries	5,732	59,509
Middle-Income Countries	18,697	103,786
Low-Income and Middle-Income Countries	24,429	163,295
East Asia and Pacific	11,135	64,284
Latin America and Caribbean Islands	8,188	61,573
South Asia	464	4,662
Sub-Saharan Africa	834	5,222
Chile	590	5,417
Indonesia	1,093	4,677
Mexico	2,634	12,477
South Africa	Not available	1,725
South Korea	788	2,844

Source: World Bank (2000: 270-1).

Table 4: Magnitude of Rent Income

State Indicator	Kuwait Libya Saudi Arabia	Algeria Iraq Iran	Syria	West Bank and Gaza	Egypt Jordan Tunisia	Israel[13]
Percentage of Rent Income to State Budget (Rent Income vs. Tax Income)	High	High	High/ Middle	High/ Middle	Middle	Low
Stability and Disposability of the Rent Income (Economic vs. Political Rents)	High	High	Middle	Low	Low	High
Rent Income per Capita (Relation of Rent Income to Population)	High	Middle	Low	Low	Low	Low
Disposability of the Rent Income for the State Bureaucracy	High	High	High/ Middle	Middle/ Low	Low	Low

Source: Beck/ Schlumberger (1999: 68).

---

[13] Of course, Israel does not participate in the petrolistic system. However, it receives a large amount of political rent from the United States of America. Per capita, Israel is by far the biggest receiver of foreign aid worldwide (World Bank 2000: 270-1).

References

Albrecht, Holger/ Pawelka, Peter/ Schlumberger, Oliver 1997: Wirtschaftliche Liberalisierung und Regimewandel in Ägypten. In: WeltTrends 16, pp. 43-63.

Amin, Samir 1982: The Arab Economy Today, London.

Beck, Martin 2001: Globalisierung als Bedrohung: Die Globalisierungsresistenz des Vorderen Orients als Ausdruck rationaler Reaktionen der politischen Eliten auf die neuen Entwicklungen im internationalen System. In: Fürtig, Henner (ed.): Islamische Welt und Globalisierung: Aneignung, Abgrenzung und Gegenentwürfe, Würzburg, pp. 53-85.

Beck, Martin 2002: Friedensprozeß im Nahen Osten: Rationalität, Kooperation und politische Rente, Wiesbaden.

Beck, Martin/ Schlumberger, Oliver 1999: Der Vordere Orient - ein entwicklungspolitischer Sonderfall?. In: Pawelka, Peter/ Wehling, Hans-Georg (eds.): Der Vordere Orient an der Schwelle zum 21. Jahrhundert, Opladen, pp. 35-55.

Beisheim, Marianne/ Dreher, Sabine/ Walter, Gregor/ Zangl, Bernhard/ Zürn, Michael 1999: Im Zeitalter der Globalisierung: Thesen und Daten zur gesellschaftlichen und politischen Denationalisierung, Baden-Baden.

Buchanan, James M./ Tollison, Robert D./ Tullock, Gordon (eds.) 1980: Toward a Theory of Rent-Seeking Society, College Station.

Elsenhans, Hartmut 1981: Abhängiger Kapitalismus oder bürokratische Entwicklungsgesellschaft: Versuch über den Staat in der Dritten Welt, Frankfurt/ Main.

Elster, Jon 1986: Introduction. In: Elster, Jon (ed.): Rational Choice, New York, pp. 1-33.

Feiler, Gil 1991: Migration and Recession: Arab Labor Mobility in the Middle East, 1982-89. In: Population and Development Review 17:1, pp. 134-155.

Feiler, Gil 1993: Palestinian Employment Prospects. In: Middle East Journal 47:4, pp. 633-651.

Ibrahim, Saad Eddin 1982: The New Arab Social Order: A Study of the Social Impact of Oil Wealth, Boulder.

Korany, Bahgat 1986: Political Petrolism and Contemporary Arab Politics, 1967-1983. In: Journal of Asian and African Studies 21:1-2, pp. 66-80.

Krasner, Stephen D. 1994: International Political Economy: Abiding Discord. In: Review of International Political Economy 1:1, pp. 13-19.

Luciani, Giacomo 1995: Resources, Revenues, and Authoritarianism in the Arab World: Beyond the Rentier State. In: Brynen, Rex/ Korany, Bahgat/ Noble, Paul (eds.): Political Liberalization and Democratization in the Arab World, Part 1: Theoretical Perspectives, Boulder, pp. 211-227.

March, James G. 1986: Bounded Rationality, Ambiguity, and the Engineering of Choice. In: Elster, Jon (ed.): Rational Choice, New York, pp. 1-33.

Murphy, Emma/ Niblock, Tim 1993: Introduction. In: Niblock, Timothy/ Murphy, Emma (eds.): Economic and Political Liberalization in the Middle East, London, pp. xiii-xvii.

Pawelka, Peter 1985: Herrschaft und Entwicklung im Nahen Osten: Ägypten, Heidelberg.

Pawelka, Peter 1993: Der Vordere Orient und das Internationale System, Stuttgart.

Pawelka, Peter 1997: Staat, Bürgertum und Rente im arabischen Vorderen Orient. In: Aus Politik und Zeitgeschichte 47:39, pp. 3-11.

Penrose, Edith 1993: From Economic Liberalization to International Integration: The Role of the State. In: Niblock, Timothy/ Murphy, Emma (eds.): Economic and Political Liberalization in the Middle East, London, pp. 3-25.

Przeworski, Adam 1991: Democracy and the Market: Political and Economic Reforms in Eastern Europe and Latin America, Cambridge.

Richards, Alan/ Waterbury, John 1996: A Political Economy of the Middle East, 2nd Edition, Boulder.

Tsebelis, George 1990: Nested Games: Rational Choice in Comparative Politics, Berkeley.

Weede, Erich 1997: Verteilungskoalitionen, Rent-Seeking und ordnungspolitischer Verfall. In: Boeckh, Andreas/ Pawelka, Peter (eds.): Staat, Markt und Rente in der internationalen Politik, Opladen, pp. 51-63.

World Bank 2000: World Development Report: Entering the 21st century, Oxford.

Zürn, Michael 1992: Interessen und Institutionen in der internationalen Politik: Grundlegung und Anwendungen des situationsstrukturellen Ansatzes, Opladen.

Zürn, Michael 1998: Regieren jenseits des Nationalstaates: Globalisierung und Denationalisierung als Chance, Frankfurt/ Main.

3

HENNER FÜRTIG

Globalization as a one-way street? The case of the Islamic Republic of Iran

Immediately after the terrorist attacks against the visible symbols of economic and financial as well as military might of the most powerful Western country, the US on September 11th, the Iranian president Khatami, his Foreign Minister Kharrazi and the entire cabinet hastened to condemn the terrorist acts and their perpetrators. Were they representatives of the same country where the first grass-root Islamic revolution of modern times took place more than twenty years ago, where an Islamic republic was established also to set an example for every Muslim in the world to follow? Was it the same country that took dozens of American diplomatic personal hostage for daring fourteen months, a country whose leadership was accused and convicted of terrorism in the famous Mykonos trial? Did they give in now to international law, to globalization as the set and framework of international development and to American leadership – not to speak of dominance? This article tries to answer these and other related questions by going more into detail and by presenting some background.

1. The Iranian revolution's universalistic approach

The Iranian revolution of 1979/80 belongs undoubtedly to the "great" revolutions of modern times. All fundamental social and political change in revolutions, be it 1789 in France or 1917 in Russia, has been characterized by universalistic efforts and the claim to have set new norms of social, political and cultural behavior with global validity. It was Crane Brinton, in his classic "The Anatomy of Revolution", who made the now universal point that these "great" revolutions "as gospels, as forms of religion, ... are all universalist in aspiration" (Brinton 1965: 196). Depending on the type of the respective revolution, it became one of their most important tasks to fight for the universal spread of either civil liberties, socialism, or simply Islam (Sick 1995: 146-7).

In this sense, the Iranian revolutionaries saw themselves obliged to explain to every single Muslim that nationalism, socialism, communism and capitalism, all Western imports, had been tried and found wanting. Instead of these Western ideologies, Islam, indigenous and comprehensible to the Muslim masses, literate and illiterate, was shown to be a viable belief system, even when opposed by a monarch who had a formidable military at his disposal and who was supported by a superpower (Linabury 1992: 33). According to Ayatollah Khomeini - the undisputed leader of the Iranian revolution - there was, therefore, only one way left for mankind to escape the negative impacts of Western and Eastern ideological imports, and that was to rely on Islam as the only indigenous worldview not affected and thus not degenerated by Western ideas and thoughts. Only Islam could stop the vicious circle of the formerly oppressed becoming the new oppressors because the eternal laws of Islam are valid for all people (Rajaee 1983: 80-1). In this sense, Khomeini never changed his credo: "Rely on the culture of Islam, resist Western imitation, and stand on your own feet" (Khomeini 1981: 304).

Without doubt, Khomeini felt himself and the Iranian revolution obliged to reintroduce Islam in the sense of Prophet Muhammad, that is as a revelation for the whole world. His universalistic approach was at least as total as he thought the West's universalistic schemes were. He firmly declared: "The Iranian revolution is not exclusively that of Iran, because Islam does not belong to any particular people. Islam is revealed for mankind and the Muslims, not for Iran...An Islamic movement, therefore, cannot limit itself to any particular country, not even to the Islamic countries; it is the continuation of the revolution by the prophets."[1]. Thus, he propagated an Islamic universalism which he saw as an alternative to Western universalism. "Why did (the Iranian revolution – H.F.) acquire global dimensions," Ayatollah Khomeini asked only to answer: "Because the world nations, especially the Islamic nation, suddenly felt that there was a shared problem between the Iranian nation and the billion-strong Muslims, which was alienation from their origin and being ensnared by the idols of arrogant powers..." (BBC 1992).

Time and again Khomeini therefore emphasized the responsibility of the Iranian Islamic revolution to spread Islam's message. "The Islamic Republic intends to implement the ordinances of the Quran and those of the messenger of God in all countries. Iran is the starting point. It intends to demonstrate to all countries that Islam is based on equality, brotherhood and unity" (Rajaee 1983: 83).

1.1 Islamic Unity

In Khomeini's view, the source of the Muslim world's problems is the estrangement from the divine path of Islam, its adoption of corrupt ways of either the East or the West and its disunity, which is partly due to the intrigues of the oppressors. Their salvation would be to return to Islam, to establish a truly Islamic government and to strive for unity in order to overcome division. "There is no difference between Muslims who speak different languages, for instance the Arabs and the Persians. It is very probable that such problems have been created by those who do not wish the Muslim countries to be united...They create the issues of nationalism, of pan-Iranism, pan-Turkism, and such isms, which are contrary to Islamic doctrines. Their plan is to destroy Islam and Islamic philosophy" (Amirahmadi/ Entessar 1993: 3).

---

[1] Ettela'at, Tehran, Nov. 3rd, 1979

Khomeini, on his part, tried to enforce the unity of all Muslims, making the *umma* the only legitimate concept of Islamic politics. He strongly denied any particular nationalism among Muslims or even Muslim nation states based on language, ethnicity or geography (Anderson 1994: 152). Thus, in the end, national boundaries would become obsolete in an Islamic society, since Islam would demand the creation of a single state (*yek keshvar-e hamegani*), uniting all people under one flag and one law (Khomeini 1980: 337). Consequently, the initial years of Iran's post-revolutionary foreign policy were dominated - apart from Khomeini - by a group of clerical leaders and laymen who considered national borders simply a heritage of colonialism.

In their opinion, the Islamic world used to be united but was later disintegrated by the two aggressive elements of Western culture, i.e. nationalism and colonialism. This led to racial and national hatred between different Muslim nations and overshadowed Islamic cultural values. By espousing the powerful "Islam does not know any borders" concept, they could well justify themselves and legitimize their actions.

Muslims all over the world were to be awakened to act according to their own benefits as seen by the Islamic Republic of Iran. "Whereas the Muslim states should gather around this center (the Islamic Republic) and incline toward Islam...they either do not pay attention or love of self...inhibits them from doing so...The Islamic Republic wishes that all Islamic countries, and their governments...would wake up from this benumbing dream."[2] Independence would be an illusion for a single Islamic country; it would only be a part of this "benumbing dream". The struggle for the unity of the *umma* therefore became an important part of official Iranian state policy laid down in the constitution of the Islamic Republic. "Based on the ordinances of the Quran, that 'Lo! that your community is a united one and I am your Lord, so worship me' (XX: 92) the Islamic Republic of Iran is to base its overall policy on the coalition and unity of the Islamic nation. Furthermore it should exert continuous effort until political, economic and cultural unity is realized in the Islamic world."[3] (Constitution of the Islamic Republic of Iran 1979: Principle 11)

Article 10 reads: "All Moslems form a single nation, and the government of the Islamic Republic of Iran has the duty of formulating its general policies with a view to the merging and union of all Moslem peoples, and it must constantly strive to bring about the political, economic and cultural unity of the Islamic world."[4] The revolution's leader often said that "nobody could defeat one billion Muslims if they were united." Thus, the Muslims and other oppressed groups

---

[2] Kayhan, Tehran, July 26, 1982
[3] Constitution of the Islamic Republic of Iran, Tehran 1979, Principle 11.
[4] Ibid, Principle 10.

and nations should cooperate in order to change the global balance of power and to put an end to their subjugation and exploitation (Hunter 1990: 40).

As mentioned before, in the early days of the revolution the entire Iranian leadership spoke with one voice in this regard. The then Speaker of Parliament, Hojjat ol-Eslam Ali Akbar Hashemi Rafsanjani, declared in a Friday prayer in 1982: "If the Islamic world would have acted on the basis of Islam and the words of the Prophet, it would be the most powerful force in the world. I don't exaggerate when I say 'the most powerful force'...Some of you may ask:' Bigger than America? More powerful than the Soviet Union? Stronger than China?' I say 'Yes!' Right now, we would have been stronger than China, stronger than the Soviet Union, stronger than America and all their satellites if we only would have been able to establish a global and united Islamic government."[5]

Victory over the Shah, seen as invincible before, seemed a "miracle" which was sufficient legitimization and an incentive to expect success not only in the region but in the whole world. Since this "miracle" only became reality after disregarding formerly valid rules and laws, the revolutionaries were convinced that they were legitimized to act beyond recognized norms of diplomacy and international law when pursuing their political aims. In the early 1980s, it was seen as a betrayal of the revolution to act merely for the benefit of Iran. To work for the domestic development of the country alone would lead to the destruction of revolutionary values and the existing model of the Islamic revolution. Therefore, continuous aggression against values dominating the existing international system and efforts to overthrow neighboring regimes were the main objectives of the Iranian leadership. For this purpose it was ready to use military force, guerrilla attacks and intelligence, and to arm the national liberation movements in order to jeopardize "non-Islamic" regimes. It would agree with national development only in the context of creating a series of revolutionary movements in Islamic nations and of threatening the international interests of the Western system.[6]

1.2. Export of the Revolution

This strategy was summarized in the conception of *sudur-e enqelab*, the export of the revolution, which became the overall credo of early post-revolutionary Iranian foreign policy (Millward 1986: 189-204). "For its part, post-revolutionary Iran saw its neighbors not as independent nation states but as parts of the Islamic world for which the 'Islamic republic' and 'Islamic revolution' had duties in mind which included what others would call 'intervention'" (Chubin 1990: 74). It was Ayatollah Khomeini once again who was most outspoken in this regard. "We should try hard to export our revolution to the world. We

---

[5] Hotba-ye namaz-e jom'e-ye Tehran. Vol. 4, Tehran 1989, p. 185.
[6] Echo of Islam, Tehran, (1996)142/143, p. 42.

should set aside the thought that we do not export our revolution, because Islam does not regard various Islamic countries differently and is the supporter of all the oppressed people of the world. On the other hand, all the superpowers and all the powers have risen to destroy us. If we remain in an enclosed environment we shall definitely face defeat."[7]

Khomeini felt the Islamic revolution was obliged to pave the way for the ultimate establishment of an Islamic world order when the *Mahdi*, the Twelfth Imam, appears. "We will export our revolution to the four corners of the world because our revolution is Islamic. The struggle will be continued until there is everywhere the call: 'There is no God but God, and Muhammad is his prophet'. As long as people are being oppressed all over the world our struggle will be continued."[8]

Khomeini repeated these ideas several times, directing them to different audiences, leaving no room for misunderstanding. For example, he told a group of Iranian youth before travelling abroad: "Today we need to strengthen and export Islam everywhere. You need to export Islam to other places, and the same version of Islam which is currently in power in our country. Our way of exporting Islam is through the youth, who go to other countries where a large number of people come to see you and your achievements."[9]

The leader of the Iranian revolution, however, did not assign this task only to the youth but considered it the duty of every Muslim citizen in his country and of all its institutions. Also, according to him, it was not exclusively the responsibility of the Ministry of Foreign Affairs to pursue these political goals. In the early days of the revolution a so-called Liberation Movements Bureau was even assigned to the Ministry to co-ordinate the efforts of exporting the revolution. To increase its importance, the Bureau was soon put under the authority of the Supreme Command of the Revolutionary Guard Corps (*Pasdaran*). For the *Pasdaran*, created as a kind of praetorian guard for the clerical regime to counterbalance the uncertain attitude of the regular forces, it became - according to the constitution - one of their most important tasks to fight for the expansion of the rule of the sharia in the world (Sick 1995: 148). Nevertheless, other individuals and organizations also continued their independent efforts to export the revolution by creating their own networks and structures.

In 1984, the Intelligence Ministry established yet another bureau from which to orchestrate Iran's Islamic activity abroad (Calabrese 1994: 144). Because Khomeini's version of the Islamic revolution did not recognize international laws

---

[7] Foreign Broadcast Information Service (FBIS), Daily Report, Middle East and Africa, March 24, 1980, V: 058, supplement 070.
[8] Rahnemudhaye Imam, Tehran 1979, p. 28.
[9] FBIS, Daily Report, South Asia, 9 March 1982, VIII: 046.

and frontiers, i.e. Islamic peoples were all one, Iran's regime felt free to use the already existing links between different religious communities across the Muslim world, and to create new ones, to establish a world-wide Islamic network with Iran at its center. Therefore, these efforts were not only directed at the region around Iran itself but at communities as far away as the Maghreb or even South East Asia, including Indonesia and the Philippines. The policy included all the means of enforcing revolutionary political and ideological ideas - arms, financial support, training, international congresses, propaganda, radio programs (Halliday 1994: 101).

Nevertheless, it should also be mentioned that Iran indeed saw itself obliged to export the revolution and to support all peoples struggling for independence and freedom, but Khomeini also reminded them that "a right is something you have to fight for. The people must rise for themselves and destroy the rule of the superpowers in the world."[10]

But not only revolutionary Islamic idealism drove the Iranian leadership to export the revolution. Pragmatic considerations also led to the conclusion that an utmost level of admiration and influence within the Islamic world might safeguard the young revolutionary state which felt exposed to many challenges.

2. Universalism between 1979 and today

The Iranian leadership soon became aware of the economic, political and military weaknesses of its Islamic Republic and had to conclude that the export of the revolution would not be accomplished in one step or within a very short period of time. Furthermore, the response to the export idea on the part of the governments of other states with a strong Muslim population was not at all encouraging. This situation helped to differentiate the Iranian leadership even further; and a more moderate and pragmatic policy began to take shape. The export of the revolution was to be situated between peaceful coexistence and opportunism. In other words, the Islamic Republic was to inflict blows to "puppet and dictatorial states" if national interests required and the situation permitted; if not, it was to continue peaceful relations.

Of course, Ayatollah Khomeini and his followers could not propagate this shift in their politics officially. But they tried to downplay the apparent threat contained in their declamatory policy to export the revolution without, however, disavowing it altogether. In late September 1982, Khomeini for example declared, "by exportation of Islam we mean that Islam be spread everywhere. We have no intention of interfering militarily in any part of the world."[11]

---

[10] Bayanat-e Emam Homeini be monasabat yekom salgerd-e enqelab. Tehran 1982, p. 5.
[11] Tehran Times, Tehran, September 30, 1982.

Furthermore, Iran got struck in a devastating war with neighboring Iraq, and became isolated in the international arena. The destiny of the revolution was at stake by the end of the eighties, and Khomeini felt obliged to do something. First, his *fatwa* against Salman Rushdie has to be mentioned here. Not only as part of a much larger Muslim effort to counter inequalities within the global system through the revitalization of Islamic particularity, but as an attempt to reinstall Iran as well as himself as leaders of the global Muslim movement. Intentionally, Khomeini presented himself as the highest Muslim authority on earth by addressing his *fatwa* not only to the Shiites but to Sunnites as well and by reminding all Muslims that Islamic law does not stop at national borders when he directed his *fatwa* against a person living outside the *dar al-Islam*.

In addition, Khomeini had to further clarify the very concept of *sudur-e enqelab*. He elaborated: "when we say we want to export our revolution we mean we would like to export this spirituality and enthusiasm we see in Iran...we have no intention to attack anyone with swords or other arms...," (Rajaee 1990: 68) meaning that to save the essence of the "Export of the Revolution"- conception the Islamic Republic of Iran should rather set an example for the Muslims of the world to follow.

2.1.Setting an Example

Its mere existence should convince Muslims of their revolutionary responsibility. It should encourage them to follow suit and topple their respective dictatorial, pro-Western and non-Islamic regimes. The revolution was to succeed internally at first, thus preparing the ground for propagating its values and objectives internationally. Success and stabilization of the Islamic revolution in Iran would inevitably influence other suffering Muslims.

The attempt to be recognized as a model by the Muslims was not new in itself but it gained momentum as the vision of an immediate export of the Islamic revolution gradually vanished. Right from the early days of the Islamic revolution, Iran had presented itself as the center of the world-wide drive for Islamic unity, as a model all Muslims should follow, as an alternative to the existing Arab/Islamic regimes.

Mohammad Javad Larijani, Deputy Chairman of the parliament's foreign policy committee, went so far as to even advocate the acceptance of the *Velayat-e Faqih* (rule of the jurisconsult) -principle by other Muslims. "...we have and have had the velayat, both during the Imam's (Khomeini's) time and during Ayatollah Khamenei's. This velayat is a righteous jurist ruling the entire Islamic nation. Muslims may not even realize that we have such a jurist ruling here, but this does not undermine the reality of this guardianship. Of course, it affects the ruling jurist's effectiveness, but not the principle. As long as this guardianship exists, the velayat is responsible for the Islamic world, and it is the duty of the

Islamic world to protect the ruling jurist...As long as our country is the seat of the true ruling jurist, we are responsible for the whole Islamic nation, and the Islamic nation is duty-bound to safeguard the Umm ol-Qura" (Mohadessin 1993: 38).

In a more general sense, A.N. Memon wrote enthusiastically: "...Iran, as an Islamic republic, has inspired numerous Muslims to advocate changes in their own governments. The Iranian Revolution has become a symbol of defiance against the West. Iran has superseded Saudi Arabia as the leading voice among many Muslims seeking an alternative to Western culture" (Memon 1995: 150).

The former Foreign Minister Velayati even used the word "Mecca" in connection with Iran's revolution to show that the center of gravity in the Islamic world had shifted to Iran. "Iran's friends and foes alike perceive Iran as the country that is the center and Mecca of the aspirations of all Muslims...Iran is a model for the fifty Islamic countries. This is because the domineering powers have not had very pleasant experiences regarding Iran."[12]

Becoming a source of inspiration and emulation for all Muslims, which was not unattainable in the Middle East and in the Persian Gulf region where Muslims are dominant and politically active, would result in increased political strength and diplomatic maneuverability for Iran. The revolutionary Iranian leadership could refer to the many miseries in the Islamic world to gain respect and sympathy. The absolute majority of Muslims around the world, including those in the oil-rich Middle East, live under conditions of economic hardship and/or political oppression. Regardless of the real Iranian influence among Muslims, the revolution had a great impact on them because it supported the anti-status quo posture of the suppressed Muslim majority. Thus its popularity was also a result of the acutely inept economic policies of the existing governments in the region (Amirahmadi 1994: 116-118).

However, apart from this and from Iran's assertion that it is the only country in the world where Islam has officially become the foundation of society and government, thus implying that it is the duty of all Muslims to support it, there were other reasons for Muslims to admire the Iranian revolution. Among them were Iran's uncompromising stand with regard to the Palestinian issue and the question of Jerusalem and its strict adherence to an independent and non-aligned foreign policy, both of which have great appeal for many Muslims.

The new strategy of setting an example became even more imminent, when Khomeini died in 1989 and with him the most important integrating personality of the revolution. Therefore, Khomeini's successor, Ayatollah Khamenei, declared: "The Islamic Revolution of Iran has taken place and was simultaneously

---

[12] Resalat, Tehran, February 15, 1993

exported throughout the world. The revolution was exported once, and that is the end of the story."[13] Hojjat ol-Eslam Rafsanjani, then speaker of the parliament and later President of the Republic, agreed with Khamenei when explaining: "The phrase 'exporting the revolution', if it is mentioned here, means that we introduce our revolution and (that) anyone who wishes to use our experience can do so. But interference and physically exporting (revolution) has never been our policy."[14]

2.2. Propagating a new bipolarity

The pragmatism of the post-Khomeini Iranian leadership has also to be seen in the light of the end of the East-West-conflict which coincided accidentally with the death of the Ayatollah. Lacking a - if only potential - counter-balancing factor in international relations, Iran saw itself directly confronted with the „Great Satan", the US and its Western allies. After a moment of consideration, Iran's leadership did not only notice the risks but the chances of the new balance of power after the end of the Cold War. It propagated a new kind of bipolarity in international politics where a revitalized and politicized Islam would replace the ineffective communism as the alternative to the West. Even in this regard, it was possible to refer to previous politics of the late Ayatollah Khomeini. Iran's revolutionary leader was satisfied by the collapse of the Soviet Empire. For him it was a proof for Islam being the one and only alternative to the Western system instead of some sort of materialism.

In January 1989, he had sent an open letter to Soviet President Gorbachev that should also popularize this „truth" among Muslims. "Your Excellency, Mr. Gorbachev, One should turn to the truth. The main difficulty of your country is not the issue of ownership, economics or freedom. Your difficulty is lack of true faith in God, the same difficulty which has also dragged the West towards decadence and a dead end. Your principal problem is a long and futile combat with God, the origin of existence and creation...It is clear to all that henceforth Communism should be sought in the museums of world political history, because Marxism does not provide any answers to the real needs of man, since it is a materialistic ideology. It is not possible to save humanity by materialism from the crisis brought about by a lack of conviction in spirituality, which is the most fundamental ailment of human society in both the West and the East" (Harney 1989: 158). The letter concluded with Khomeini asking Gorbachev „to seriously study Islam" (Rajaee 1990: 76).

Later, the Iranian leadership continued to separate the post-Cold War world into two camps, "the world of arrogance i.e. the materialist West and the world of

---

[13] Kayhan Hava'i, Tehran, April 4, 1993.
[14] BBC SWB, op.cit., February 3-4, 1993.

Islam."[15] This perception was also shared abroad i.e. in the Islamic as well as in the Western world. Musa Saleem, director of the Islamic Institute in London, wrote for example: "Like the communist system whose inevitable demise came sooner than expected, the time is fast approaching for the demise of the Western system as we know it. We know of no other system than the Islamic system to replace it. Sooner, rather than later Islamic values and ideals penetrate into Western culture and governments in varying degree. We predict this will happen within twenty five years" (Saleem 1993: 4). And Graham Fuller asserted: "With the collapse of communism, no other coherent set of beliefs dispersed among people over a wide geographic area has emerged to pose a systematic critique of the West as strongly and clearly as has radical Islam" (Fuller/Lesser 1995: 2). Anyway, for the Iranian clerics it was important that the Islamic Republic should be recognized as the center of the Islamic pole.

Thus, even years after his death, Khomeini's legacy of the overall universalistic nature of Iran's foreign policy is still valid. As one of the basic marks of its identity, the Islamic Republic cannot afford to conceal it. If an Islamic foreign policy is a reflection of Islamic belief, having a global mission with a message for all the people of the world and thus not being able to accept limits or remain bounded within the framework of national, regional, ethnical or geographical structures, how can the responsibility of an Islamic state than be limited to its borders? But, as mentioned before, Iran's leadership had to learn its lessons, and was forced to adapt its foreign policy objectives to the real world.

2.3. Efforts to create an "Islamic" foreign policy

In the decade between 1979 and 1989, when the majority of the Iranian revolutionaries felt themselves to be a part of the mighty revolutionary wave, no one really noticed the overall declamatory character of Khomeini's foreign policy statements or dared to ask questions about commonly recognized Islamic propositions concerning international relations. But as soon as the situation in Iran began to normalize, both politicians and clerics painfully felt the widening gap between the pursuit of Islamic foreign policy and the pressure to secure the interests of Iran as a nation-state in a world becoming more and more complex. In particular, diplomats and members of the Foreign Ministry were asking questions as to how Islamic foreign policy could be handled in detail.

With increasing frankness they accused the religious jurists of Iran of not providing sufficient and satisfactory answers despite the importance and sensitivity of the issue (Ghazvini 1996: 780-796). Contemporary *fuqaha* and Islamic scholars would either deal with foreign policy matters in a very cursory manner or would pursue extremely idealized principles impossible to implement in the

---

[15] Deputy Foreign Minister Besharati in a radio interview. BBC SWB, ME/1169A/5, September 5, 1991.

present world such as collecting tribute (*jezya*) from those who refuse to convert to Islam, rejecting present borders between countries, insisting on the religious duty of directing others to do good or enjoining others not to commit anti-religious deeds.

According to Iranian foreign policy specialists, also "befriending God's friends (*tawalee*) and avoiding God's enemies (*tabaree*) is not possible in the foreign policy arena due to conflict with existing international law and the interests of certain powers.

On the other hand, those directly involved in Iran's day to day foreign policy do not feel themselves legitimized to call their pragmatism Islamic foreign policy. Be that as it may, in contemporary Iran both its clerics and diplomats seem to have reached at least one common denominator in the seven basic principles that should not be left out in a foreign policy claiming to be Islamic. These are:

- Protection of Dar al-Islam. Both clerics and laymen within the Iranian leadership have agreed upon the protection of the Islamic system as the most important and fundamental principle in the foreign policy of Islam. Thus, the Foreign Ministry and the diplomats are obliged to keep this vital principle in mind with all their activities and should not move towards a practical path that undermines it.

Glory, Protection of Independence and Rejection of Dominance. The second important and basic principle in the foreign policy of an Islamic government should be the glory and the authority of Islam and its government. The experts among the Iranian politicians know that the relevant texts on this principle were compiled and arranged when the Muslims were at the height of their power, when their domain was spreading, and other states were conquered by them. Thus, the principle reflects the honor and glory of the Islamic state at a time of powerful presence in the global arena. Under present circumstances, the Iranians are therefore concentrating their foreign policy efforts on the second part of the principle, i.e. the rejection of dominance by non-Muslims (*nafiye sabil*). It forbids any relations that lead to the dominance of foreigners over the destinies of Muslims such as giving concessions, specific powers or exclusive economic and commercial rights that promote foreign dominance. Articles 152 and 153 of the Islamic Republic's Constitution refer especially to this principle. According to most clerical leaders of Iran, the principle of *nafiye sabil* is one of the fundamental commands and rules of Islamic jurisprudence and has priority over other rules (Shakuri 1982: 387). But despite the importance of this principle, there is an ongoing dispute among the Iranian leadership over the feasibility of implementing *nafiye sabil* under the conditions of an accelerating globalization, leading to "mutual dependence among countries" and making "concepts such as independence and absolute (national) sovereignty obsolete...in the not too distant future" (Ghazvini 1996: 786).

Interest (Maslahat). The third principle is grouped around the rules of ability (*vos*), no harm (*la zarar*) and avoidance (*taqiyeh*). The "vos"-rule connotes the fulfillment of one's duty according to one's ability. The "la zarar"-rule means choosing the easier way if the more difficult one implies the possibility of losses (Alavi 1994: 4). The "taqiyeh"-rule suggests going along with an opponent in order to ward off harm and injury (Ansari 1994: 11). There is a deep rift within the Iranian leadership on the question of whether *maslahat* primarily refers to the Islamic Republic of Iran or the whole Muslim *umma*, on the extent of "vos", the amount of noticeable "zarar" and the necessity of "taqiyeh" in the contemporary era. In general, Iran's acceptance of UNSCR # 598, which lead to a cease-fire with Iraq in 1988, is seen as a convincing example of applying the *maslahat*-principle by the Iranian government.

Establishment of Relations, Coexistence and Cooperation with other Countries. According to the present Iranian leadership, there is no other way to implement the above mentioned major principles than to establish cooperative relations with other countries, in order to avoid isolation, strengthen the Islamic state, and relay its message to the people of the world. The IRI should have an active and authoritative presence in the global arena.

Support for the Rights of the Muslims and the Oppressed throughout the World. According to Article 154 of the Iranian constitution, every citizen of the country and all its institutions are obliged to "support the righteous struggle of the down-trodden in face of tyranny all over the world" (Amini 1985: 7). The Iranian leadership is sure that all its relations with Muslim and non-Muslim opposition movements throughout the world are legitimized by this principle, including material and ideological support. Although the Iranian leaders dealing with the country's foreign policy are well aware that their uncompromising attitude towards the rights of the *umma* and the world's oppressed has fostered their prestige among Muslims, they also know that such a policy has many harmful effects for Iran, too. Because their support for political movements in other countries often provokes strong pressures and boycotts from the governments of those countries, Iran has to consider the pros and cons of the various foreign policy principles, especially that of *maslahat*.

Invitation and Propagation (*da'vat*). In Islamic jurisprudence, there is no major disagreement among the *ulama* on the obligatory nature of *da'vat*. But the Iranian clergy has not reached a final conclusion as to whether this obligation should be imposed on each and every individual in society (Shakuri 1982: 360). Some of them definitely believe that *da'vat* has priority over other principles in foreign policy, both in terms of timing and value (Qaderi 1989: 226). In that sense, it would be impossible to direct the responsibility for the propagation of and invitation to the Islamic faith exclusively to specialized organs such as propaganda, cultural and media organizations. Therefore, given the sensitivity and importance of propagation and the Qoran's emphasis on it, most of Iran's *fuqaha* consider it one of the foreign policy principles of the Islamic Republic and thus one of the main duties of the country's diplomacy. Seyyed Ali Qaderi, for example, stated: "The first social duty of any prophet after mission is invitation - this principle constitutes the essence of Islam's foreign policy...Avoidance of invitation not only confronts Dar al-Islam with the danger of extinction, but also carries punishment in the next world" (Qaderi 1989: 228).

Gaining the Endearment of Others. The principle of giving financial or non-financial assistance to other countries should not be confused with the fifth principle, i.e. the support of Muslims or oppressed people. This seventh and last approved principle intends rather to gain the affinities of other countries or to moderate their views in relation to the Islamic Republic of Iran and its policies (*ta'lif qolub*). Donations or interest-free loans to countries like Syria, North-Korea, Sudan or the former PDRY can be seen in the light of this principle (Shakuri 1982: 501-514).

Although these principles of the Islamic Republic's foreign policy have been agreed upon by the majority of the country's leading personalities, there is still no common opinion about their relative ranking.

Especially diplomats know that the realization of Islamic ideals and sacred objectives, such as support for the rights of the Muslims and the deprived, and invitation and propagation, is a dangerous responsibility, with its own particular effects, for instance the threat of becoming isolated. Thus, none of them is really sure whether the efforts to realize one or more of the above mentioned principles might harm others. Iran's foreign policy is therefore caught in a trap between pretension and reality.

"Should Iran pursue what it wants through the promotion of national liberation movements in the manner done by the communists or should it engage in plotting coups d'État as was practiced by the US or other Western powers," asked Mohammad Javad Larijani, head of the Majles' Foreign Policy Committee, only to continue: "The answer to both options is clearly and forthrightly negative...our understanding of the Islamic renaissance values its generative potential *within* various countries" (Larijani 1996: 756). Compared with Khomeini's approach, which envisioned a complete merger of all Muslims within an organic *umma*, the new approach suggested that the Iranian government handle the issue flexibly and be more sensitive to the adverse impacts of this objective. The post-Khomeini foreign policymakers - at least within the government - no longer subscribed to the utopia of a Muslim world without national frontiers. They advocated instead greater and greater Muslim solidarity. "Theoretically, this reflects a shift from a monist concept of Umma to a more complex and pluralistic concept in which the principle of ethnic and national difference...is respected" (Afrasiabi 1994: 203).

3. Interrelations between Iran's version of universalism and globalization

There is enough reason to declare that the Iranian revolution utilized globalization and contributed to its spreading simultaneously. Even as early as in 1978/79, Khomeini and his aides used the advanced technology of their time, the tape recorder, to give instructions via the 80.000 mosques of Iran. But this perception comes in a retrospective view only. It is rather unlikely that the Iranian revolutionaries knew the word "globalization" when they toppled the Shah in 1979 since they support the majority opinion – in today's Islamic world and in the West alike – that globalization is a phenomenon resulting from the Western victory in the Cold War.

But it is important to notice that, from the beginning they considered the West to be the dominant global power and therefore responsible for all the existing injustices, inequalities and misfortunes in the world. By trying to impose norms of political, economic, military and even cultural behavior on mankind, the West was suppressing - according to their view - any development in the world that went against its interests. This opinion did not change substantially until today when Iran stresses the point that globalization - regardless of its economic, technological or cultural forms – is basically a one-way street i.e. an uneven and asymmetric process favoring Western interests and fostering Western superiority. Therefore, Muslims should dissociate themselves from the globalization process at least or better resist it.

Wasn't it Ayatollah Khomeini who wrote as early as in 1983 in his last will and testament: "Among the gravest conspiracies...has been the plot to alienate colonialized countries and make them look to the West...as their model. So much so that those nations eventually lost their self-esteem and their trust in their own cultures...(concluding) that their countries could not but become independent...More saddening, however, is that the (West has) checked the progress of the nations whom (it) attempt(s) to make consumption-orientated, and install a fear in us of (its) technological advancements and of (its) satanic power and destroy our self-confidence. This sense of self-nothingness and this feeling of dullness is inculcated in us by the big powers served to make us distrust our own knowledge and expertise and capacity in all areas and let us simply try to imitate the West...blindfoldedly,...even though (this) might be totally absurd and ridiculous..."[16]

And in an interview with the journal of the Revolutionary Guard he added: "(The West) claims that civilization, science and development are peculiar to (it) and they - especially Western and more recently American - are the 'superior

---

[16] Imam's Final Discourse. The text of the political and religious testament of the Leader of the Islamic Revolution and the Founder of the Islamic Republic of Iran, Imam Khomeini. In: The Iranian Journal of International Affairs, Tehran 1 1989, 2/3, pp. 328-329.

race' while others are of lower races; therefore, their progress is the result of their 'noble race' and these other people's backwardness stems from their being an imperfect race. (They)...are still on the way to perfection which, after millions of years, will gain proportional perfection; therefore, the effort for our own progress is useless... In other words, we don't have anything and must beg everything from either East or West, be it science, civilization, law or development."[17] Khomeini insisted on changing this situation.

Encouraged by his legacy the present Iranian leadership is trying to amalgamate the universal mission of the Islamic revolution with globalization by altering the very nature of the latter. Why should globalization always be a one-way street? Wouldn't it be worth while to establish an Islamic "counter-globalization" when globalization itself is not more than a framework for "permanent Western approaches to export its value-system throughout the world" (Sanjar 1989: 34, 59). The Iranian efforts were thus simple counter-measures to Western pressure.

The „counter-globalization" would be focussed at the Quran and its message i.e. the permanent endeavor of mankind "to respond...by fulfilling both its external project of building a righteous social order and its internal project of drawing humans nearer their Maker" (Eaton 1993: 31). In the process of „counter-globalization" all the questionable elements of Western globalization would be replaced by a genuine Islamic offer based on justice, contentedness and egalitarianism. According to Iranian Muslim thinkers the Islamic world should not tolerate the condescending Western attitude any longer which describes every non-Western model of modernity and/or globality as "localism" or as a revitalization of local sensibilities. On the contrary, the secular materialism of Western modernity with its predominance of reason vis-à-vis ethics and morality should give way to Islamic modernity based on faith, patience, sense of proportion, and compromise. In this sense, „counter-globalization" would not be anti-modern as assumed by many Western critics but an alternative or "co-construction of modernity" (Piscatori/ Eickelman 1996: 192) emphasizing the non-materialist dimension of progress. "Islam...places materialism within a wider context of divine purpose; it also shows the ephemeral nature of a civilization devoid of spiritual content" (Kamal Pasha/ Samatar 1996: 196). The Islamic "counter-globalization" deserves its name since it is directed at the entire globe. It is an attempt "to create at the global level a new *Gemeinschaft*..." (Turner 1991: 178) an attempt to organize the Islamic community, the umma, in a „global state" to fulfill its divine obligation "to lead the world;..." (Issawi 1998: 15).

This is not the place to discuss the practicability of the „counter-globalization" which is questioned even by many Muslims. But the Islamic Republic of Iran

---

[17] Message of Revolution (Islamic Revolution Guard Corps), Teheran 1983, 21, p. 6.

cannot renounce the project since it is one of the main pillars upon which it is based.

4. Summary

Iran's opposition to the West and its set of social, legal, ideological, cultural and behavioral norms and values continues. In this sense, the Islamic republic's leadership is also opposing globalization which is perceived as a one-way street fostering Western dominance all over the world, not simply a paraphrase of imperialism but its perfection.

Due to both interior and exterior reasons the Islamic Republic of Iran cultivates its pretension of constituting the one and only countable alternative to the West and globalization. By proclaiming leadership of the *umma*, Iran puts itself at the center of a counter-globalization in the name of universal Islam.

The heterogeneity, or better, duality of the Iranian leadership originating – more or less by accident – from the course of the revolution was developed into a sophisticated policy. In the framework of this policy, President and government are responsible for moderation, diplomacy and adaptation of Iranian foreign policy goals to international law whereas the supreme leader and the clerical institutions take care that these "official politics" do not deviate from the basic goals of the Islamic revolution. Thus, it did not come as a surprise when Iranian supreme leader Khamenei - in a meeting with 400 veterans of the Iraq-Iran war – declared shortly after President Khatami had condemned the terrorist attacks against the US that Iran will not at all support any Western i.e. American military measure against its Afghan Muslim brothers, and when Khamenei rejected the American formula that everybody who is not with us in this special situation, is against us by insisting instead that Iran is the enemy of terror as well as of the US.

It was not before September 26th, 2001 when the call "margh bar Amrika (death to America)" coming from 400 veterans' throats was transmitted by Radio Tehran.

References:

Afrasiabi, Kamran L. 1994: After Khomeini. New Directions in Iran's Foreign Policy, Boulder.

Alavi, Ahmad al- 1994: Al-Taqiyeh fi Rihab al-'alamein al-Sheikh al-A'zam al-Ansari wa al-Sayyid al-Imam al-Khomeini (Taqiyeh in Sheikh al-Ansari and Imam Khomeini's thoughts), Qom.

Amini, Ehsanollah 1985: Siyasat-e Khareji-ye Hokumat-e Eslami (The foreign policy of the Islamic government), Tehran.

Amirahmadi, Hoshang/ Entessar, Nader 1993: Iranian-Arab Relations in Transition. In: Amirahmadi, Hoshang/ Entessar, Nader (eds.): Iran and the Arab World, London, pp. 1-18.

Amirahmadi, Hoshang 1994: Iran and the Persian Gulf: Strategic Issues and Outlook. In: Zanganeh, Hamid (ed.): Islam, Iran, & World Stability, New York, pp. 110-132.

Anderson, Stuart K. 1994: The Impact of Islamic Fundamentalist Politics within the Islamic Republic of Iran on Iranian State Sponsorship of Transnational Terrorism, Ann Arbor.

Ansari, Mohammad al- 1994: Al-Taqiyeh, Qom.

BBC 1992: Summary of World Broadcasts (SWB), Reading, ME/1300A/8, 10 February 1992.

Brinton, Crane 1965: The Anatomy of Revolution, New York.

Calabrese, John 1994: Revolutionary Horizons; Regional Foreign Policy in Post-Revolutionary Iran, London.

Chubin, Sepehr 1990: Iran and the Persian Gulf States. In: Menashri, David (ed.): The Iranian Revolution and the Muslim World, Boulder, pp. 73-90.

Constitution of the Islamic Republic of Iran, Tehran 1979.

Eaton, Richard M. 1993: Islamic History as Global History. In: Adas, Michael (ed.): Islamic & European Expansion; The Forging of a Global Order, Philadelphia, pp.1-36.

Fuller, Graham E./ Lesser, Ian O. 1995: A Sense of Siege; The Geopolitics of Islam and the West, Boulder.

Ghazvini, Ali 1996: On the foreign policy of Islam: A Search into the Juridical Dimension of Iranian Foreign Policy. In: The Iranian Journal of International Affairs, 7:4, pp. 780-796.

Halliday, Fred 1994: The politics of Islamic Fundamentalism: Iran, Tunisia and the challenge to the secular state. In: Ahmed, Ali S./ Donnan, Hastings (eds.): Islam, Globalization and Postmodernity, London/ New York, pp. 91-113.

Harney, Desmond 1989: The Iranian Revolution Ten Years On. In: Asian Affairs, 20:6, pp. 153-164.

Hunter, Shireen T. 1990: Iran and the World; Continuity in a Revolutionary

Decade, Bloomington.

Issawi, Charles 1998: Cross-Cultural Encounters and Conflicts, Oxford.

Kamal Pasha, Mustafa/ Samatar, Ahmad I. 1996: The Resurgence of Islam. In: Mittelman, J. H. (ed.): Globalization: Critical Reflections, Boulder, pp. 187-202.

Khomeini, Ruhollah 1980: Kashf-e Asrar, Tehran.

Khomeini, Ruhollah 1981: Message to the Pilgrims. In: Algar, Hamid (ed.): Islam and Revolution; Writings and Declarations of Imam Khomeini, Berkeley, pp. 301-305.

Larijani, Mohammad J. 1996: Iran's Foreign Policy: Principles and Objectives. In: The Iranian Journal of International Affairs, 7:4, pp. 754-772.

Linabury, Gary 1992: Ayatollah Khomeini's Islamic legacy. In: Amirahmadi, Hoshang/ Entessar, Nader (eds.): Reconstruction and Regional Diplomacy in the Persian Gulf, London/ New York 1992, pp. 33-44.

Memon, Abdullah 1995: The Islamic Nation; Status & Future of Muslims in the New World Order, Beltsville.

Millward, William G. 1986: The Principles of Foreign Policy and the Vision of World Order expounded by Imam Khomeini and the Islamic Republic of Iran, in: Keddie, Nikkie R./Hooglund, Eric (eds.): The Iranian Revolution and the Islamic Republic, Syracuse, pp. 189-204.

Mohadessin, Mohammad 1993: Islamic Fundamentalism; The new global threat, Washington D.C.

Piscatory, James/ Eickelman, Dale F. 1996: Muslim Politics, Princeton.

Qaderi, Ali 1989: Tarh-e Tahqiq-e Mabani-ye Siyasat-e Khareji-ye Eslam (Research Proposal for the Foundation of Islam's Foreign Policy). In: Majallat-e Siyasat-e Khareji, 8:1, pp. 218-236.

Rajaee, Farhang 1983: Islamic Values and World View. Khomeyni on Man, the State and International Politics, Lanham etc.

Rajaee, Farhang 1990: Iranian Ideology and Worldview: The Cultural Export of Revolution, In: Esposito, John L. (ed.): The Iranian Revolution; Its Global Impact, Miami, pp. 63-80.

Turner, Bryan S. 1991: Politics and Culture in Islamic Globalism. In: Robertson, Roland/ Garrett, W. (eds.): Religion and Global Order, New York, pp.161-181.

Saleem, Musa 1993: The Muslims and the New World Order, London.

Sanjar, Ibrahim 1989: Nofuz-e Amrika dar Iran: Bar-rasi-ye siyasat-e khariji-ye Amrika va ravabet-e ba Iran, Tehran, pp. 33-59.

Shakuri, Ali 1982: Osul-e Siyasat-e Khareji-ye Eslam (Principles of Islam's Foreign Policy). In: Feqh-e Siyasi-ye Eslam (Islam's Political Jurisprudence), Vol. 2, Tehran, 588 pp.

Sick, Gary 1995: Iran: The Adolescent Revolution. In: Journal of International Affairs, 49:1, pp. 145-166.

4

SONJA HEGASY

Double Standards in Reverse. The Debate on Cultural Globalization from an Arab Perspective[1]

1. Introduction

The idea that globalization levels cultural specialties and differences is subject of a heated debate both in academia and in the feuilletons around the globe. Expressions of discomfit and fear of lost identity can be witnessed everywhere. Losers and winners of globalization, apologetics and harsh critics are found in the North as well as in the South. Following, I look at a contribution to the debate by a well-known Egyptian intellectual, Sherif Hetata, who arguably exemplifies a significant position in the broad spectrum of the discussion on cultural globalization. Even secular authors like him or Gamil Mattar, Burhan Ghalyun, Samir Amin, Ahmed Abdallah display a disdain of globalization processes in conferences and monographs which is reflected in the Arab press. I deliberately leave out the discussion on economic and social effects of globalization to reduce the inflationary use of this term slightly. But also within the debate on cultural globalization there are quite different definitions from McDonaldization to hybridization and its secondary literature is vast. Nevertheless I propose to look at a critical position towards cultural globalization which is significant within the range of reactions to globalization in the Arab World. I apply a shorter temporal definition for the term 'globalization' which regards it as a process beginning at the end of the 20th century due to a third technological revolution which allows for an even "faster exceleration of places, peoples and processes" (Giddens) after the invention of steam power and the personal computer.

I chose an author with a Western education (psychologist), someone who is economically well-off, who has no restrictions of movement, who has access to an English-speaking audience and who does not adhere to a religious group. Still he writes in a volume on 'The Cultures of Globalization' edited by Fredric Jameson and Masao Miyoshi: "What the World Bank calls *structural adjustment* is a potential economic genocide" (Jameson/Miyoshi 1998: 276). Sherif Hetata designs a picture of the "masters of the global economy" (Hetata 1998: 276) who invade Egyptian society to a degree even he himself cannot refute. He claims that an economic substructure subordinates every societal area to the logic of market capitalism. Culture serves these masters to continuously expand the market and to destroy any resistance. I will argue that this debate is not determined by Arab culture or religion but by the Fanonian rhetoric of the "wretched of the earth". I intend to extract the main arguments against globalization and try to trace them

---

[1] A text read before and after the 11th of September

back to their origins. Therefore, I propose to concentrate on Hetata's text and quote it a little bit more extensively in order to substantiate my argument.

Originally, I regarded this essay as a contribution to the debate centering around the question whether globalization unifies or heterogenizes different cultures of the world. Reading Hetata's text again after September 11th, 2001 can give us insights into a better understanding of the reactions emanating from the Middle East after the attacks.[2]

2. Globalization-Americanization

Sherif Hetata begins his contribution 'Dollarization, Fragmentation, and God' with a personal account of his youth in Egypt under British colonial rule: "Educated in an English school, I discovered that my English teachers looked down on us. We learned Rudyard Kipling by heart, praised the glories of the British empire, followed the adventures of Kim in India, imbibed the culture of British supremacy, and sang carols on Christmas night" (Hetata 1998: 273). As a young medical student it was not difficult for him to discover the connection between health and poverty, colonialism, class, race and the price of cotton. But the male authorities - father, president, god - forbid him to make such connections. Today, Hetata continues, we are witnesses of an unknown concentration of capital and technology in the hands of a few in the North. This accumulation depends less on natural resources or labor (which the South could easily provide) but on technology based on the intensive use of knowledge (which is - according to his argument - not accessible for the South).

Here, we encounter the first common reasoning of the debate: The new economic world order is made responsible for the exclusion of the Arab world from knowledge-based technologies ignoring that most Arab states deliberately either started very late or very selectively to introduce for instance national access to the internet for reasons of control over the media.[3] Such a justification leaves out the fact that in contrast to natural resources, knowledge-based technologies are relatively independent of ways of transportation, the climate or political upheavals and therefore offer especially to developing countries an economy which is based much less on incalculable risks. High-value-added software can be produced in Banglahore as well as in Silicon Valley. And the implosion of communication costs through the internet opens up many opportunities for developing

---

[2] I presented a shorter version of this paper twice: once in June 2000 at the 'Institut für Weltgesellschaft' of the University of Bielefeld and on October 14th, 2001 at the 'Internationales Zentrum' of the University of Tübingen. Both times I was very grateful for the questions and remarks by the audience. I would also like to thank Jan-Georg Deutsch from the Centre for Oriental Studies in Berlin for his comments.
[3] To boost Internet use in Egypt, Hosni Mubarak supported a nation-wide project with free Internet access since January 2002. Egypt started to have full Internetservices since 1993. Today, half a million users are registered. (FAZ, 12.2.2002) In the whole Arab world the number edges towards four millions (http://www.nua.ie/surveys/how_many_online/index.html).

countries especially when the next generation of mobile phones will be available which allows easy access to the internet without a complete telephone infrastructure. But Hetata - as many Arab authors - only sees a free market spreading which plunders developing countries like the Spanish Armada or the slave trade under innocent terms as: aid, free trade, loans, development etc. Therefore, he even calls the SAPs genocide.[4]

In order to illustrate how the media manipulate global consumer behavior, Hetata lets us know that his own son[5] - who is a film director - started at the age of 25 to smoke two packs of Marlboro a day. Likewise, he is shocked about himself, because he started at the age of 71 to wear Jeans and hear rock music. We might wonder what is the essence of such a statement in Jameson's volume? Does he want to tell the reader that his education failed or that neo-colonialism cannot be defeated or that Marlboro tastes better then the local Egyptian brand Cleopatra or that even leftist artists like to surround themselves with Western status symbols? At the latest since Horkheimer and Adorno (Adorno/ Horkheimer 1944) we know of the artificial creation of needs through advertisement and television as a means of compensating for one's own alienation. But for Hetata the global Americanization in its quest for more and more consumers is responsible:

"To expand the global market, increase the number of consumers, make sure that they buy what is sold, develop needs that conform to what is produced, and develop the fever of consumerism, culture must play a role in developing certain values, patterns of behavior, visions of what is happiness and success in the world, attitudes toward sex and love. Culture must model a global consumer." (Hetata 1998: 277)

Logically, if Hetata does not claim the freedom and enlightenment to choose and decide for himself which products he likes to eat or hear, he does not grant this right to anybody else, not speaking of those with lesser education. He, for example, gives the account of a marriage in the Egyptian country side which was very "un-traditional" with the bride wearing a white wedding dress and the couple eating a wedding cake after driving around in a hired Peugeot car. Hetata does not regard this as an increase in choices for the Egyptian peasant as well as for the American peasant, who can now decide whether he wants to play Elvis at his wedding or Cheb Khaled. He does not recognize the emergence of an innovative hybrid culture. Globalization-Americanization is not only something which is

---

[4] It is of course well known that the classical Structural Adjustment Programs (SAPs) first hit the poor since they cannot survive without state subsidies but we are not talking of processes comparable to the genocide in Ruanda or other recent systematic massacres.
[5] Born in 1965 in New York Atef Hetata is the son of Sherif Hetata and the famous medical doctor as well as writer Nawal Saadawi. In 2000 he directed the film 'al-Abwab al-mukhlaka' (Closed Doors).

imposed from the outside but also absorbed from inside. This is part of the truth which Arab intellectuals refuse in their discourse on cultural globalization.[6]

Hetata cites several studies in order to underlie his argument of the destructive effect of television on children in Europe and the US: "...all this change in the notion of beauty, of femininity, of celebration, of happiness, of prestige, of progress happened to my peasant friend and his bride in one generation. The culprit, or the benevolent agent, depending on how you see it, was television [...]. Through these TV advertisements, the young boy or girl will have assimilated a whole set of values and behavioral patterns, of which he or she is not aware, of course. They become a part of his or her psychological (emotional and mental) makeup." (Hetata 1998: 278) "To kill, one has to learn at an early age, or at least that's the best way. If you are brought up to be human and kind, the chances are that you will not kill later or unless under very exceptional circumstances. The cartoons shown to children in the United States are one example of how you can develop a culture of violence with all it implies." (Hetata 1998: 279).

I mention such concrete examples from Hetata's text to deepen our understanding of one of the most strongly and widely felt sentiment among many Arab people. Hetata goes on to accuse the commercial media of transforming women in every corner of Egypt into sex objects. To lump the reduction of women to sex objects together with the effects of cultural globalization seems to me quite a-historical. The institutionalization of the monogamous family and the control over female sexuality through the invention of forbidding pre-marital sex to women has much more to do with the definition of women as lavish sex objects than the selling of Western beauty products in the Delta since the 1990s a.d. The introduction of sexual double standards within the family is not a contemporary phenomenon.

Hetata's next attack aims at French publishing houses whom he portrays as serving Northern cultural hegemonic interests. "French publishing houses are past masters at this art, aided and abetted unfortunately by North African Arabs or Africans living in France. The modern novel produced in the South, especially if it deals with the problem of our age, with the reality behind relations between North and South, with gender and class, is not considered suitable for cultural consumption in the North. The area of translation should be exposed to serious and systematic cultural studies in conferences, in academia, and in scholastic research." (Hetata 1998: 286). The defamation of Arab communities living outside of the Arab world is a recurrent theme in the anti-globalization debate. But it leaves out that many (esp. young) talented Arab writers are forbidden to publish in Arab countries or hindered to write in Arabic so the only way we know of

---

[6] Here he is of course not alone: Every country has its globalization critics like Benjamin Barber in the US, Viviane Forrester in France or Maria Mies in Germany who follow this line of thinking.

them or their works is through Western publishing houses. World literature and world music are conserving some of the best contemporary Arab artists for the global audience (Hanan al-Sheikh, Ahdaf Soueif, Naguib Mahfuz, Algerian raï singers or Iranian filmmakers). One of the most famous novels by Mahfuz ('The Children of our Quarter') is still black-listed in Egypt due to objections by the Azhar university.[7] Hanan al-Sheikh's 'Women of Sand and Myrrh' is not available in many Arab countries and Ahdaf Soueif has only a selection of short stories and articles available in Arabic thanks to the General Egyptian Book Organization. Still her two lengthy and literary renowned novels 'In the Eye of the Sun' and 'Map of Love' which has been shortlisted for the 1999 Booker Prize are not obtainable in Arabic yet. Whom Edward Said deemed as "one of the most extraordinary chroniclers of sexual politics now writing" has not found a translator and this does not seem to be only a financial question. Rather Ahdaf is accused of being immoral and of tarnishing the image of Egypt - the main argument given by any ruling elite in many Third World countries when being confronted with critical cultural works.

To make sure that all of these works can be seen, read and heard in Egypt and not only at the American University in Cairo which is regarded as the imperialist thorn in the heart of Cairo a local elite which includes and not excludes these creations per definition (with the pretext that these authors are writing in English or meanwhile living abroad) is needed. This experience is no longer a single one but shared by a whole generation of young Muslims who generate their own narratives.[8]

Cultural globalization not does not reduce cultural production and choices even if Arab critics want to make us and their societies believe so. Local cultures are being globalized but not unified. How can we otherwise explain global trends which did not have the support of global merchants or television channels like Raï-music or open-source software? These phenomenon do not appear in Hetata's arguments. Globalization has brought about a geographical as well as mental intrusion of the peripheries into the metropolis. Trespassing boundaries is its first and foremost characteristic. Or as Wolf Lepenies put it: "There are only hybrid cultures. This fact alone makes the clash of civilizations prophecy appear unrealistic." (Lepenies 1997: 12) Denying blended cultures and one's own contribution to a globalized world rather has a self-destructing effect. What Edward Said calls "adversarial internationalization" is an unintended creation springing

---

[7] This does of course not mean that it is not available in nearly every Egyptian household in an edition from Beirut or other Arab cities.
[8] It is no accident that recent films by young Muslim directors often tell us the story of expatriate communities in France (al-Medina, 2001 by Youssef Nasrallah; Wesh wesh, qu'est-ce qui se passe?, 2002 by Rabah Ameur Zaïmeche), the US (America so beautiful, 2002 by Babak Shokrian) or Canada (L'Ange de Goudron, 2002 by Denis Chouinard).

out of a conflicting encounter between two adversaries: the post-colonial world and the quasi-imperial world. The former enemies have now become rivals. The result is a cultural amalgam of scholarly works posing some of the most interesting contemporary intellectual challenges. Quite in contrast to Hetata, Said proudly takes up the position of a "third world intellectual" living in the West who has been "deeply affected by the remarkable outpouring of literature and scholarship emanating from the postcolonial world, a locale no longer "one of the dark places of earth" in Conrad's famous description, but once again the site of vigorous cultural effort." (Said 1990: 28, 29) The emergence of the post-colonial as an authoritative one is a part of the globalization processes which cannot be denied. In the course of events following the attacks on the WTC and the Pentagon, intellectuals and artists from the so-called "periphery" have e.g. become political authorities and their opinion is in demand. One just needs to remember the debate triggered off through the article 'The Algebra of Infinite Justice' by the Indian writer Arundhati Roy in the German daily *Frankfurter Allgemeine Zeitung* commenting on the attacks of September 11th (FAZ, 28.9.2001).[9] Roy dared to write that Osama Ben Laden is the dark twin of George Bush but one should not forget that neither of the two is more acceptable than the other: "But who is Osama Bin Laden really? Let me rephrase that. What is Osama Bin Laden? He's America's family secret. He is the American President's dark *doppelgänger*. The savage twin of all that purports to be beautiful and civilized. He has been sculpted from the spare rib of a world laid to waste by America's foreign policy: its gunboat diplomacy, its nuclear arsenal, its vulgarly stated policy of "full spectrum dominance", its chilling disregard for non-American lives, its barbarous military interventions, its support for despotic and dictatorial regimes, its merciless economic agenda that has munched through the economies of poor countries like a cloud of locusts." (Roy 2001) In Germany, this provoked several critical as well as sympathetic responses among them a comment in a popular magazine by the most famous German newscaster, Ulrich Wickert, who in the course of events had to excuse himself for his position on German television. Here we can see the intrusion of the periphery right into the center of every living room.

The Egyptian writer Ahdaf Soueif gives us another example of this path. After the attacks she was asked to write four lengthy articles for *The Guardian*. On September 15th, 2001 she wrote that "the nation that once said "give me your poor, your weak, your hungry" needs to look at itself through the eyes of the

---

[9] It is important to note that Roy voiced her opinion in the conservative FAZ and not in some leftist newspaper with a much smaller circulation. In 1996 Roy had published her first novel 'The God of Small Things' which instantly became a global success. It was translated into 18 languages and awarded with the prestigious Booker Prize for Fiction. By January 1999 3,5 million copies had been sold worldwide. In India though the novel was censured and regarded as an attack on public morality. Currently, Roy is facing a court trial in india.

world's dispossessed." She heavily criticized the US by stating: "You could almost say that US officialdom, the media and Hollywood dreamed this nightmare into reality." Words which cannot be classified as "what the West wants to hear" as Hetata reproaches Arab intellectuals in the West. On October 9th, she explained in *The Guardian* what kind of a TV station al-Jazeera was. On November 6th, she was send from London to Cairo to report about Arab reactions towards Tony Blair and the British engagement in the American "War against Terrorism" where she again countered the image that Arab citizens had been rejoicing over what had happened in New York. Finally, in December 2001 she was send to the occupied territories to write a two piece article on the Palestinian situation. Although her voice had been audible in the arts for quite some time[10], she only started to articulate a current political point of view after September 11th.

There are few who defend Soueif's writing against allegations that they are "not part of Arab literature at all" (*Cairo Times* 30.4.1998) and who see her contributions in the end as inherently Egyptian - a hybrid result of a life which is not a singular experience any longer but which reiterates the biography of a certain class. Part of this experience includes undoubtedly writing in English rather than in Arabic.

The competitiveness of non-Western cultural products is rising to a degree which is being perceived as a challenge to the Western cultural canon. The center is regarded as no longer able to generate innovation alone. "Thus a literature has now come into being that can no longer be traced to established traditions of reading and writing. It is a new kind of cross-border 'creative-writing' that is forcing its way from the periphery into the centers of the West. It is penetrating the Anglo-American megacities and the trans-national metropolitan areas - New York, Toronto and London - with their aggressive mixed cultures." (Lepenies 1997: 10). The powerful body of post-colonial literature testifies of the periphery's growing self-confidence and its vivacity. Lepenies' argument that since the Booker Prize went to Salman Rushdie in 1981, "the prize was won by two Australians, a half-Maori, a South African, a woman author of Polish descent, a Nigerian, and a Japanese ..." might be a weak argument since these writers are often enough regarded as token representatives of the Third World and the awarding of such prizes is regarded as dependent on a certain distribution key but it is at least a hint to the productivity of the "peripheral cultures".

Hetata carries out another intellectual spin when it comes to analyzing the popular Islamist movements in the region. He rightly identifies them as protest movements against the cultural hegemony of the West. But paradoxically the leaders of the fundamentalist groups are in his point of view also allies of the

---

[10] Her first narrative was published in 1983.

global economy: "They propagate a culture that believes in fate, in obedience, in not questioning, in believing that happiness or unhappiness, wealth or poverty are apportioned by Allah, and so people should accept whatever lot is theirs. What better ally does the global economy want? And if they come to power in Algeria or in Egypt after a period of adjustment, just as before, all will be well." (Hetata 1998: 283)

This is a surprising hypothesis since Europe supported to stop a democratic process so fundamentalists could not come to power in Algeria which was re-garded as a confirmation of Western anti-Muslim sentiments. Hetata even sees the fact that Sheikh Omar Abdel Rahman is - as he puts it - "safely in jail here in the States away from the clutches of Mubarak's police" as part of the global coalition between globalization-americanization and Muslim fundamentalism.

According to Hetata the process of globalization divides, confuses and fragments people. "They can think, but only in the way that the global powers want them to think. The global economy, the global culture, must exercise an undivided rule. And if people think, they must think in a way that will keep them from finding out what they have in common." (Hetata 1998: 283) If we take the internet as the materialization of globalization, we encounter the opposite: People are not di-vided, confused and fragmented - they virtually come together from all over the world to send 100.000 e-mails within 24 hours to protest against a human rights abuse. It offers them the possibility to find people with the same health problem all over the world and to exchange solutions within minutes or to unite in order to increase the pressure on national politics.

If these processes are so disturbing, what are Hetata's proposals for resistance? Edward Said rightly pointed to the important scholarly endeavour originating in the Indian subcontinent under the heading of *Subaltern Studies*, to denominate a whole area of research designed to decolonize science. One may smile about French radio stations which are obliged since 1996 to play not more than 60% of foreign music but here a country resists cultural americanization (as it does as well in other spheres) and it fights for a part of its cultural peculiarity and inde-pendence. This proves that their is a consensus between the political elite and society to introduce counter-measures in order to protect the cultural heritage. A country needs an elite which recognizes the value of its cultural products and sees the necessity to interfere into the market. Why should a country in the South not introduce measures of cultural protectionism? It is not a question of costs.

3. Where is Africa?

Cultural double talk *à la* Hetata looks as follows: He starts with criticizing Afri-can art festivals in the North accusing them of being "disparate samples brought to entertain and delight without any reference to the societies, the problems, the miseries they represent and the factors behind all this, including relations with the North." Such art festivals together with so-called world literature which is being chosen for translation are in his eyes good examples of how the North is only interested in displaying the "exotic" and the "strange" (Hetata 1998: 286). Half a page later he proudly mentions that a film of his son won prices in Spain, France, England, Canada and elsewhere. Again, we discover that the references he chooses are the centers of the Northern hemisphere. Why does he not mention the film festivals in Ouagadougou, Alexandria, Cairo or Cartage? Are they not distinguished enough? Hetata freely chooses the Western metropolis as his scale and overarching framework deliberately leaving out what is happening in the South. He complains that there is no South-South cooperation but inconsistently orients himself to the North. Not only that he misses out on the importance of Arab and African cultural production, but he reproaches those Arab artists who display their work in the North as token Arabs who "help the North to appropriate the culture of the South, instead of letting the "other" in the South speak for themselves." (Hetata 1998: 289) He ascribes no role to those whom Peter Berger called the 'transnational intelligentsia'. Hetata just identifies them as parasitic intermediaries who serve the Western *goût*.

Why does Egypt only import American soaps and no African or Latin American ones? Why can we see the filmfestival of Ouagadougou in Berlin but not in Cairo? Why are there no "authentic" African art festivals in Cairo if there exists such a thing? I propose that the answer is: because there is a much more vibrant interest in the South from the North than between Southern countries even if the Northern interest is only *à la mode* at the time.

In times of shifting real and virtual boundaries, Africa is no longer a continent but a concept as Ulrich Beck argues: "Africa is not a fixed geographical magnitude, not a separate place on the globe, but a *transnational idea and the staging of that idea..* [...] Where is Africa to be found in a world society with porous frontiers? In the ruins that the colonial masters have left behind in Africa? In the big-city shapes of an only half-modernized Africa? In the African four-star hotels? On organized safaris? In the 'back to the roots' hopes and illusions of Black Americans? In the books about Africa that are written in Western universities? In the Caribbean? [...] This Africa [the African carnival in Notting Hill], or counter-Africa, is in the strictest sense an 'imagined community'; it serves to break down and overcome the alienation of Afro-Caribbean groups in Britain. We could say that 'there is Africa' in Notting Hill." (Beck 2000: 27) It is not merely some token-Africans ingratiating themselves with Western images as Hetata posits but a community which tries to answer a question, which is gaining urgency in the processes of globalization: "What and where is 'Africa' within a transnational social space?" (Beck 2000: 28)

4. Self-Exclusion from the Global Village

Rudolf Stichweh showed that the rise of the term 'exclusion' in the 1990s occupied two theoretical concepts: It replaced theories which use 'class' in order to describe social inequalities and it took the place of the concept of poverty. Different degrees of sharing social goods are related to graded degrees of exclusion from society. Stichweh points out that poverty is not only meant economically but also in terms of closeness to the decision making centers. Someone who is poor has no access to the respective centers and therefore is excluded which perpetuates his or her marginal position. Authors like Hetata use the term 'exclusion' in this new sense describing their societies as being excluded by the process of globalization which results in poverty and the withering away of one's own voice. But Stichweh refutes the idea that whole societies are being excluded from the world society. He uses a physical analogy in order to illustrate the connection between exclusion and global society. The image of a universe with 'black holes' is intended to counter the idea of included and excluded societies as a whole. He proposes to look at globalized functional systems which are being fed from everywhere (economy, literature, law) and in each of which we can find areas of exclusion, i.e. black holes, but not whole societies which are excluded in all their diversity.

Furthermore, Hetata's approach leaves out that the term 'exclusion' always denotes interaction. One needs to ask more specifically who excludes the Arab world from the global society? Thus one discovers that it is a process with actors on both sides of the divide, in the North and the South, with progress and setbacks. The role of the news channel *al-Jazeera* during the American "War on Terrorism" has proven that Arab journalists can establish a counter-public even in times of "globalization-americanization at war". Today *al-Jazeera* is part of (i.e. included into) the global media players. Attempts to discredit *al-Jazeera* after having shown videos of Osama Ben Laden have not been fruitful. No journalist working on the Arab world may from now on disregard its authoritative voice. The satellite telephone as part of the technological revolution connected with globalization has catapulted news reporting from an Arab perspective into every American home. Exclusion may therefore actively and critically be countered. Disregarding these phenomena does not prompt exclusion but self-exclusion. Constituting identity through self-exclusion is a widespread form of reaction, but one should be aware of the prize a society is paying for this strategy. Moreover, the rhetoric of self-exclusion is a dubious intellectual exercise. It partly prepared the ground for the nearly unanimous reaction in the Arab World regarding the attacks on September 11th, 2001. Talking of a 'society under attack', Arab public opinion was instantly thinking of itself and not of the New Yorkers.

The reiteration of the theories of dependency, world capitalism and imperialism does not only indicate a strong neglect of internal actors and factors, but also disregards a whole set of literature which emerged since the eighties, written by ardent former proponents of the dependency school, who revised their own model of a binary world divided into center and periphery (see Menzel 1992, Senghaas 1982). To reproduce this discourse of the sixties without recognizing the new dimensions of globalization furthermore offers a convenient explanation for stagnation and exploitation to the authoritarian regimes in the Middle East. Intellectuals become willing henchmen of the ruling elite leaving their skeptical and critical attitude from a certain distance aside. Anti-globalization seems to serve as a new form of nationalism which ingratiates with power and authority.

My argument is not that globalization-winners may not sympathize with globalization-losers, but that opinion leaders should not reproduce the old dichotomy of center and periphery since this division no longer exists. Such a discourse orients public opinion towards a fake enemy.

5. Digression

I am not opposed to Hetata's mode of intervention but I find it difficult to accept that he does what he rejects at the same time, namely using the West as supreme frame of reference and denouncing anybody else who does so from the bride of his farmer friend to any Arab intellectual in Paris. I miss consistency in Hetata's writings when he measures his works or the oeuvre of his son in accordance with Western criteria while downgrading any other Arab intellectual who expresses him- or herself in the West. Furthermore, Hetata's dichotomy cannot attribute any positive role to Western cultural mediators even if they use their freedom to publish Arab writers whose works are forbidden or disregarded in their homeland. Finally, I think it is a failure to leave out strategies of resistance and alternative cultural policies, be it in the field of cinema, television and literature or simply a call for boycotting Western fora as other Arab intellectuals do.[11]

Then again I ask myself whether he might only be doing what Edward Said called breaking the "code of politesse and ritual calmness" imposed by Western research norms because Hetata voices an urgent political concern: "...scholarship and politics are more frankly connected because all these writers, as intellectuals from the Third or non-Western world, feel themselves to be writing as representatives of a political freedom and accomplishment as yet unfulfilled, blocked, postponed. To misinterpret the historical force of such statements, discourses, and interventions from the Third World, to call them (as Conor Cruise O'Brien once did) the whine for sympathy of formerly colonized peoples, to dismiss them as emotional and subjective *cris de cœur* of strenuous activists and partisan politicians rather then the "objective writings" of real scholars, is to attenuate

---

[11] See e.g. Fatema Mernissi's booklet "Why I will not go West in 2002".

their force, to misrepresent their value, to dismiss their enormous contribution to knowledge." (Said 1990: 47) Hetata goes into the same direction when he portrays himself as "incapable of understanding cultural processes and the role culture plays if I do not locate it in the power struggle, in the movement of gender and class, rulers and people." (Hetata 1998: 284) But I very much object to his exemption of local elites and their extremely ambivalent role. And I would like to ask him whether he is really identifying power and powerlessness in the right place?

6. Conclusion

After 200 years of interaction and integration between Arab and Western societies, a majority of Arab intellectuals now displays a distinct resistance against globalization. This position is credible out of four reasons: It comes in a time of severe identity crises which demands for a clear demarcation line and defining oneself as the victim of a global onslaught helps to rally people together. In this context it is also a resort to a new form of nationalism. It reflects a paradox feeling of refusal of Western cultural products which is combined with the desire to share in. Finally, it reflects a "clash of non-synchronous processes" (Willms, SZ 18.10.2001). Meanwhile their own position reflects the hybridization of cultures which they criticizes so heavily. But the transnational identity which has emerged and transferred part of the Arab societies into the global context is ignored by them. In my point of view, they turn a blind eye to the gains of cultural globalization and the richness of recent Arab production. And in doing so they continue a project of the West which they refute deeply inside namely the exclusion of modern Arab and Muslim artists. Although they could feel represented by "cultural ambassadors", like Ahdaf Soueif and others, a feeling of deprivation prevails which breeds a defensive stance. The majority of authors participating in the debate on cultural globalization dispose of a considerable neglect of the reality of cultural production. They are not willing to identify their own role in this process or see themselves and other citizens from the South as actors. Alternatives or strategies of resistance are rarely proposed, even though the authors regard themselves as enlighteners. The frame of reference is not the marginalized Arab or Muslim, but the dominated poor.

It is a "self-enclosed approach", as Peter Berger rightly remarked and one needs to add 'self-excluding' and 'self-contradictory' as well, which is "immune to empirical refutation". Berger characterized this approach as "shaped by a particular mixture of neo-Marxism and so-called literary theory, which began as an intellectual fashion in France and has become a dreary orthodoxy in American academe. There was not a single dissenting voice [in Jameson's volume, SH]. This makes for exhaustion in any reader not already committed to this approach."

The Arab debate centers around neo-colonialism, anti-Americanism and anti-Zionism rather then global diffusion, diversity and decentralization. It disposes of a cultural pessimism which goes back to leftist intellectuals in the sixties. We encounter the old lamentation over violence on television, the power of the multi-national cooperations, the misleading promises of advertisements or the seduction of the youth, but no debate about cultural globalization and its characteristics. Hitherto unknown phenomena, which have emerged in the course of globalization, like the "super-powered individual" (according to Friedman individuals like Osama Bin Laden) or the exchange between people regardless of social, geographical or economical barriers, are neglected by these authors. Especially young Muslim women experience the later phenomenon, when they for the first time in their life talk to a male person without patriarchal supervision via internet. They welcome this transcending communication - and it is neither in Egypt nor in Saudi Arabia a rare pass-time.

The asymmetric picture drawn by these critics is counter-emancipatory since there seems to be no way out of globalization-Americanization although local groups in other regions of the world effectively protect their culture. The lumping of both terms together is the crux of understanding the problem. Americanization can be resisted; globalization not.

The role of local elites as part of a movement in the region which counters the negative ecological, social and cultural effects of globalization is left out - quite to the contrary this elite only gives an account of its own "un-voluntary" merger with American consumer behavior. The simplistic polemic about Americanization moreover neglects the esthetic and ethnic heterogeneity of American mass culture itself. What is called 'glocalization' by Roland Robertson and others shows that "no country transfers American imports, without adapting it to its own cultural conditions. The idea that 'Americanization' simply means the leveling of cultural differences is false. It is rather a process of never-ending differentiation of cultural facts - though certainly on the basis of a universal standardization." (R. Herzinger in DIE ZEIT, 2.1.2000; transl. SH)

What is attacked and rightly so are the double standards in the West which have undermined any moral credibility and authority of the West: "In 1996, Madeleine Albright, then the US Ambassador to the United Nations, was asked on national television what she felt about the fact that 500,000 Iraqi children had died as a result of US economic sanctions. She replied that it was "a very hard choice," but that all things considered, "we think the price is worth it." Albright never lost her job for saying this. She continued to travel the world representing the views and aspirations of the US government. More pertinently, the sanctions against Iraq remain in place. Children continue to die. So here we have it. The equivocating distinction between civilization and savagery, between the 'massacre of innocent people' or, if you like, 'a clash of civilizations' and 'collateral damage'. The sophistry and fastidious algebra of Infinite Justice. How many dead Iraqis will it take to make the world a better place? How many dead Afghans for every dead American? How many dead children for every dead man? How many dead mujahideen for each dead investment banker?" (Roy 24.9.2001)

But the answer to this should not be 'double standards in reverse', as I have called this essay. I think that a majority of Arab intellectuals fuel an anti-globalization/ Americanization sentiment with intellectually dishonest arguments when it comes to cultural production. For one, they leave out how local cultural production is treated in the region and how it sees light through Western media. And secondly, they personally make use of globalization processes without giving credit to them. Many of them depict globalization as cultural imperialism. This consensus clearly emerged after the September 11th events. They were interpreted as a (justified) result of a merciless globalization process.[12] The attacks generated admiration not because of malicious joy but because people felt that someone was mastering globalization here in all its aspects: technically by the elegance of the planes, economically by speculating at the New York Stock exchange and culturally through "their" elite students who had successfully studied in the West. In this sense, the fact that Mohammed Atta and his companions had blended in so well in German and US-American society and had even obtained honorary degrees plays an important role in understanding the common reaction of the Arab streets. Reading Hetata's text again after September 11th, this paradox and bitter feeling towards processes which one is not sure whether they in- or exclude oneself, stands out even clearer.

I know that by now I have posited several normative statements but still I very much hope to enter into a dialogue with Dr. Sherif Hetata even if some of my arguments are formulated at point range. Not from a scientific but from a political point of view, I ask myself whether it would not be more appropriate to defend Egypt's rich hybrid culture rather than ignoring it. Cross-cultural encounters and trespassing boundaries are frequent and forceful in the Arab world.[13] There are reasons to be afraid of globalization, indeed, but these are not the reasons which Hetata wants us to believe. Strategies of resistance can be manifold and are surely not restricted to industrialized countries.

---

[12] One just needs to remember that in the beginning the anti-globalization movement was among the possible suspects for the attacks.
[13] In dealing with the problems of female Arab writers who publish in the West, Amal Amireh writes: "Even though reviewers tend to represent whatever Arab women writer they happen to be reviewing as a "lone voice" and a victim of Arab censorship, there is really no dearth in talent. The literary historian Joseph Zeidan lists 480 Arab women writing between the 1880s and the 1980s. Last year [1995], 150 women writers and 26 publishers from throughout the Arab world converged on Cairo for the first Arab Women Book Fair, which exhibited more than 1500 titles." (Amireh 1996).

References

Adorno, Theodor/ Horkheimer, Max 1991/1944: Dialektik der Aufklärung. Philosophische Fragmente, Frankfurt/ Main.

Amin, Samir/ Ghaliun, Burhan 1999: Kultur der Globalisierung und Globalisierung der Kultur, Damaskus.

Amireh, Amal 1996: Publishing in the West: Problems and Prospects for Arab Women Writers. In: al Jadid, 2:1,
www.aljadid.com/features/ 0210amireh.html

Ashcroft, Bill et al. 1989: The Empire Writes Back. Theory and Practice in Post-Colonial Literatures, London.

Beck, Ulrich 1997/ 2000: What is Globalization?, Cambridge.

Berger, Peter 1999: In the Faculty Club. In: The Times Literary Supplement 5029:8.

Friedman, Thomas 1999: The Lexus and the Olive Tree, New York.

Fürtig, Henner (ed.) 2001: Abgrenzung und Aneignung in der Globalisierung: Asien, Afrika und Europa seit dem 18. Jahrhundert, Berlin.

Gosh, Amitav 1996: The Calcutta Syndrome, New Delhi.

Hegasy, Sonja 2001: Globalisierung und Technologietransfer im Nahen Osten. In: Henner Fürtig (ed.): Islamische Welt und Globalisierung: Aneignung, Abgrenzung, Gegenentwürfe, Würzburg, pp. 251-271.

Hetata, Sherif 1998: *Dollarization, Fragmentation, and God.* In: Fredric Jameson/ Masao Miyoshi (eds.): The Cultures of Globalization, Durham, pp. 273-290.

Jameson, Fredric/ Miyoshi, Masao (eds.) 1998: The Cultures of Globalization, Durham.

Al-Kholy, Ossama (ed.) 1998: The Arabs and Globalization, Beirut.

Lepenies, Wolf 1997: Has the Europeanisation of the World Ended? New Challenges for the Old Continent. In: D+C 5, pp. 8-12.

Mattar, Gamil 1999: *Globalization... Unavoidable and Stupid* (Arabic) In: Wighat Nadhar 9:Juli, pp. 46-52.

Menzel, Ulrich 1992: Das Ende der Dritten Welt und das Scheitern der großen Theorie, Frankfurt/ Main.

Roy, Arundhati 1996: The God of Small Things, London.

Roy, Arundhati 2001: The Algebra of Infinite Justice, New Dehli, 24.9.2001. published in *Frankfurter Allgemeine Zeitung* under the tile 'Wut ist der Schlüssel', 28.9.2001.

Said, Edward 1990: Third World Intellectuals and Metropolitan Culture. In: Raritan: A Quarterly Review IX: 3, pp. 27-50.

Senghaas, Dieter 1982: Von Europa lernen. Entwicklungsgeschichtliche Betrachtungen, Frankfurt/ Main.

Soueif, Ahdaf 1995/1983: Aisha, London.

Soueif, Ahdaf 1992: In the Eye of the Sun, London.

Soueif, Ahdaf 1999: Map of Love, London.

Stichweh, Rudolf 1997: Inklusion/Exklusion, funktionale Differenzierung und die Theorie der Weltgesellschaft. In: Soziale Systeme 3:1, pp. 123-136.

5

IVESA LÜBBEN

Globalization and the Rediscovery of *Morality* – Some Remarks on the Reconstruction of Popular State Discourse in Third World States. The Case of Egypt.

1. Introductory remarks

Discussing the notion of *morality* within the context of the discourse of *globalization* one could expect two things: That the following reflections deal with aspects of cultural, moral-based responses to a presumed danger of foreign elements which infiltrate autochthon national cultures and value-systems, or that it will examine local reactions to the uniformity of the global consumerists culture that has been described as the MacDonaldization of the world (Barber 1996). However, the focus of this essay will be on another, sometimes neglected aspect of globalization: How authoritarian Third World or Middle Eastern rentier-states use cultural notions to reconstruct their legitimatory discourse in order to counterbalance the undermining of their power through global processes. In this sense the following research is not dealing with culture, but with power techniques, or in other words: with a mechanism with which the state tries to achieve a minimum of ideological consent among different social strata or political currents. The ideological hegemony of the state has always been an important factor in stabilizing state-power which in the long run and even under the most repressive regimes can never be based on force alone.

Any discursive strategy of the state, however, is linked to culture. State discourses borrow from existing intellectual and popular, political and religious discourses. They integrate cultural symbols and rituals, refer to existing value systems, develop them, regroup them, reformulate them, or drop them if they are no longer convenient. They integrate new concepts in order to facilitate social or political alliances, integrate forces and exclude others from the social consensus, and to give legitimacy to their own power. The following presentation is an attempt to explore this idea around the concept of *morality* that crystallized as a central notion in the Egyptian legitimatory discourse at the turn of the millenium. Up till now Egypt claims to be an important intellectual center of the Middle East. Therefore ideological developments in Egypt might be indicative for other Middle Eastern rentier-states as well, although this still has to be proven or refuted in other case studies.

Although Egypt - unlike the Gulf states - does not depend on oil-revenues as an exclusive source of income, it still is a typical Middle Eastern rentier-state[1]

---

[1] For the theoretical discussion about the *Rentier-state* see Schmid (1991).

which is affected by the integration into global structures in a very specific way, as we shall see. Egypt's main financial resources originate from non-productive and non-renewable foreign transfers: Oil, Suez-Canal revenues, tourism, transfers of Egyptian labor-emigrants, and foreign aid. Egypt receives second to Israel the highest western aid per capita. Egypt went through a series of structural reform programs in the 1990s that implied the privatization of most of former state enterprises, of which many were eventually closed down, an agrarian counter-reform which replaced customary hereditary tenancy with limited contracts of lease, and the liberalization of housing. As a consequence, hundreds of thousands of workers lost their jobs and an estimated 900 000 peasants had to leave their land.

2. The Globalization-Dilemmas of the Rentier-State

The literature on globalization has repeatedly hinted at the fact that the sovereignty of the national state is undermined by two related forces (Benhabib 1999, Breidenbach/ Zukrigl 2000, Beck 1999). *Firstly,* the economic and financial globalization and the integration of national capitals into global capital structures which are beyond the control of national governments, and, *secondly,* the cultural and social fragmentation and the disintegration of national identities: "The worldwide movement of capital, information, viruses, news, and trends across national borders undermines sovereignty and creates a new and unpredictable global environment in which nation-states often are not actors, but victims, recipients and not movers.... These problems of integration on the global level correlate with the increasing decay of the mechanism of social integration within the nation-states. As the power of nation-states deteriorates on the international level, their ability to act as an integrative factor within their societies also diminishes" (Benhabib 1999: 28 – translation by the editor).

Thus, globalization results in the decreasing ability to integrate social forces within in the borders of the national state. In the Western world this leads to new forms of transnational integration on one hand and privatization of formerly political functions on the other hand. This process is accompanied by new forms of internal and transnational social and cultural integration and by the discussions about the redefinition of the political functions of the state. New local and transnational identities emerge which are not necessarily related to nation-states. There are transnational discussions among intellectuals, social activists, and politicians about the meaning of global values, and even anti-globalization movements organizes themselves in global networks as a nucleus of an emerging global civil society.

All this does not represent a threat to the capitalist mode of production, as the western financial capital still profits most from this integration, this time on the transnational level, as the restrictions of national social and financial legislation are progressively shed.

For third world rentier-states, however, national integration represents the basis and precondition for economic reproduction. It is the state-class – the symbiotic alliance of the bureaucratic state and a non-productive comprador-bourgoisie – through which the non-productive financial transfers are internally distributed in an authoritarian way. It functions as conveyer belt between international capital and their national economies. Any threat to the political and economic functions of the state or to its legitimacy will automatically affect its chances to generate rents and its position as the ruling class.

The increasing economic integration of non-democratic Third-World-States into global economic structures confronts their ruling regimes with three dilemmas of legitimization:

The dilemma of political legitimization: The ruling state classes have an interest in integrating their national economies into global capital and financial structures in order to have their own share of the global rent. At the same time, however, they fear that part of the discourse about civil society and about universal, global values – as for example the debate on democratization or on human and minority rights – could undermine their own authoritarian structure of power.

The social dilemma: The structural reform programs which are forced on most Third World countries by international monetary and trade agencies like the IMF, GATT or WTO in order to subsume them under the rules and logic of international financial capital, have resulted in the marginalization of large parts of the population. This places increasing stress on the legitimization of the regimes that approved the implementation of the reform packages. The recourse to native values and notions has to be seen as one of the reactions to stabilize the ideological hegemony.

The dilemma of sovereignty: The policy of privatization of the formerly state-owned sector, the opening of capital and commodity markets, the adoption of western patterns of consumption, education etc., undermine the social construct of national identity and the claim of sovereignty of the state itself. As a reaction, the state tries to reconstruct a distinct national identity by referring to cultural characteristics and peculiarities, but without contradicting the economic and political mechanism of globalization.

3. The Dual Discourse of Legitimacy

In order to overcome these dilemmas, the Egyptian regime made use of a dual ideological discourse serving different social and political clienteles.

First: With an Islamic pietistic discourse emphasizing obedience to the ruler as an Islamic duty, the regime tried to convince the broad masses of population which were the main losers of globalization to behave loyally towards the state. At the same time this discourse was meant to undermine the hegemony over the

Islamic discourse of competing Islamic forces whose opposition had started to represent a real threat to the regime from the late 70s. This opposition comprised a moderate trend represented by the Muslim-Brotherhood, whose grass-root influence had grown immensely, as well as radical groups, that had declared the armed *jihad* against the state which they perceived as *infidel*.

Second: A secular discourse based on the principles of enlightenment was intended to link intellectuals and left-wing opposition forces to the regime and to promote a modern self-image abroad. This second point became even more important since human rights and women's issues have increasingly become part of the agenda of international development agencies.

This duality of discourse went hand in hand with a split between the discourse producing institutions or, as Althusser had called it, the *Ideological State Apparata* (Althusser 1973).

The production of the Islamic discourse was the responsibility of state controlled Islamic institutions *al-Azhar*[2], the *Mufty* of the Republic and the Ministry of Religious Endowments (*awqaf*). This discourse was disseminated by a broad network of mosques[3], as well as *Azhar*-linked Islamic schools, popular *fatwa*-committees[4] and Islamic mass media.

On the other hand, the Ministry of Cultural Affairs was considered as the leading and most outspoken producer of the secular discourse of the state transmitting this discourse to the intellectual elite.

Both, the Islamic and the secular state-discourses, existed relatively independently from each other. More importantly: both discourse producing institutions assumed that they were the only relevant producer of state discourse and ideology, and that the ideology produced by them represents the true self-understanding of the state, while the other is only of secondary importance. Furthermore, both of them assumed that it was basically up to them to push back the

---

[2] The al-Azhar university, founded in the 12th century under Fatimid rule, up to the present day is considered to be the highest theological authority in Sunni Islam. It disposes over a broad network of decentralized institutions like the approximately 6000 religious schools. Under Nasserist rule the *Azhar* was put under direct state control. Since then its head, the director of the University and all members of the Islamic Research Academy, the body that is responsible for supervising the conformity of laws with Islamic rules, are appointed by the President of the Republic.

[3] there are 24.000 state controlled mosques in Egypt. Since the second half of the 1990s, the new Minister of Religious affairs Hamdi Zaqzuq began to subject the 30 000 private mosques to strict governmental control. Since then, only preachers with a governmental license are allowed to give Friday sermons and to organize religious lessons. The themes and main arguments of the sermons are dictated by the Ministry. In order to collect money the mosques have to get a license from either the Ministry of Social or Religious Affairs.

[4] The *fatwa*-committees, that exist in every main city, are some kind of *shari'a*-based popular juridical committees with consultative function open to any Muslim who wants the opinion of Islamic jurisprudence concerning private and social questions, mostly concerning marriage, inheritance etc.

extremist Islamic ideologies which seriously threatened the ideological hegemony and legitimization of the state in the 80s and early 90s. This discursive coexistence could continue as long as the discourses were used on different occasions, directed to a different audience, and as long as they did not have to relate to each other, so that the contradictions between the legitimatory ideologies of the state did not become obvious and the ideology-producing institutions did not enter into public competition. This came to an end in summer 2000 when Islamic forces initiated a campaign against the publishing policies of the cultural ministry.

It was triggered by the re-editing of *A Banquet of Seagrass*, a novel by the Syrian writer Haidar Haidar, by the Ministry of Cultural Affairs. In his book, Haidar presented a self-critical evaluation of the experience of the Arab left. In this context he assessed the role of religion in a critical way, thus infuriating Adil Husain and other leaders of the *Socialist Workers Party*, a formerly Nasserist party, which in the 80s turned to an Islamic platform and formed an alliance with the Muslim-Brotherhood. The party started a harsh campaign against the minister of culture, Faruq Hussni, reproaching him for publishing anti-Islamic literature, and instigated student demonstrations and nation-wide public meetings.[5] The newspaper of the party spoke of a *conspiracy against Islam* and claimed that the minister of culture was an apostate who had to pay with his life for his deeds (*al-Sha'b*, 28.4.2000).

This was not the first campaign against a novel by Islamic forces. During the 90s, Egypt had seen several campaigns against books, films, and intellectuals in the name of Islam. In 1992 the secularist author Farag Foda was murdered by radical Islamists. Three years later Nasir Abu Zaid, a linguistic professor was driven into exile after he was forcefully divorced from his wife because of his controversial linguistic interpretations of the Qur'an. And during the 90s, al-Azhar put dozens of books on the index because of their presumed anti-Islamic content, among them works by the winner of the Nobel Prize Naguib Mahfuz and the famous Moroccan author Muhammad Shukri. What was different this time was that a non-governmental organization, the Labor Party, not only succeeded in gaining the support of all other Islamic opposition forces but also of large parts of the Islamic state establishment. Thus the commission for religious affairs of the *majlis al-sha'b*, the Egyptian parliament, large parts of *al-Azhar* including their head Shaikh Sayyid Tantawi and the director of the university Ahmad Umar Hashim, and even officers of the security police, which was sent out to squash the student demonstrations, openly supported the point of view of Islamic opposition.

---

[5] The strange point about the campaign was the fact that the Lebanese edition of the book had been on the Egyptian book-market for years without any objection even by the Islamic forces (Fawzi/Lübben, 2000).

The conflict between the Islamic opposition and the cultural minister was thus transferred into a conflict between the different ideological apparatuses of the state itself: between the secular cultural ministry on one hand and the religious apparatus, above all *al-Azhar*, on the other hand. Both sides tried to mobilize support among the parliamentary and non-parliamentary opposition in order to enforce their respective position inside the state apparatus. While cultural minister Faruq Hussni was supported by the left, human rights organizations, the intellectual elite and the cultural committee of the ruling *National Democratic Party* (NDP), *al-Azhar* was not only supported by the Islamic forces but also by the so-called liberal *Wafd Party*, by parts of the Nasserits, and even by the religious committee of the NDP.

Although in the short term the confrontation was ended by forcefully squashing the demonstrations and freezing all activities of the *Labor Party* and its mouth-piece *al-Sha'b*, it still had other, more far-reaching consequences: It made the inconsistencies and contradictions of the state discourse visible to the public and threatened to undermine the authority of the ideological legitimization and hegemony of the state. The opposition had succeeded in penetrating and splitting the power apparatus. This made the reformulation of state discourse an urgent necessity.

4. The Reformulation of the State Discourse and the Notion of Morality

This reformulation of the state discourse was centered around the notion of *morality*, *morality* not in a sense of a whole set of social and political morals and ethics, but *morality* in the very narrow sense of personal behavior, of moral sexual *morality*, of *sexuality*. At first glance this notion seems to be very vague, very narrow in comparison with the all-embracing former *big ideologies* such as Egyptian Nationalism, Nasserism, Socialism or even Islamism, ideologies that tried to integrate the different social strata into one all-embracing national project. *Morality* does not seem to have any relevance for the social order, for the political systems or for the economic options.

But as the French philosopher Michel Foucault has stressed in his work *The History of Sexuality*, *sexuality* has an immense significance as a power technique exactly because of its private character. This power technique is structured, organized and legitimized by respective discourses on *sexuality*. Although the concrete definition of *sexual morality* varies depending on time and locality, on situations and social groups which make use of it, it creates a mechanism of inclusion and exclusion into the discursive consensus that represents the basis of power. According to Foucault sexuality *"appears as an especially dense transfer point of power: between men and women, young people and old people, parents and offspring, teachers and students, priests and laity, an administration and a population. Sexuality is not the most intractable in the power relations, but rather one of those endowed with the greatest instrumentality: usefull for the greatest number of maneuvers and capable of serving as a point of support, as a linchpin, for the most varied strategies"* (Foucault 1983: 103). The reason is that *"disciplining of the body [is like] the regulation of the population"* (Foucault 1983: 147).

The actual occasion for the reformulation of the state discourse, the *discursive event* as Foucault would have called it, was again a publication by the Ministry of Culture. On the 2nd of January 2001, Jamal Hishmat, a member of parliament of the Muslim-Brotherhood presented a parliamentary inquiry concerning the publication of three novels by the Ministry of Culture that presumably contained pornographic scenes.[6]

But this time the reaction of Cultural Minister Faruq Husni was completely different than half a year earlier during the dispute over the *Banquet of Seagrass*. The criticized books were immediately withdrawn from the market. Within only two days all employees who were responsible for the publication – all of them well-know intellectuals – were fired. Husni declared that his ministry refuses to publish pornography: „The policy of the government does not allow the publication of anything that hurts religious feelings and undermines *morality*." (*Middle East Times*, 13.-19.1. 2001).

Some intellectuals criticized the ministry for this dramatic turn-around under what they presumed was the pressure of the Islamists. But the fact that Faruq Husni himself confessed that he ordered much more than what was originally asked for by the parliamentary faction of the Muslim-Brothers – an opinion that was shared by the Jamal Hishmat himself and other members of his faction, who were rather astonished themselves - suggests that there was more at stake than the question of making concessions to pressure from parliamentary opposition forces or a possible parliamentary compromise, especially if we take into consideration that the Egyptian parliament mainly plays an acclamatory role. The renewed debate on cultural policies coincided with the attempt by the regime to restructure the relationship between the state and the Islamic opposition on one hand and the secular and Islamic opposition on the other hand. This seemed to be necessary after the Muslim-Brotherhood emerged as the strongest opposition force from the parliamentary elections of November 2000 in contradiction to all expectations and predictions. In spite of the massive intervention by the state in the electoral process, the Brotherhood gained 17 seats, more than all other oppo-

---

[6] At stake were the novel *Qabl wa Ba'd* (Before and After) by Tawfiq 'Abd-al Rahman in which a retired state-employee looks back on his life. The story is interlinked with memories of his affair with an emancipated women called Qadriya. The second novel is *Ahlam Mamnu'a* (Forbidden Dreams) by Mahmud Hamid that deals with an Egyptian journalists coming back for holidays from the Gulf and remembering his sister who was violated and later killed by her father to reconstitute the *honor* of the family. The third novel is *Ibna' Khata' Romansia* (Sons of a Romantic Error) by the psychiatrist Yasir Sha'aban, a surrealistic psycho-drama on death and Eros.

sition parties together. This proved them to be an important social and political actor whom the state had to take into consideration in the future. Until then, the regime had mainly used means of criminalization and exclusion to prevent the Muslim-Brothers from gaining influence, which due to the new quasi-legal parliamentary existence – the Muslim-Brothers are officially illegal – would now no longer work. So the regime turned to a new strategy of partially co-opting the Brotherhood into the political system without opening up new spaces of political action for them.

The precondition of this co-optation was a minimum degree of harmonization of state discourses, because the regime feared that the Muslim-Brothers could win the support of parts of the religious state apparatus if the former discursive dichotomy continued. This would undermine state unity.

It was President Mubarak himself who during his traditional speech to Egyptian intellectuals on the occasion of the opening of the Cairo book-fare on January 25th named the basic elements of the new ideological consensus, thus explicitly supporting the role of the Cultural Ministry:

First: Democracy and freedom of opinion and thought are the basis of intellectual and academic freedom and creativity.

Second: The intellectuals bear the responsibility for the preservation of „our deep-rooted traditions, our culture and our identity."

Third: Creative freedom does not mean absolute freedom. It has to act within the framework of law and is limited by Islamic values and Islamic moral.

Fourth: It is the duty of the state to protect society from any breach of this framework. The ministry of culture is a governmental institution, which is controlled by parliament and public opinion, while private publishers are controlled by society and the judiciary (*al-Ahram*, 26.1. 2001, *Ruz a-Yusif*, 27.1.-2.2. 2001).

Although at first glance this appears simplistic, there is a well defined discursive strategy underlying these principles. On one hand it aims at integrating parts of the discourse of the secularist opposition by saying to the intellectuals: *We are supporting freedom of creativity*. On the other hand it promises the Islamists: *We will protect morality*. At the same time it defines the mechanism of constitutional integration when it says: A*ny violation of the principles, any surpassing of the line of demarcation set by the notion of morality will be sanctioned by institutionalized bodies and procedures*.

There are two remarkable points in this strategy:

First: The basis of the process of harmonization is not *Islam* as it used to be but *public morality*. It might be presumed that this is a concession to secular forces.

But there seems to be another reason. *Morality* represents a *discursive field* that can more easily be controlled than the field of *Religion* or *Islam*. A possible discourse of *Islam* would have covered a much larger *discursive field* whose demarcation lines would be difficult to define and thus to control. It would have given the chance to opposing forces specially from Islamic circles to challenge the state's power of definition and to add new themes in the name of Islam to the ideological agenda, like questions of social justice in Islam, corruption, discussions of Islam and democracy, etc. This hypothesis is supported by the fact that the new parliamentary group of Muslim Brothers put forward more than 100 questions and interpellations within the first month after the formation of the new parliament, most of them linked to social and educational problems. All of them had been completely ignored, except the one concerning the publications by the ministry of culture.

Second: The leading role of restructuring the legitimatory state discourse was delegated to the Ministry of Culture and not to any of the Islamic institutions. Thus the state intended to exclude the Islamists also on the institutional level from participating in the reformulation of discourse. On the other hand, the cultural ministry was more inclined to co-opt the left and the organization of the civil society on the basis of the new discourse than religious institutions would have been.

These calculations proved to be correct. The harmonization of discourse turned out to be an appropriate instrument of political integration under the hegemony of the state. On one hand it led to an unambiguous approval of the constitutional order and even to the recognition of the regime by the Muslim-Brothers. „Our *jihad* is a democratic *jihad* on the basis of the Egyptian constitution. This constitution gives the state the task to guarantee public morals," declared Jamal Hishmat.[7] And Abd al-Min'em Abu al-Futuh, another leading figure of the Brotherhood, said during a talk-show on the *al-Jazeera* TV channel: „The [Egyptian] state is an Islamic state, the [Egyptian] government is an Islamic government. We don't enter any competition about the question who is a better Muslim. Our problem with the government is the lack of public liberties and social justice, it is not a religious problem".[8]

On the other hand, the new state discourse was also supported by the main intellectuals and ideologists of the organized left. Some of them are even said to have actively participated in the reformulation of the state discourse as for instance Salah Issa, the chief-editor of the al-Qahira, a cultural weekly and mouthpiece of

---

[7] During a personal interview with Jamal Hishmat on 5th of January 2001.
[8] By telephone intervention during an interview with Jamal Hishmat in the program al-Ra'i al-Mu'akis on 18th of January 2001 on the *Jeezira*-TV-Chanal.

the cultural ministry[9], or Rifa'at Sa'id, secretary-general of the left-wing *Ta-gammu-Party*. „Freedom has its limits in the rights and freedoms of others", said Rifa'at Sa'id during a controversial discussion organized by the literary maga-zine *Adab wa Naqd* about the new cultural policies. „Everything that hurts my freedom, my body, my *morality*, my *rationality* is an attack against my freedom. Literature has not the right to attack the *moral* values of the society. To protect religion from being humiliated can not be equaled or confused with the limita-tion of intellectual freedoms."[10]

5. Redrawing Moral Borders between *Us* and the *Other*

As we have seen, one of the functions of *morality* was the internal harmoniza-tion of former antagonistic discourses or a discursive integration. There is a sec-ond function closely linked to the first: the external demarcation between the *I* from the *Other*, the self-affirmation of identity.

Foucault has described in his above cited *Histoire de la sexualité*, how *sexuality,* before it became an instrument of societal control, had been instrumental for the self-affirmation of the rising bourgeoisie of the late 18th and 19th century to dis-tinguish itself from the aristocracy. Foucault traces back the establishment of a *dispositive of sexuality*[11] and comes to the conclusion that it was not the working classes that were the first to be subdued under the strict control of their sexual body in order to facilitate the exploitation of their labor as is usually presumed. The first on whom the mechanism of the new dispositive was enforced was the bourgeoisie itself, the members of the bourgeois family, specially the wives and the children[12], while the popular classes for a long time had succeeded in escap-ing from its harsh regime. Only later with the campaigns for the *moralization* of society and the medical and juridical control of all forms of perceived *perversion* was this regime extended to the whole body of the bourgeois society. By, as he calls it, *autosexualization* (Foucault; 1983:124) it *[the bourgeoisie] "provided itself with a body to be cared for, protected, cultivated, and preserved from many dangers and contacts, to be isolated from others so it would retain its dif-ferential value"* (ibid: 123), *„This class must be seen rather as being occupied, from the mid-nineteenth century on,, with creating an own sexuality and forming*

---

[9] Since the end of the 1980s, a growing integration of the left into the clientelist pyramid of the rentier-state can be observed. In this process an important part of the intellectuals of the tradi-tional left found their way into the regimes think tanks and cultural institutions. The new left was integrated by the NGO-sation of the Civil Society (see Kassem; 1999: 107 and Fawzi/ Lüb-ben 1996).

[10] Rifa'at Sa'id during a seminar organized by the literary magazine of the *Tagammu'*, *Adab wa Naqd*, on which he tried to defuse the criticism of the new policy of the cultural minister by party intellectuals (Fawzi/ Lübben 2001).

[11] According to Foucault, the term *dispositive* comprises power institutions as well as power regulations, i.e. laws (Foucault 1983: 106).

[12] Foucault reminds us that the discourse of the *hysteric wife* and the fear of the *onanism* of the adolescent that has to be protected by a whole army of pedagogues finds its origin in the bour-geois family in the early 19th century (Foucault 1983: 105f).

a specific body based on it, a "class" body with health, hygiene, descent and race" (ibid: 124)

The emphasis on the body should be undoubtedly linked to the process of growth and establishment of bourgeois hegemony. The sexually controlled body represents the *symbolic capital of the bourgeoisie*: *There was a transposition of the different forms of the methods employed by the nobility for making and maintaining its caste distinction; for the aristocracy has also asserted the special character of its body, but this was in the form of blood, that is the form of antiquity of its ancestry and of the value of its alliances. The bourgeoisie on the contrary looked to its progeny and the health of its organism when it laid claim to a specific body. The bourgeoisie's "blood" was its sex"* (ibid.: 124)

As *sexuality*, inclusively the whole dispositive of institutions and procedures of control that are implied, had been used by the bourgeoisie to affirm its new class identity, it is now used by the rentier-state in order to reaffirm its own cultural and national identity to counter the corroding effects of cultural globalization. The discourse of *moral values* as a more discrete paraphrase for *sexual morality* serves as demarcation line of the field of power of the state. It redraws national borders on a cultural, behavioral and discursive level in view of the growing disintegration of the nation-state and national economies and its incorporation into global economic structures. In this sense it becomes an ideological weapon to give meaning to the continuous dominance of the state-class and the ruling regime.

The Egyptian president Mubarak himself pointed at these two contradicting but intertwined tendencies during the above mentioned discussions with the Egyptian intelligentsia at the book fair 2001, when he stressed that Egyptian nationalism does not contradict the fact that parts of the national sector are sold to foreigners. Those positions would not agree with the spirit of time. He demanded that all the talk about protection of national property be relegated to the *Museum of History*. On the other hand he warned against a conspiracy to destroy Egyptian culture and stressed the necessity to protect the authentic values against the challenges of globalization.[13]

We find the same argument more clearly expressed by Kamal Baha al-Din, the Egyptian Minister of Education. In this function he is considered to be the official mainly responsible for the reproduction of state ideology, as education implies the ideological formation of future generations.

In a book titled *Nationalism in a World without Identity – The Challenge of Globalization* he presents the following argument: The West is dominated by *technopoly* as he puts it. This had led to the breakdown of morals, to the split of

---

[13] see *Ruz al-Yusif* 27.1. 2001.

the family, to growing violence and growing suicide rates. Youth has to be presented an alternative against this culture originating from the outside world by strengthening the pride in their roots and values. Baha al-Din suggests that more weight be given to religious and national education, which are closely linked to each other. Nationalism (*wataniya*) is the protective fence, the framework which has to be filled with moral values.

"It is our task to promote the feeling for our own identity, loyalty and pride in our own roots and values. We must give coming generations a convincing alternative to the alien culture." (Baha al-Din 2000:153). The immunity of the youth has to be strengthened, so Kamal. They should be enabled to select external information, to separate the wheat from the chaff. „We have to strengthen their ability to refuse everything contradicting our religion, our culture, and our values and at the same time to profit from the information and thoughts that are useful for us, and from science, that links us with progress and the future. We have to be able to speak the language of the third millennium without using offensive expressions." (ibid: 154)

6. The Practical Consequences of the *Discourse of Morality*: The Queen Boat Affair

There are rituals, institutions, procedures, or *dispositives of power* that evoke ideological discourses in order to justify or legitimize particular policies, like for example discourses of security that justify certain practices of the police or the intervention of the army, or discourses about hygienics in order to justify certain health policies etc. This seems to be the normal case. But there are also practices whose only or main function is to give credibility to discourses and thus suggesting a unity between ideology and practice. What happened as a consequence of the formulation of the *discourse of morality* is an example of the latter case.

On May 11th, 2001, fifty-five men were arrested on the *Queen Boat*, a floating restaurant on the Nile in central Cairo that was known as being a gay hang-out. The men were put on trial before the State Security Court, which was originally established for offenses against state security on the basis of the emergency laws, which have been in force since the assassination of President Sadat more than 20 years ago. The men were accused of practicing homosexuality. During custody they were tortured, they were forcefully medically examined in order to prove that they had anal sex, and they were publicly denunciated in a large media campaign. Later it was discovered that there is no law prohibiting homosexuality, so the State Security Court and the State Prosecutor had to construct other legal charges against them, mainly focusing on the charge of practicing *habitual debauchery with men* founding their indictment on law No. ten from 1961 that prohibits prostitution and public indecency. The main defendant, Sharif Farahat, was also accused of *contempt for religion* and of founding an illegal religious sect that falsely interpreted Islam, a legal charge that can be punished by up to five years of imprisonment. The State Prosecutor claimed that the men had considered themselves followers of the prophet Lot, that they made the medieval poet Abu Nawas, who was famous for his erotic poetry, their prophet, and that Sharif Farahat had baptized his followers in the Dead Sea. By this the men had offended the basic fundamentals of Islam, as Ashraf Hilal, the State Prosecutor argued, adding that "Egypt will not be used for the defamation of manhood and will not be a hub for gay communities"(al-Ahram Weekly,22.-28.11. 2001).[14] Finally on November 28[th,] Farahat was condemned to five years imprisonment, the second defendant Mahmud Allam got three, and 20 others two years. There is no possibility of a formal appeal against any judgement by the State Security Court.

The whole *Queen Boat Affair* turned out to be a further move in constructing the new morally-based state-discourse. Although homosexuality has on the formal level always been publicly condemned and was considered as being outside of the accepted norms, informally it always had been practiced and was implicitly tolerated in popular culture. This fact was more or less ignored by the formal institutions of the state which refrained from any official prosecution of homo-sexuality. For them it simply did not exist.

It seems that the main reason behind the prosecution and trial of gays was to put the mechanisms of the new *discourse of morality* into action, to develop it further, and to put it explicitly into a context with the discussions about globalization. The *Queen Boat Affair* and the discourse that developed around it were used to further strengthen the idea of a presumed difference between *us* and the *others*. In a large media campaign homosexuality was described as a cultural phenomenon of the West that is enforced onto the *global citizen* through international media, UN-conferences like those on population or women, and development agencies.[15] The only therapy to this moral decline would be to strengthen authentic cultural values and the institution of the family. The masculine patterns as positive models should be emphasized by enhancing the role of the father in the education of male children. The mothers should stick to the pedagogic rules of Islam. This would be the best remedy against the spread of homosexuality, as, for example, the sociologist Ahmad Mahgub of the Egyptian Sociological and Criminological Research Institute (*al-Ahram al-arabi*, 25/8/2001) argues.[16] And the vice-president of al-Azhar University, Taha Abu Kuraisha, requested pub-

---

[14] see on the campaign and the process also of al-Ahram Weekly 17.-23.5. 2001, 23-29.8. 2001, 13.-19.9 2001 and the Cairo Times 12.-18.7. 2001, 26.7-1.8. 2001, 23.-29.8. 2001, 13.-19.9. 2001.

[15] Some even suspect a Zionist conspiracy. Jewish companies tried to organize Egyptian youth in secret gay-circles, in order to threaten the national existence of the country, argues Ahmad Tala'at Ahli, an Egyptian representative in the WHO (al-Ahali 10.3. 2001).

[16] Mahgub cites the Sunna-rule „Teach them with seven, if necessary beat them with ten, and separate them in bed" as the most effective prophylactic remedy against homosexuality.

licly that this sort of crime should be wiped out by all means, claiming that the Qur'an would administer capital punishment in such cases (ibid.).

To give even more credibility to its anti-gay campaign Egypt put itself on the forefront of conservative Islamic and Catholic states that tried to prevent any mentioning of the gay question during the UN-AIDS-conference that took place in New York parallel to the *Queen-Boat Affair*. The draft document of the conference had asked for additional protective and prophylactic measures for specially endangered social groups in the national AIDS-campaigns, such as drug addicts, prostitutes and gays. National governments were also requested to respect the rights of gays and lesbians within their national constitutions, which caused an outcry by some Islamic countries. Ahmad Abu Gheit, the leader of the Egyptian delegation to the conference, declared that there is no compromise for the Islamic world concerning homosexuality. Only if all articles treating this question as a human rights issue were deleted from the final document, would the Islamic block approve of it (*al-Hayat*, 27.7. 2001).

The campaign against homosexuals was further used in order to prevent the discourses of the international civil society from penetrating the Egyptian public debate. Specially after international human rights organizations, among them Amnesty International, sent protest resolutions to the Egyptian authorities, they were most heavily attacked by the official and semi-official press, which questioned the universality of the international human rights movement as a whole.

"The appeal by Amnesty is a mere masquerade. It makes obvious that they [Amnesty] are suffering from a vacuum of values. The organization has astonished everybody when they described the prosecution of homosexuals as violation of human rights. They don't want to understand that there are fundamental differences concerning values between us and them.... If they see homosexuality as a personal freedom, we see it as a violation of values and religious principles. For us it means espionage and violation of national security. It seems to be impossible that we ever meet ", wrote the allegedly liberal *Ruz al-Yusif*, a political weekly with close contacts to the regime. It further demanded that "any future appeal of this organization has to be analyzed very thoroughly, preferably with a lie-detector."(*Ruz al-Yusif*, 22.6. 2001)

The campaign against homosexuals added new elements to the *discourse of morality*:

First: The rejection or at least the questioning of the concept of individual human rights.

Second: The characterization of the international human rights movement and its demand for principles of a global civil society as expression of cultural imperialism.

Third: The conservation of authentic moral principles is presented as a matters of national security.

Particularly with the argument of a presumed cultural imperialism the regime succeeded in stabilizing its support of the left-wing *Tajammu'*-Party and in gaining a new consensus with large parts of the local human rights movement, thus neutralizing both. With this the regime regained ideological hegemony: It was able to define the concept of Human Rights within the national discourse. Egyptian human rights groups during the last years had repeatedly and with the support of international human rights organizations instigated discussions about the alleged torture of political prisoners, women's rights, and the situation of Egyptian Copts. These arguments were taken up by the American Congress that - to the annoyance of the Egyptian government - threatened to make foreign aid to Egypt conditional on the respect of religious minority rights.

"If permitted we would like to ask one question: Are there any international organizations behind these young people that provide them with money and other means in order to spread vice and moral decay among the youth?," asked *al-Ahali* the mouthpiece of the *Tagammu'* –Party and continues: "Can it really be the task of NGOs to defend the right of homosexuals? ... How is it possible to build a strong and virtuous wall against this trend that corrodes religion, the values and concepts, the moral of the youth of our Egypt protected by God?" (*al-Ahali*, 10.3. 2001) Nuri Abd al-Raziq, secretary-general of the Afro-Asian Solidarity Organization, claims that gay rights are the top priority of the agenda of western NGOs, who try to enforce this agenda onto the Arab world. By this they try to destroy the fabric of the society. There would be no organization in the Arab world that would defend rights of homosexuals in the name of freedom, claims Abd al-Raziq in al-Ahali. (ibid.)

Hafiz Abu Sa'ada, secretary-general of the Egyptian Organization for Human Rights denies completely that the prosecution of homosexuals is a human rights issue his organization should care about: "We work on behalf of our people. Therefore we can't contradict the basic convictions and values of this people by defending a group of homosexuals, or let us say, of prostitutes. It is not a case of violation of Human Rights. It is a case of prostitution."(*al-Ahram al-arabi* , 25.8. 2001) Also Nigad al-Borai, another well-known human rights activist, supports the argument, saying that the *Queen Boat Affair* is a matter for the vice police and not for human rights organizations. "If human rights organization would adopt the case they would soil the concept of human rights. But this is not the first time that they [international human rights groups] don't respect our cultural specifities. There were similar discussions concerning death penalty", says Bora'i, defending death penalty as a cultural particularity. (*Ruz al-Yussif*, 22.6. 2001)

By stressing the notion of cultural imperialism in the described context, the rentier-state succeeds in transforming the critique against the economic globalization into a critique against the global civil society. This happened precisely at a moment when this *global civil society* started to play a role as a critical social actor to counterbalance the negative effects of economic globalization, be it through the international anti-globalization movement or through international NGO-networks dealing with women's, human rights, ecological, housing or other issues. Thus, the Egyptian critics of globalization are being isolated from potential allies in the international anti-globalization movement and from any discussion about the international civil order and the place of human rights in it.

7. Conclusions

In his prison books Antonio Gramsci has introduced the idea an *ideological war of positions*. On this idea Gramsci based a strategy of a step-by-step conquest of a hegemonic ideological position by the workers' movement in pre-World-War II Italy. In this *ideological war of positions* it is the Egyptian state that succeeded in re-conquering ideological positions from the opposition: from the Islamists it re-conquered key elements of the religious discourse. And by their explicit recognition of the Egyptian constitutional system the Islamic main-stream movement provided religious legitimacy to the political system as well as to the ruling regime. On the other hand, the organized left gave up main elements of its secular and implicitly anti-religious ideology in favor of a conservative discourse of *morality* which is compatible with central Islamic notions. But this harmonization of political discourses does not necessarily mean the end of the power struggle among different political forces or between the ruling regime and its opposition. However, unlike earlier, this struggle is no longer about the enforcement of one discourse at the expense of another. It is about the question who represents the discourse and consequently who is legitimized to exercise power based on this. It is much easier for the traditional power-apparatus of the state to control this conflict.

The notion of *morality* has become the starting point of a new form of populist ideology, whose function is integrating contradicting social groups and strata by confronting them with the threat of a culturally, *morally* different *Other*. But unlike the populist ideologies of the post-colonial era, which generally were ideological expressions of the attempt of economic emancipation from world market structures, this new ideology of a *moral* populism is separated from its economic basis. The emphasis on cultural and moral differences goes hand in hand with the economic integration into global economic structures.

But still the question remains: Does the discourse of morality represent a way out of the legitimatory dilemma that was described in the introductory remarks?

We think that it can only be transitory – although the term *transitory* can apply to historically long periods.[17]

The discourse of *morality* is not an ideological concept embracing and integrating different aspects of social existence within a consistent system of meaning, in a kind of *Weltanschauung*. The notion of morality is the smallest common denominator. In a way, it expresses the recognition of the ruling state-class that there is no concept, that there is no perspective, that there is no *national project* either in the framework of globalization, or as an alternative to it.

Sexuality, or the concept of *sexual morality,* was initially a concept that was applied by the rising bourgeoisie to itself. Only later, after the bourgeoisie had established itself as ruling class, did it start to generalize it as a power mechanism to control society as a whole. With this it could achieve a certain degree of credibility. But this is not the case when the notion of *morality* is applied in third world rentier-states of which Egypt has been an example. This can be seen on a daily basis in the yellow press, which is full of stories about scandals of the nouveau riches, who exist in a kind of legal and normative vacuum. During the last decade, the state-class has started to retreat into separated spaces: clubs, shopping malls, five star-hotels, private schools, and separated, privately protected housing areas that escape social and sometimes even legal and political control.[18]

The homogenization of discourses exists only on the surface. The duality continues as a duality of the meaning of the discourse and the question to whom it is applied. It continues as a duality of life experience and of everyday culture, which is the expression of the social heterogeneity among the political, economic and cultural elites of the rentier-state who have succeeded in profiting from the integration into the global system, on the one hand, and the popular strata on the other, which have been marginalized by the globalization process. In the future, this growing social gap will most probably lead to new legitimatory crises.

---

[17] *Transitory* is meant here in a qualitative sense as it is not able to solve the underlying dilemmas that led to the contradictions of the old discourse.
[18] This phenomenon is actually discussed under the headline of the so-called *gated communities*, that has started to spread more and more in Middle Eastern countries: closed, privately administrated residential areas with own shopping and recreational facilities and exclusively private services from security to education and health services, and to which only members and authorized persons have access.

References

Althusser, Louis 1973: Ideologie und ideologische Staatsapparate. In: Althusser, Louis 1973: Marxismus und Ideologie, Berlin.

Baha al-Din, Hussein Kamal 2000: al-wataniya fi alim bala hauwiya - tahadiyat al-aulama, Cairo.

Barber, Benjamin R. 1996: Jihad vs. McWorld. How Globalism and Tribalism are Reshaping the World, New York.

Beck, Ulrich 1999: Was ist Modernisierung, Frankfurt/ M.

Benhabib, Seyla 1999: Kulturelle Vielfalt und demokratische Gleichheit – Politische Partizipation im Zeitalter der Globalisierung, Frankfurt/ M.

Breidenbach, Joana/ Zukrigl, Ina 2000: taNZ DeR kuLtUReN – Kulturelle Identität in einer globalisierten Welt, Hamburg.

Efferding, Wieland/ Eckard, Volker 1986: Societá Civile, Hegemonie und Intellektuelle bei Gramsci. In: Das Argument, Theorien über Ideologie, AS 40, Berlin.

Evers, Hans-Dieter, Schiel, Tilman 1988: Strategische Gruppen – Vergleichende Studien zu Staat, Bürokratie und Klassenbildung in der Dritten Welt, Berlin.

Fawzy, Essam/ Lübben, Ivesa 1996: Fünf-Sterne-Demokratie – Wie die Zivilgesellschaft Ägyptens Opposition ausschaltet. In: Blätter des iz3w, No. 213, Freiburg.

Fawzy, Essam/ Lübben, Ivesa 2000: Zensur und Inquisition in Ägypten – Das Dilemma des ägyptischen Legitimationsdiskurses. In: INAMO No. 23/24, Berlin.

Fawzy, Essam and Ivesa Lübben 2001: Ägypten und die öffentliche Moral. In: INAMO Nr.25.

Foucault, Michel 1983: The History of Sexuality, London.

Gramsci, Antonio/ Riechers, Christian (ed.) 1977: Philosophie der Praxis, Frankfurt/ M.

Kamal al-Din, Hussain 2000: al-wataniya fi alim bala hawiya – tahdiyat al-auwlama, Cairo.

Kassem, May 1999: In the Guise of Democracy – Governance in Contemporary Egypt, London.

Markaz al-Dirasat al-Siyasia wa al-Stratejia fi al-Ahram 1996: al-Hala al-Dinia fi Misr 1995, Cairo.

Schmid, Claudia 1991: Das Konzept des Rentierstaates – Ein sozialwissenschaftliches Paradigma zur Analyse von Entwicklungsgesellschaften und seine Bedeutung für den Vorderen Orient, Münster/ Hamburg.

6

ALENA V. LEDENEVA

Non-Transparency and Globalization: Russia's Unwritten Rules.[1]

Globalization makes the distinction between transparent and non-transparent economies much more evident. Not only the global financial capital 'avoids' the non-transparent economies these can also be identified by their non-compliance with international standards in accounting or principles of corporate governance. Non-transparent economies are often regarded to be the threat to the world's financial stability and are hard to predict. Just as the August 1998 crisis overturned the expectations of the Russian boom, the quick post-1998 recovery of the Russian economy came as a surprise too.[2] It has almost become a commonplace that 'nothing is as strong or as weak in Russia as it seems' and the need to understand how the Russian economy really works is as urgent as ever.

In order to make Russia's economy transparent, one should understand it on its own terms. In other words, rather than looking only at what does not work in Russia and why, one should concentrate on what does work and how. An example will illustrate such an approach best. The ineffectiveness of the rule of law in Russia is one of the main obstacles to Russian economic and political development. Not only does the weak rule of law deter much needed foreign investment in the Russian economy, it also undermines efforts to rein in acute problems such as capital flight, tax evasion, and abuses of corporate governance. Following our alternative perspective, one should ask 'If the rule of law does not work in Russia, then what does?'

A tentative answer can be found in popular wisdom: 'Russia is a country of unread laws and unwritten rules'. Or, as they say, "the imperfection of our laws is compensated for by their non-observance" (*nesovershenstvo nashikh zakonov kompensiruetsya ikh nevypolneniem*). It is not that the requisite components of the rule of law are absent in Russia; rather, the ability of the rule of law to function coherently has been diverted by a powerful set of practices that has evolved organically in the post-Soviet milieu. Adopting a perspective of 'unwritten rules' and understanding how they work can help to make the rules of the game in Russia more transparent and therefore subject to positive change and reform.

Given the scale of the informal economy in Russia, there is no shortage of examples that illustrate how 'unwritten rules' operate. Tax evasion and tax bargaining alone provide an excellent ground for studying the informal order of

---

[1] For a full version see pamphlet by Alena Ledeneva 2001.
[2] Real GDP growth in 1999 – 3.2 per cent; in 2000 – 7.7 per cent; in 2001 – 5.2 per cent. The Economist Intelligence Unit Country Report.

things. In the corporate sector, the most damaging for the transparency of the new Russian economy are practices based on the so-called 'corporate identity split' and false reporting. What this means is that firms insulate themselves by at least two front companies and create various shell-firms or scam-firms, which are organized in a sophisticated financial networks. Specially established off-shore companies conduct financial transactions in order to reserve profits for the insiders' club of shareholders or managers. Unwritten rules also prevail in regulating non-monetary exchanges and help fighting business and political wars.

All of these phenomena of the new Russian economy share an important feature: agents at all levels employ practices that have come to be known as extralegal or informal. These practices are to a large extent responsible for the non-transparency of the 'rules of the game' in the Russian economy, mainly because they are regulated by what is referred to as informal arrangements, unwritten codes or unspecified rules. All these are elusive in nature and need further clarification.

1. The rules of the game

Let us start with the notion of the 'rules of the game'- a phrase which is rather often taken for granted. Douglass North has defined institutions as the 'rules of the game in a society or, more formally, humanly devised constraints that shape human interaction' (North 1990: 3). He distinguishes between formal and informal types of constraints, with both being components of institutions. 'They [Institutions] are perfectly analogous to the rules of the game in a competitive team sport. That is, they consist of formal written rules as well as typically unwritten codes of conduct that underlie and supplement formal rules, such as not deliberately injuring a key player on the opposing team. And as this analogy would imply, the rules and informal codes are sometimes violated and punishment is enacted. Taken together, the formal and informal rules and the type and effectiveness of enforcement shape the whole character of the game' (North 1990: 4). According to North, the 'difference between informal and formal constraints is one of degree. Envision a continuum of taboos, customs, and traditions at one end to written constitutions at the other' (North 1990: 46). Informal constraints are defined by the codes of conduct, norms of behavior and conventions. Underlying these informal constraints are formal rules, but these are seldom obvious and immediate source of choice in daily interactions. Formal rules include political (and judicial) rules, economic rules and contracts and determine formal constraints. That informal constraints are important in themselves (and not simply as appendages to formal rules) can be observed from the evidence that the same formal rules and/or constitutions imposed on different societies produce different outcomes (North 1990: 36).

Unwritten rules should not be confused with informal rules. Although the literal sense of being 'written' or 'unwritten' can actually be an interesting dimension of the analysis of formal and informal constraints, this is the dimension I chose to ignore. What I want to explore here is the intuitive sense of the idiom unwritten rules – unwritten rules as meta-rules or rules about the rules.

In this sense, unwritten rules are neither formal nor informal. If we use North's competitive team sports analogy again, unwritten rules are about the mastery of the game, including the skill of the players and the knowledge they possess of the game. Unwritten rules prescribe how formal and informal constraints can be circumvented or partially enforced. If the counterpart to informal rules is formal rules, the counterpart of unwritten rules is the 'rules of the game' as a whole.

The meta- nature of unwritten rules can be explained by distinguishing between rules and rule-following. Rules make one's behavior regular, recognizable and understood. Knowing a rule, however, does not imply an ability to follow it, or mastery of it, just as knowing a recipe does not assure practical skill in its implementation or knowing the literal meaning of a word does not automatically mean that one will use it correctly in context. In Wittgenstein's terminology there are practices of 'rule-following' (i.e. being able to continue the sequence of numbers 2, 4, 6, 8,...) that are distinct from rules interpreted, explicated and understood (i.e. an ability to figure out the formulae of this sequence). In a classic example of chess playing, Wittgenstein shows that certain mastery and expertise can only be achieved by dealing with constraints in practice.

A distinction between a rule and mastery of the rule can be illustrated by the metaphor of driving. To drive 'properly', one has to know not only formal (traffic rules) and informal rules (conventions would differ, say, in Russia, Italy and UK) but also to be able to apply them as required in appropriate contexts (follow formal rules in one situation and informal in another). The mastery of switching fluidly between the formal and informal rules; of manipulating both and of knowing how to negotiate oneself out of trouble implies some particular expertise:

- *Unwritten rules are the know-how needed to 'navigate' between formal and informal sets of constraints, and to manipulate their enforcement to one's own advantage.* Without being articulated, they 'prescribe' which rules to follow in which context and 'set' the best approach for getting things done. Applying one formal rule rather than another, using restrictions (quotas, filters etc.) and small print, enforcing some decisions but not the others are examples of how constraints can be mediated. The focus of unwritten rules is not on constraints *per se*, as in case of formal and informal codes, but on the enabling aspects of those constraints. To put it more bluntly, unwritten rules define the ways of circumventing constraints, both formal and informal, of manipulating their enforcement to one's own advantage and of avoiding penalties by combining the three elements of the rules of the game creatively.
- If we distinguish between organizations as enforcing mainly formal constraints and social networks as enforcing mainly informal constraints,

unwritten rules regulate the ways in which organizations and networks interact. In other words, they shape the interaction between organizational principles and kin- and friendship ties. For example, the ways in which old-boy networks or nepotism permeate modern institutions are guided by unwritten rules. Soviet *blat* (Ledeneva 1998) – a widespread use of personal networks for obtaining goods and services in short supply – is a classic example of unwritten rules, by which resources of the formal distribution system were siphoned into informal networks of the 'gatekeepers'. *Blat* was functional for the Soviet system as it helped in lubricating the rigid constraints of the formal economy. In present-day Russia, unwritten rules bridge the formal and informal sectors of the economy, prevail in areas vacated by the state but not yet filled in by the civil society thus deforming both organizational and network principles.

- Unwritten rules exist in all societies, but predominate (and even become indispensable) in those *where enforcement, formal and informal rules are not synchronized and do not constitute coherent rules of the game.* North shows that when people perceive the structure of the rules of the system to be fair and just, transaction costs are low and enforcement costs are negligible, which helps the efficiency of the economy. When people perceive the system to be unjust, the costs of transacting go up. In other words, if one cannot follow both formal and informal sets of rules coherently, this will be reflected in their merger and certain patterns of rule-following or unwritten rules. It might be tempting to think that unwritten rules are generally disadvantageous for the system. This is only true, however, if the rules of the game – formal and informal constraints and their enforcement – were tied to the public interest and were beneficial to economic performance. As this has not always been the case in Russia, the impact of unwritten rules is rather ambivalent.

2. Unwritten rules: an invisible hand

Reliance upon unwritten rules is an outcome of the loopholes in legislation, plus the inefficiency of formal rules and their enforcement, on the one hand, and people's lack of respect for formal rules on the other. Traditionally distant and skeptical attitudes to the law create a fundamental problem of public governance and limit the constituency for the effective institutional framework, essential for a market economy. To overcome Russia's dependency on unwritten rules means breaking free from the following chain reaction:

The 'rules of the game' in the economy are non-transparent and frequently change, because the existing legal framework does not function coherently. Some key building blocks of a transparent market system, such as land code, anti-corruption legislation, and a functioning banking system, are not in place and basic market institutions such as open competition, property rights, and transparent corporate governance do not work as they should. The incoherence of formal rules forces almost all Russians, willingly or unwillingly, to violate them and to play by rules introduced and negotiated outside formal institutions.

Anybody can be framed and found guilty of some violation of the formal rules, as the economy operates in such a way that there is always something to be caught for. For example, everybody is forced to earn in the informal economy to survive - a practice that is punishable, or could be made so. Businesses are taxed at a rate that forces one to evade taxes in order to do well. Practices such as embezzlement of state property or tax evasion become pervasive. Inside state institutions, a whole family of corrupt practices such as bribe-taking and extortion in the granting of licenses etc. has been prevalent. The fairly ubiquitous character of such practices makes it impossible to punish everyone.

Due to the pervasiveness of the offence punishment is bound to occur selectively on the basis of criteria developed outside the legal domain. While everybody is under the threat of a punishment, the actual punishment is 'suspended,' but can be enforced in principle at any time. The principle of 'suspended punishment', by which certain freedom and flexibility did exist, but could be restricted at any moment worked well in the Soviet system. It brought about the routine practice for authorities to switch to the written code only 'where necessary'. A similar tendency is noticeable at present and apparently for the same reasons: formal rules are insufficient to operate fully on their own and it is not feasible to catch everybody.

Unwritten rules come into being to compensate for the defects in the rules of the game and to form the basis for selective punishment. Violation of unwritten rules can result in enforcement of written ones, which paradoxically makes it more important to observe the unwritten rules rather than written. This in turn feeds back into the non-transparency of the 'rules of the game' in the Russian economy.

Unfortunately, these attributes of the system seem not to have changed much during Russia's transition to a market economy. In the same way that the planned economy was not really a planned economy and was actually run with help of *tolkachi* ('pushers'), *blat* and other informal arrangements operating according to unwritten rules, the market economy today is not really a market economy. This is due primarily to the key role that unwritten rules still play in the system.

If the functioning of the economy depends on unwritten rules, how can their significance be reduced without cutting down the branch on which one is sitting?

Western aid programs have funded ambitious macroeconomic reforms aimed at 'shocking' Russia into a functioning market economy and foreign investors have attempted to introduce and apply Western business practices and norms within the Russian context. Despite these external efforts and the internal political will to change the foundations of the system, it turned out not to be an easy task. Unwritten rules have long been a powerful invisible hand within Russian political culture and their presence is unlikely to melt away.

In 1990s', unwritten rules surfaced as the opportunistic and manipulative use of formal constraints and the possibility of building corporate strategies on such basis. In order to get routine business tasks accomplished companies, firms and enterprises are often compelled to secure a 'roof' (*krysha*), or to employ individuals and private security services companies skilled at both navigating Russia's complex financial and legal spheres and mastering the so-called informal negotiation techniques. The former implies professional expertise in the tax code, licensing requirements, insolvency law, accounting and banking procedures in combination with the necessary know-how to manipulate these codes to the firm's advantage. The latter refers to sophisticated intelligence-gathering capacities and the informal use of blackmail files (*kompromat*), including copies of bank statements, currency transfers, business and real estate transactions, and other official documents as well as general correspondence, personal information and unofficial transcripts of telephone conversations of discrediting nature.

Rather than restricting their activities to 'traditional' tasks such as physical protection and informational security, private security services in Russia have become the *de facto* administrative force of the present economy: their extra-legal activities enable Russia's imperfect institutional framework to operate. Representatives of security agencies facilitate interactions with both state bodies and with other economic agents, including business competitors, organized crime groups, and protection agencies. The transaction costs incurred by private security services, pervasive corruption and high-risk environment undermine the solvency of small firms in competitive markets and serve to maintain the unwritten rules which benefit those interested in keeping transaction costs high.

Thus, the participation of security agencies in 'solving problems' and enforcing the outcomes is both enabled by, and is a contributing factor to, the chronic weakness of the Russian rule of law. In light of the state's inability to perform its functions (regulation of competition, enforcement of legal agreements, overseeing financial deals and property relations, etc.), private security agencies have stepped into the void to become the arbiters of justice and the guardians of Russia's unwritten order.

Will Russia be able to break free from the dependency on unwritten rules? We should not be pessimistic about it. But in order to reduce the prevalence of unwritten rules in the economy and to make the latter more responsive to market stimuli, it is not enough to simply change the formal constraints. It is crucial to influence the system of informal constraints and to target those unwritten ways in which these informal constraints divert, redefine and enforce the formal ones.

Otherwise it will be impossible to prevent an endless string of frustrations in the course of further reforms in Russia.

3. Can Russia's unwritten order be changed?

In theory, the significance of unwritten rules can be reduced in three ways. First, the rules of the game and the principles of their enforcement have to be made clear for economic agents so that economic success wouldn't be dependent on the mastery of unwritten rules. That is to say, the formal and informal rules have to be observable and enforceable on their own, and spheres regulated by the formal and informal rules have to be separated. Second, the selective nature of enforcement has to be acknowledged as unavoidable, exposed and dealt with on a long-term basis. A disinterested role of the state is a prerequisite of such change. So far state institutions have been too closely involved with business and interest groups.[3] Third, the significance of unwritten rules can be reduced by better accommodation of different sets of interests. In other words, a 'zero-sum game' mentality should give way to an understanding that success at one level does not necessarily mean failure at another. For example, Russia's entrepreneurship could be made to operate in a more socially productive manner and the regional and the federal levels of economy could be coordinated better.

In the economy of a size of the Russian one, these suggestions sound unworkable but they constitute an important set of criteria for a fundamental change and an increase in transparency of the economy. In parallel with changes in formal rules, I would argue, it is also important to think of alternatives to the top-to-bottom patterns of implementation of yet another wonderful reform. Instead, the target might be to invoke processes on a grassroots level, which will create prospects for spontaneous change from below and bring eventual decline in significance of the unwritten rules. The following practical steps can be instrumental in this respect.

The *formal constraints* notoriously associated with extra-legal practices have to be identified and revised, as was done with the tax code. Equally important, non-working legislation has to be identified and abolished. A long-term commitment to the impartial enforcement of the revised formal constraints should be in place. Establishing channels for the 'from below' feedback about these formal rules and their enforcement can help to find ways that would potentially minimize the

---

[3] Some measures to counteract these tendencies are starting to take place under the Putin's administration. According to the First Deputy Prosecutor-General Yurii Biryukov, approximately 18,000 officials were charged with economic crimes in 2000, including more than 1,000 Interior Ministry officials, 120 customs officials, more than 20 tax police officials, 30 judges, and 10 prosecutors [ITAR-TASS, quoted from *RFE/RL*, 5:30, Part 1, 13 February 2001]. Addressing hearings in the Duma in November 2001, Deputy Interior Minister Yevgenii Solovev said over 10,000 officers have been put on trial since the beginning of the year, "Izvestiya" and ORT television reported on 22 November. Among those officers, 2,700 have been sued for corruption [Quoted from RFE/RL Newsline 5:222, Part I, 26 November 2001].

need for informality in the system. Otherwise the situation with good but not working legislation will be repeating itself.

The *informal constraints* tied up with the legacies of the command system and traditional patterns such as patronage etc. should be targeted. This can be done by introducing public debate on the role of informal constraints, by demonstrating how the rule of law is a more advanced form of social contract etc. Such a campaign might involve spelling out openly the legacies of the Soviet era and explicitly acknowledging the grip of path dependency. Financing opinion polls, research, educational literature, TV informational programs and popular advertising would help to bring about an awareness of unwritten rules and to make Russian economy and society transparent first of all to itself.

A framework set out to enhance motivation of *social actors*, professionalism and good management at every level will facilitate a major change. People in Russia have an enormous potential for ingenuity, which is now 'wasted' either on outwitting the system. This potential can be a source of positive change if synchronized with the interests of the economy as a whole. The growing demand for the rule of law among entrepreneurs suggests that in certain sectors, at least, there is a desire for behavior and standards that diverge from previous norms. Long-term efforts are required to introduce standards of professionalism and management substituting for the informal order of things. Training programs for managers of different levels are essential to maintain such efforts.

'Modernizing' *social networks* can reverse their impeding impact on the economy. Instead of diverting the economy's dominant functions and processes, social networks can help organize and facilitate them, once their subversive role in the economy is limited. These 'modernizing' measures should be aimed not only at creating and developing new networks, but also at transforming existing networks into healthier, more open and inclusive ones. Professional networks have to cease being personalized, closed up and exploitative of institutional resources. In order to suggest specific ways of transforming social networks one has to look into the conditions that generated their undesirable features in more detail.

Finally, *outside influences* and organizations can play a substantial role in transforming the setting for the unwritten rules. On a company level, investors, lawyers and consultants can act as 'role models' by introducing new practices and norms into the Russian economy. However this transfer of standards has not operated as hoped thus far and most Russian businessmen are convinced their Western counterparts operate as the Russians do. According to one Western lawyer working in Russia, the behavior of Western firms is not identical to their behavior at home, mainly due to widespread stereotypes, such as: (a) Russia is another planet, no rules apply; (b) There is no law in Russia; (c) One can't enforce one's contractual rights; (d) One never wins in Russian courts; (e) One can't do business in Russia if unprepared to give bribes.

Although these stereotypes might not be totally untrue, it is regrettable that business ethics and international standards become compromised. According to the Economist, the top financial companies and accountancy firms of the world are implicated in various controversial affairs in Russia.[4] At a smaller level, the lack of flexibility towards the Russian business environment on the side of outsiders and their refusal to become adept in using unwritten rules can result in them experiencing intense frustration, economic losses and even personal harm.

It would be fair to suggest that the dilemmas of such choice should not be loaded on an individual investor. To create an investment climate in which such dilemmas do not exist is a matter of internal political will and effort. The pressures from both the international business community and multilateral institutions like the IMF for the diffusion of International Accounting Standards (IAS), OECD and EBRD for the adoption of good corporate governance practices, etc. are necessary but far from sufficient factors. It remains to be studied, when and under which circumstances political players might collaborate to demand and economic players might support an action by the state substantially to promote measures for the improvement of transparency and accountability. Articulation of unwritten rules and focused efforts of the policy-makers to transform them can be an important indicator for monitoring the development of an effective and 'transparent' market economy.

---

[4] For examples, see 'The Smell Test: Western financiers hold their noses when they do business in Russia', *The Economist*, 24 February 2001, pp. 113.

References

Ledeneva, Alena 1998: Russia's Economy of Favours: Blat, Networking and Informal Exchange, Cambridge University Press.

Ledeneva, Alena 2001: Unwritten Rules: How Russia Really Works, published by Centre for European Reform, 2001: *info@cer.org.uk; www.cer.org.uk*.

North, Douglass C. 1990: Institutions, Institutional Change and Economic Performance, Cambridge University Press.

7

ANDREY S.MAKARYCHEV

Globalization as an Intellectual Puzzle: Discourses and Practices of Russian Elites

1. Introduction

The general confusion over globalization challenges which Russia has to face was best expressed by Sergey Karaganov's confession that it is very much unclear what Russia has to do with globalization (Karaganov 2000). Russian elites' perception of globalization is a mix of resistance and adaptation, archaic phobias and newly emerging utilitarian approaches. The whole issue of dealing with the global world is the battlefield between different domestic platforms which are to be analyzed in this paper. This uncertainty and conflictuality brings us to studying intellectual dimension of globalization. What matters with this point of view are different ideas, concepts, approaches, worldviews – all what forms the country's intellectual capital.

Yet the space of Russian political discourse is very much fragmented. On the one hand, it still bears the legacy of great power heritage. Very frequently, as soon as Moscow elites start to speak about globalization, the main issues to arise are NATO enlargement, US-Russian relations, geopolitics, disarmament and other security matters which traditionally are part of diplomatic and "high" foreign policy discourse. This trend – obviously inherited from the Soviet past - was clearly discernable in major projects aimed at analyzing the globalization paradigm for Russia and implemented by two Moscow-based think tanks – Gorbachov Foundation and the Council on Foreign & Defense Policy. Clearly missing in those and other endeavors were domestic dimensions of Russia's transformation which are usually discussed separately of globalization paradigm.

On the other hand, there is another significant tendency which in 1990s became ostensibly inward-oriented, focusing on domestic actors and their intrinsic interests at sub-national levels. This gave birth to mushrooming regionalist studies all across Russia.

What is obviously missing is an analysis of global changes through the prism of major domestic opinion makers. In our view, globalization in Russia has to be primarily discussed among its domestic home actors, both federal and regional. "Mediascapes" and "ideascapes" are among those notions that identify the loci and foci of the process of intellectual thinking about globalization, including changing attitudes to information, appearance of new lifestyles, cultural codes and meanings, etc. Global themes – unfamiliar to most of Russian intelligentsia only a decade ago - are emerging in the domestic political discourse, and new forms of communication among writers and students of world politics have unfolded (Segbers 2001: 4-24). All these new phenomena in Russia's intellectual life might eventually pave the way to creation of new set of rules, norms and principles that might constitute the institutional foundation for country's acceptance of basic logic of globalization.

2. Globalization as Russia's Domestic Problem: Federal Perspectives
2.1. Globalizers

There is a fertile ground for pro-globalist discourse in Russian academic milieu, since the biggest part of major think tanks and public policy research institutions are either sponsored by Western grant institutions, or participate in international research projects based on distance networking, sharing ideas and intellectual capital across borders.

Universities and Academia possess their own resource base for going global. First, many universities are islands of free political discourse and agents of liberal thinking. "Even in a republic where an authoritarian situation flourishes, where in essence a regime of dictatorial power has been established, we speak openly about those things that are happening in the republic as well", says Dr. Midhat Faroukshin from Tatarstan (Kishkovsky 2000: 4). This makes universities very important actors in Russian politico-academic complex. As Raymond Struyk pointed out, their goals extend well beyond those of a conventional educational institution; "these organizations often wish to become actively involved in policy prescription and in program implementation and evaluation" (Struyk 1999: 77).

Second, universities are gateways to the cyberworld. The Open Society Institute paid for establishing 33 internet centers in non-central universities all across Russia.

Third, cooperation with foreign partners makes Russian universities and research centers more independent from Ministries and public authorities in financial terms, thanks to grants and technical resources. Since 1999, the Soros Foundation runs the so-called "Megaproject" which lays the basis for networking liaisons between leading Moscow universities and their regional partners. In 2000 the Carnegie Corporation of New York launched a similar program for establishing Centers for Advanced Study & Education in several non-central universities (Tomsk, Voronezh and Ekaterinburg) to develop a network of scholars beyond the main academic hubs of Moscow and St Petersburg (The Challenge 2000: 13-14).

All these efforts are undoubtedly geared towards integration of Russian universities and think tanks into the international academic community, and the forming a new generation of Russian political and intellectual leaders with a sense of strategy for global development. Raymond Struyk reported that Russian public policy research institutions are the largest in Eastern Europe and are growing the most in terms of staff size and budgets (Struyk 1999: 89).

There is no wonder that Russian globalists in general are very much in favor of Western version of globalization, with networking relations and changing roles of the state in its core. Globalists argue that globalization undermines the "island mentality" (in the words of Viktor Kuvaldin's) which is one of the preconditions for Russia's abandonment of the Communist legacies.

Sergey Markov, Executive Director of Moscow-based Association of Centers for Political Consulting, shares the idea of rapid unfolding of a "common human-kind", and even of a "world government" consisting of a web of international financial institutions, supra-national organizations and some national govern-ments (Markov 2000: 43-46). Hence, if Russia wants to become part of the global world, it has to integrate the internationally dominant norms into its inter-nal development. Dmitri Trenin suggests that globalization for Russia means "building Europe" within its own border. There is no longer an option of with-drawing into "Eurasia", he suggests (Trenin 2001: 320). The same approach is shared by Alexei Podberiozkin, the head of the left-oriented "Spiritual Heritage" think tank, who suggested that Russia has to learn how to gradually incorporate the core elements of globalization into the everyday life of people (http://scenario.ng.ru/printed/problem/2001-05-16/1_problem.html).

Globalists also make extensive use of economic arguments. Ernest Kochetov points out that globalization has to be perceived in terms of growing geo-economic and geo-financial interdependencies. "Infatuation with geopolitics", in his opinion, has to be terminated for the sake of future development. Thus, Rus-sia has to learn how to use geo-economic instruments to find its appropriate place in the world increasingly shaped by emerging "ethno-economic systems", each based on specific set of values, cultural norms and principles of existence (Euro-Atlantic, Islamic, Slavic, Finno-Ugrian and other "systems") (Kochetov 1999: 200-242, 278). In this sense, building the global world is a very competi-tive and demanding enterprise. In search for its geo-economic niche, Russia has to be ready to beat its opponents and rivals. To strengthen the country's geo-economic potential, the government has to give special treatment to Russian transnational companies, which are considered to be Russia's vehicles to the global world. At the same time, many experts suggest that particularly the non-state (intellectual and human capital) resources are the main Russian assets for survival in the era of globalization (http://www.ptpu.ru/issues/1_01/9_1_01.htm).

Thus, Russian supporters of globalization – unlike many of their counter-parts in the West – treat it basically as a "promise", not as a definite result. They deem that the world is still very much fragmented (socially, culturally, politically, and economically), and global forces are not prevailing over local ones. The segregation between world actors (both states and non-state agents) are not being destroyed but modified. Globalization and its economic foundation - post-industrialism - are explained by Mikhail Ilyin and Vladislav Inozemtsev as a culmination of modernity, and not as its negation (Ilyin/ Inozemtsev 2001: 9-12). At the same time, there is a recognition that globalization might be reversed. In this sense, it is not an automatic, "objective" and politically neutral movement. Rather it is man-made and dependent on people's interests and resources. The pro-globalization elites in many countries (including Russia) have to face the challenge of "a majority inimical to progress" (Ilyin/ Inozemtsev 2001: 19).

Yet there is a deep perceptional split among globalists in Russia. One part of them, the optimists, do believe – like Ernest Kochetov does – that Russia has all prerequisites and chances to become one of the pivotal centers of global world and even offer a new model of civilization and development. Russian globalists are not inclined to equate globalization with Westernization, and do not seem to believe that the West has at its disposal the most adequate answers to the most acute developmental challenges. They overwhelmingly are in favor of further democratization of international relations to include a greater variety of decision makers.

Others are much more skeptical about Russia's might and power. Globalists do admit that Russian economy is not ready to meet the competition challenges, except for several industrial sectors (armaments, food and mineral resources). Hopes for large-scale foreign investments in Russia in 1990s have eventually faded (Human Development Report 2000), which undermined some of initial illusions about the fruits of globalization. Yet even harsher appraisals are being heard. Vladislav Inozemtsev, for example, argues that "Russia has definitely missed its chance to join the group of post-industrial leaders" (Inozemtsev 2001: 58). The same view is shared by Valentina Fedotova who deems that Russia keeps staying beyond the global world, and lacks any chances to enter post-industrial phase (Fedotova 2001: 92-93). Interestingly enough, such gloomy perspectives do not push these intellectuals to the camp of anti-globalists. They still are very positive about globalization even though it does not bring tangible results for Russia in particular, at least not for the current generation.

2.2. Alarmists

Opponents of globalization follow quite different approaches. Professor Valentin Bazhanov describes their conviction in the following way: The belief in uniqueness of Russia pushes the country to the periphery of the world process. The idols of the past tend to revive and block the boundary between Russia and outer world" (Bazhanov 2001). Lack of conceptual clarity leads to futile attempts to "achieve the unachievable": both "protect Russian producers" and "attract foreign capital".

The strongest group among Russia's anti-globalist/ alarmist coalition is intellectual stream called "Eurasianism". This agglomeration politically teams up with a wide range of Russian patriots and nationalists (from Alexander Barkashov to Vladimir Zhirinovsky and Gennady Ziuganov). All of them take it for granted that globalization is widely used by foreign countries to impose their domination over Russia. For instance, Sergey Romanov, Moscow diplomatic officer, argues that countries bordering with Russia are a potential threat to Russia's "national interests", eager to apply propaganda tools, increase their "unproportional presence in certain spheres", skip the federal and local regulations, and even change the ethno-demographic balance in Russia's border regions (Romanov 2001: 110). Sergei Kortunov, Rustem Nureev and others posit that Russia is the opponent of the West in global development matters, and is not supposed to copy Western developmental standards (Kortunov 1997: 34-35, Nureev 2001: 111-117).

Alarmists usually start with pointing to the deficiencies of the current world order. Some of their strongest arguments are:

- Inefficiency of global financial organizations in dealing with developing and underdeveloped nations. Some are convinced that international financial architecture is obsolete and inadequate, if not corrupted, and is doomed to failure.

- Lack of transparency in IMF and World Bank dealings with Russia.

- Failure of the Western policies in Iraq, the Balkans and Afghanistan (Novoe Vremia 2001).

At the same time, the Russian version of anti-globalism contains a number of other highly dubious assumptions as well:

Partly, anti-globalization pathos stems from misunderstanding and misreading of the basic world trends. Thus, left-minded economist Sergey Glaziev builds his concept on the assumption that all over the world the state is becoming economically stronger and more dominating. Based on this highly disputable point, he denies in principle the feasibility of such ideas as economic freedom, liberalism, and deregulation. In his opinion, these are basically the criminals who want the state to give up some of its functions (Minutes of the IX Assembly of the Council on Foreign and Defense Politics). Another misperception is that globalization will lead to "complete disarmament", as suggested by the economist Nikolay Shmeliov (ibid: 59).

Another frequently used point is that globalization is an exclusively elite-driven process (Alexander Panarin). For the elites of post-industrial countries, globalization is a means of escape from the control of national constituencies and of forming its own trans-national "exclusive club" of top-level decision makers (Vesti online 2001). Others use much tougher language to characterize the globalization agents – like "clan-like system", intrinsically aggressive and alien to Russia (http://www.e-journal.ru/p_euro-st1-15.html). Hence, the critics presume, globalization undermines the foundations for people's sovereignty and democracy – a thesis which is also very popular among Western anti-globalists (http://www.imperativ.net/imp8/sav1.html). In their circles, globalization is equated with world-wide concentration of power and increasing possibilities to control the human lives (http://sobor.mastertest.ru/print.asp?id=1889). Many Russian political analysts believe that globalization inhibits grass roots activity through the "implantation" of certain political choices into mass conscience. One of them, Stepan Sulakshin, assures us that because of globalization Russia is being ruled by international organizations through sophisticated financial machinery (Sulakshin 1998: 64-08).

Russian anti-global isolationists – basically those raising cultural issues – think that globalization brings moral and mental slavery and therefore has to be fended off. Thus, Boris Erasov, senior researcher at the Institute for Oriental Studies, argues that the general impact of the standards of Western civilization upon non-Western countries is harmful (http://scenario.ng.ru/printed/expertize/2001-03-14/1_unification.html). Most of Russian Orthodox church thinkers tend to believe that globalization is incompatible with Russia's traditional religious mentality.

A number of authors of the so called national patriotic stream (for example, Alexander Zinoviev, Vadim Kozhinov and some others) equate globalization with "information totalitarianism" (http://www.futurerussia.ru/conf/forum_infosociety.html). Those who adhere to the "Eurasianist" ideology think that the globalization will inevitably lead to the appearance of a "world government" which establishes complete control over the citizens. As a confirmation of these intentions, the introduction of individual taxpayer numbers is frequently referred to (http://www.e-jurnal.ru/euro-st1-14.html). This reaction reveals Russian "fundamentalists'" deep fear of new external influences that lead to greater accountability and transparency (Itogi 2001). Nevertheless, their positions are rather influential not only in religious circles but in the academic community as well (Miasnikova 2000: 3-8). An important part of the alarmist discourse argues that globalization leads to growing religious solidarity which might be detrimental for Russia (alleged "Afghanistan – Chechnia – Kosovo" linkage) (Primakov 2000).

Some thinkers assume that globalization will open up Russian industries and regions to foreign capital which is eager to establish its protectorate or economic dominance over the country (http://www.nasledie.ru/oboz/N08_99/8_11.HTM/). Seen from this angle, globalization is associated not with interdependence, but mainly with growing social and economic differentiation of regions (both subnational and supra-national). "Open society" idea, according to this logic, is a tool for opening up domestic markets for much stronger and more experienced international competitors (http://www.nasledie.ru/oboz/N08_00/08_15.HTM). There is a wide spread fear – overwhelmingly unsubstantiated – that Russia's entry into WTO might lead to further discrimination of Russian producers and speed up bankruptcies of Russian enterprises due to the access of foreign to the Russian market. The conclusion is that globalization is an impediment for Russian economic recovery (Ivanov 2000: 12-18). As an alternative to globalization, which offers no perspectives for Russia, Mikhail Deliagin proposes to foster regional integration (probably within the CIS framework) (Deliagin 2001: 97).

The general idea of all alarmists is that Russia needs strong protection against globalization (http://ekg.metod.ru/pub/inoe-2001-koghinov-prn.html). Alarmists and isolationists share a deeply rooted disbelieve in the adaptive possibilities of Russia as a part of the global world. Alarmists adhere to the unjustified and even dangerous idea of Russia's perennial "peculiarity" which is usually an euphemism for its backwardness and inability to compete internationally (Birzha 2001: 8). In fact, what they propose is the conservation of weakness under the multiple guises of "stability", "national security imperatives", or "defense of national producers". For example, the adaptation of the international accounting standards, the precondition to Russia's entry into WTO, is absolutely indispensable for fighting corruption. Those arguing against this measure, in fact impede anti-corruption initiatives (http://www.ng.ru/printed/politics/2001-04-21/3_vto.html).

What is also peculiar for all anti-globalists is that they believe that the process of globalization is masterminded and managed by some sort of international power elite which of course is far from being true. Russia's resistance to globalization is seen as a battle against "new totalitarianism" exemplified by Western bankers, media barons, and the world oligarchy. In order to resist these "evils", Russia in this perspective needs to be a well integrated state (may be even a unitary one), based on economic self-sufficiency, protectionism, tremendous military power and an indigenous state ideology.

One of the weakest points in the anti-globalists argumentation is the thesis that the real centers of decision making for Russia are to be found not within Russian ruling circles but mainly abroad. This misperception becomes even more obvious in the light of the failure of Western powers' attempts to secure Russian transition and to assist with building workable and transparent democratic institutions. Seen through the prism of the wars in Chechnia and former Yugoslavia, it is hard to disagree that the Western countries have only a partial influence over Russia's foreign and security policies, and even a more limited impact on Russian domestic policies.

Third, many Russian enterprises are unable to get access to foreign markets because their products are not adequately certified or because they fail to provide adequate information about their operations and finances. This creates a false impression of "isolation" from the world mainstream, and provokes anti-globalization reactions. In Sergey Kirienko's words, "free market competition is good for domestic operations", not for international ones (http://www.pfo. ru/main/news.phtml?id=2743). For example, the local car makers (GAZ, AvtoVAZ, UAZ) in alliance with some of the governors (that ones of Nizhny Novgorod and Samara oblasts) and the federal district authorities (Sergei Kirienko) have pressured the federal government to raise the customs tariffs for second hand foreign cars (http://www.polit.ru/printable/423515.html). This decision was taken in defiance to public opinion polls that clearly demonstrate that 80 per cent of "Volga" cars consumers are unsatisfied with its quality (MK v Nizhnem 2001: 21). Another controversy is that creating exceptional conditions for a specific industry did not make WTO authorities happier, since other sectors might wish to extend this practice, which would certainly make the whole economic policy of Russia less compatible with the international standards. This case is a good illustration of the fact that ideas do matter and change the policy making milieu.

Fourth, some parts of the regional business communities are afraid that the entry of the foreign companies into the Russian markets will disadvantage and marginalize local producers. Alexander Kuznetsov, the owner of "Elektronika" chain of department stores in Nizhny Novgorod, has complained that foreign competitors are able to sell their merchandise with 5-10% discount, which damages local business (Gorod i gorozhane 2001: 12). In the insurance business as well there are fears of "intrusion" of foreign competitors into regional markets (Russian Regional Report 2000).

The *fifth problem* is relations with the federal authorities. The regional actors try to make their voices heard in the center – with mixed results, however. Regional metal makers, for example, have complained that the central government does not take into account their interests to get a better trade agreement with the United States to provide better access to the American market for the steel producers (AK&M Press Conference 1999: July).

The governors repeatedly complain that the center impedes the international projects of regions. Thus, Igor Farkhutdinov, chief executive of Sakhalin, has confessed that "Sakhalin-1" and "Sakhailn-2" projects were not applauded in Moscow. In his words, for Far East provinces to become an integral part of Asia Pacific economic milieu, the national foreign economic legislation has to be eventually liberalized (Gubernskaya Rossia 2001).

By the same token, Nikolay Fiodorov, the President of Chuvashia, has accused the federal bodies (in particular, the Ministry of Foreign Affairs) in impeding contacts of Russian regions with the Council of Europe. The regional authorities, which in his opinion are placed under stronger public control and hence are more trustful than the federal institutions, have to be allowed to play more decisive roles in implementing social and humanitarian projects with European partners (AK&M Press Conference 1999: February).

Sixth, old misperceptions die hard. Thus, Leonid Polezhaev, the governor of Omsk oblast, launched a campaign for "spiritual security" which was meant to do away with foreign religious missionaries and "foreign propaganda" in the media and educational institutions (http://www.svoboda.org/programs/CH/2001/CH.042801.shtml).

 Kamchatka governor Mikhail Mashkovtsev and the mayor of Petropavlovsk-Kamchatskii Yurii Golenischev (both Communists) have commented on September 11, 2001 terrorist attack on New York and Washington as justifiable "punishment" of US government for its foreign policy conduct (Kommersant Daily 2001).

4. Conclusions. Do Ideas Matter?

The focus of domestic political debates in Russia is gradually changing. While old lines of ideological opposition (between "communists" and "democrats", or "left" and "right") are fading away and are getting blurred, new antagonisms unfold, including that one dividing "globalists" and "anti-globalists". Though the globalization debate is a rather new element in Russia's discourse, it already has started drawing new demarcation lines in political and intellectual circles.

Despite all peculiarities of Russian domestic reactions to the challenges of globalization, it is feasible to identify those theories of international relations originating in the West that would roughly correspond to each of the groups described above.

Globalists in Russia basically stick to post-positivist way of thinking. Many of them are constructivists in a sense that they accept the extraordinary role of intellectual (ideas), human (know how and technical expertise) and symbolic (reputation, image) capital in building overseas communications. Globalists are also in a significant degree inspired by "complex interdependency" approach.

Anti-globalists overwhelmingly adhere to traditional state-centric (Realpolitik) paradigm, with special emphasis on national security and balance-of-power issues. Nationalist rhetoric reveals a strong impact of geopolitical and neorealist worldviews. This makes Russian anti-globalists very much different from their Western counter-parts that are under strong influence of anarchic ideas and anti-state slogans of leftist background. The Russian anti-globalism is shaped by strongly conservative political identity, while Western anti-globalism is an ideology of social revolt and revolutionary protest.

Perhaps, the ideas of those taking *compromising (middle-of-the-road) positions* originate from a wide variety of ideological sources. This is a broad coalition that includes sympathizers of neofunctionalism (focusing on "technical" trans-border cooperation), "English school" (recognizing the gradual emergence of "international society" with its norms and principles), neoliberal institutionalism, and moderate versions of trans-nationalism (in terms of at least understanding the role of non-state actors in the global world).

In the regional discourses it is much harder to find any certain connections with existing world politics theories. Regional intellectual communities are still in the process of discovering of advantages and disadvantages of globalization, and need some more time to form their own coherent visions of being parts of the "global village".

References

AK&M Press Conference 1999:
http://www.akm.ru/rus/press-club/990218report.stm, February 18.

AK&M Press Conference 1999:
http://www.akm.ru/rus/press-club/990730report.stm, July 30.

Apletin, Pavel 2001: Peredovoi krai bol'shogo biznesa (The vanguard of big business). In: Birzha, No. 12, April 5, p.6.

Bazhanov, Valentin 2001: Vozrozhdenie arkhetipov? (The revival of archetypes? Anti-globalization trends and factors in Russia): http://scenario.ng.ru/printed/problem/2001-06-10/1_revival.html

Birzha 2001: No. 9, March 15, p.8.

Deliagin, Mikhail 2001: Puti Rossii v odnopoliarnom mire (Russia's Ways in Unipolar World). In: Megatrendy mirovogo razvitia (Mega-trends of the World Development), Moscow: Ekonomika, p. 97.

Fedotova, Valentina 2001: Modernizatsia i globalizatsia (Modernization and Globalization). In: Megatrendy mirovogo razvitia (Mega-trends of the World Development), Ekonomika, Moscow, pp. 92-93.

Globalizatsia 2001: varianty dlia Rossii (Globalization: Options for Russia), Round table proceedings, St.Petersburg: "Rosbalt" Information Agency and "Club 2015", September 28.

Gorod i gorozhane 2001: No. 34, August 21, p. 12.

Gubernia 2001: No. 36, August 31, p. 2.

Gubernskaya Rossia 2001: No. 12 (32), April 2, p.2.

Human Development Report 2000: Russian Federation 2001

Ignatov, Alexander 2000: A Strategy of Globalization Leadership for Russia: http://www.ripnet.org/strategies/religions/globalization.htm

Ilyin, Mikhail / Inozemtsev, Vladislav 2001: Vvedenie (Introduction). In: Megatrendy mirovogo razvitia (Mega-trends of the World Development), Ekonomika, Moscow, pp. 9-12.

IMEMO RAN 1998: Rossia i vyzovy na rubezhe vekov (Russia and its challenges between two centuries), Moscow, p.14.

Inozemtsev, Vladislav 2001: Neizbezhnost monopoliusnoi tsivilizatsii (The Inevitability of Unipolar Civilization). In: Megatrendy mirovogo razvitia, p.58.

Itogi 2001: March 27.

Ivanov, N. 2000: Globalizatsia i problemy optimal'noi strategii upravlenia (Globalization and the problems of optimal management strategy). In: Mirovaia ekonomika i mezhdunarodnie otnoshenia, No. 3, pp. 12-18.

Karaganov, Sergey 2000: Mezhdunarodnie otnoshenia v usloviakh globalizatsii (International Relations Under Conditions of Globalization): http://www.svop.ru.

Kishkovsky, Sophia 2000: A Bright Future for Russian Higher Education. In: Carnegie Reporter, Summer, p. 4.

Kochetov, Ernest 1999: Geoekonomika, Vek, Moscow, pp. 200-242, 278.

Kommersant Daily 2001: No. 166, September 13, p.3.

Kortunov, Sergei 1997: Kakaya Rossia nuzhna miru? (Which Russia is needed for the world?). In: Pro et contra, winter, pp. 34-35.

Markov, Sergey 2000: Yugoslavskiy krizis i noviy morovoi poriadok (Crisis in Yugoslavia and New World Order). In: Kulik, Anatoly (ed.): World Order After The Balkan Crisis. New Realities of the Changing World. Conference Proceedings, November 1-2, 1999, Moscow, Russian-American Academic Exchange Alumni Association "Professionals for Cooperation", pp.43-46.

Miasnikova, L. 2000: Globalizatsia, ekonomicheskie prostranstva i setevaia nesvoboda (Globalization, economic spaces and networking non-freedom). In: Mirovaia ekonomika i mezhdunarodnie otnoshenia, No. 11, pp. 3-8.

Migranian, Andronik 2001: Rossia: ot khaosa k poriadku, 1995-2000 (Russia: from chaos to order, 1995-2000), Moscow Public Science Foundation, Research Paper No. 128, pp. 405-407.

Minutes of IX Assembly of the Council on Foreign and Defense Politics (2001): March 3: http://www.svop.ru.

Ministry for Economic Cooperation and Development 2001: Federal'naia tselevaia programma "Elektronnaia Rossia" na 2002-2010 gody, Project, Moscow.

MK v Nizhnem 2001: April 26 – May 3, p. 21.

National News Service Web site 2001: http://www.nns.ru/interv/int4026.html

Neklessa, Alexander 2001: Ordo quadro: prishestvie postsovremennogo mira (The Coming of Post-modern World). In: Megatrendy mirovogo razvitia (Mega-Trends of the World Development), Ekonomika, Moscow, p. 151.

Novoe Vremia Journal Web site 2001: http://www.newtimes.ru/newtimes/artical.asp?n=28&art_id=1255.

Nureev, Rustem 2001: Iskat' svoi osobyi put' (In Search for Our Own Path). In: Megatrendy mirovogo razvitia, Ekonomika, Moscow, pp.111-117.

Primakov, Yevgenii 2000: Statement at the working group of the Council on Foreign and Security Policy, December 19: http://www.svop.ru.

Remchukov, Konstantin 2001: Sleduet li prislushivat'sa k sovetam MVF (Shall We Heed the IMF Advices). In: Nezavisimaya gazeta, March 16.

Romanov, Sergey 2001: Paradiplomatia evropeiskikh granits i Rossia (Paradiplomacy of European borders and Russia), Nauchnaya kniga, Moscow, p.110.

Russian Regional Report 2000, 1:16, September 6.

Segbers, Klaus 2001: Institutional Change in Russia. In: Segbers, Klaus (ed.): Explaining Post-Soviet Patchworks. Volume 2: Pathways from the past to the global, Ashgate etc. pp. 4-24.

Struyk, Raymond 1999: Reconstructive Critics. Think Tanks in Post-Soviet Block Democracies, Washington, D.C.: The Urban Institute Press, p.77.

Sulakshin, Stepan 1998: Izmena (Treason), Political Centrist Development Foundation, Moscow, pp. 64-68.

The Challenge 2000: Academic Freedom in the Former Soviet Union. In: Carnegie Reporter, Summer, pp. 13-14.

Trenin, Dmitri 2001: The End of Eurasia: Russia on the Border Between Geopolitics and Globalization. Carnegie Moscow Center, p. 320.

Valuev, Vasily 2001: Internatsionalizatsia rossiiskikh regionov i globalizatsia kak vzaimno obuslovlennie protsesy (Internationalization of Russia's Regions and Globalization as Mutually Dependent Processes). In: Vestnik RAMI, No. 1, pp.21-23.

Vesti Online 2001: http://www.vesti.ru/printed/994846456.html.

Yuriev, Alexander 2001: Summary of presentation at the conference "St. Petersburg: From Future to Present", St. Petersburg State University, May 22-24.

8

ANDREI SHASTITKO

Anti-globalization under transformation: administrative barriers in Russian economy at the turn of the millenium[1]

1. Understanding globalization and transformation

Formally, Russian economy is under transformation for more than ten years. This period is characterized by trade liberalization, mass privatization, and numerous attempts to provide macroeconomic stability. The background for this process is the globalization of economic processes in the world. What are the problems of embedding Russian economic reforms in the context of globalization? Where are obstacles for matching of transactions on national, inter-regional and intra-regional levels with tendencies of globalization? What might and should be done to prevent negative consequences of anti-globalization and the shrinking geographical range of trade in the Russian economy?

As a first approximation, in economic terms, globalization means the emergence of a system of a world markets for goods and services based on international division of labor, information and unified and/or coordinated basic rules of the game. The boundaries of particular product markets or product groups, (under a given closeness of substitutes)[2] depend on transportation and transaction costs. The concept of transaction cost goes back to the famous article of Ronald Coase "Nature of the Firm" (Coase 1937) and has been widely used for last three decades. Ronald Coase used this concept for explanation of the firm as a substitute of the market (price mechanism). Further developments of the New Institutional Economics led to other interpretations of transaction costs. A general definition of this concept (correlated with key aspects of institutions) runs like this: Costs of coordination of economic activities and resolution of distributive conflicts in the world of scarce resources. However, this general definition is not operational. A more operationalized interpretation of this concept contains the following elements: cost of search because of the unavailability of information necessary for decision-making, contracting, measurement of valuable dimensions of goods and services, opportunistic

---

[1] This text has been prepared on the basis of the paper "Rent-seeking in the Regions: Bureaucracies and Administrative barriers" elaborated for the project "Transformation and Globalisation" implemented in 1998-2000 and funded by Volkswagen Foundation.
[2] As is known, most products are differentiated. For this reason theorists are confronted with the problem of identification of a particular good. In fact it means there is a set of goods which might be considered as a close substitutes. Closeness of substitutes depends on the level of cross price elasticity of demand on one good with the respect to price changes of another good.

behavior[3], property rights specification and enforcement (Barzel 1989, Bromley 1989: 95, Furubotn/ Richter 1991: 9, Kapelyushnikov 1990: 29-1, Wallis/ North 1987: 96).

Before the concept of transaction cost was introduced, boundaries of markets had been considered as a dependent variable of transportation cost. Transportation costs, ceteris paribus, depend on the technology of transportation.

Development of transportation technology is a very important factor in widening the geographical boundaries of the market. At the same time the dynamics of transaction costs may provoke reverse processes. Russia in transition is a suitable case for the analysis of tendencies which are not compatible with the patterns of globalization, a good illustration of the shortcomings of the Washington consensus regarding the degree of attention to the development and the design of new institutions (including rules enforcement). In Russian economic literature, the key element of these institutional aspects recently has been described as "administrative barriers". Studies of the World Bank have shown that the quality of institutions as formal and informal rules and enforcement mechanisms is even more important for economic performance than the quality of macroeconomic policy or value of human capital (Chhibber A. et al. 1997, Keefer/ Shirley 2000: 88, 94, Stiglitz 1998).

Thus, there is a causal chain partially borrowed from Adam Smith's explanations of the welfare of nations. It demonstrates the significance of institutions. *First*, welfare depends on productivity of labor in particular, and productivity of factors of production in general. *Second*, productivity of labor (factors of production) depends on the degree of specialization. But, *third*, specialization results from the social division of labor. The degree of the division of labor depends on the scope of market. *Fourth*, the scope of market is constrained by transaction costs depending on the structure of institutions. Thus, institutions are key elements in explaining the resolution of co-ordination and distributive problems.

According to New Institutional Economics institutions are humanly devised formal and informal rules of the game which are complemented by enforcement mechanisms. The last element transforms rules as simple sets of prescriptions on permitted or prohibited actions to constraints in the situation of choice for each actor.

To avoid an oversimplified correlation between the scope of markets, institutions and transaction costs, it is important to stress two points. *First*, not only the total amount of transactions costs matters but also the structure and distribution of

---

[3] According to Williamson's definition (Williamson 1996: 378), opportunism is self-interest seeking with quile, to include calculated efforts to mislead, deceive, obfuscate, and otherwise confuse.

these cost among economic agents (Shastitko 1999: 164-168). *Second*, because of a whole variety of exchanges dimensions the meaning of transaction costs as such is ambivalent from the perspective of economic efficiency. In some dimensions decrease of transaction cost is desirable to achieve Pareto-improvement, but in other dimensions decrease of transaction cost may lead to worsening the allocative features of the economic system, as in the case of cartels, for example. Thus, the design of new institutions (and, consequently, transaction costs) and perspectives of institutional changes has an obvious efficiency dimension related to the distributive nature of institutions.

Coming back to the meaning of the globalization, it might be regarded as the emergence and reproduction of a network of economic, political, social relations throughout the world and consequently the emergence and reproduction of the global social system. The increasing density of these relations and the intensification of mutual dependencies are also essential characteristics of globalization. In more detail, this aspect will be considered below.

For purposes of our analysis, globalization might be considered as a complex, versatile process of development of a unified economic space.[4] It is not only the result of deliberate actions of political and economic actors but also an unintended result, a by-product of ongoing transactions among numerous economic agents from different parts of the world. By the economic space we mean arena for repeated transactions between economic agents with an infrastructure containing common elements (for example, rules of the game with enforcement mechanisms). Through these transactions goods and resources move from one part of the world to another. We use concepts of globalization and united economic space as a key concepts, but simultaneously there are obvious difficulties of identification of its invariant contents. Thus, there is necessity of an explicit definition to operationalize the above mentioned concepts.

There are various ways to do so. The obvious one is to consider globalization and reverse processes in terms of distance of exchanges as a part of the organization of production. The most important dimensions are geographical, temporal and social, as it was mentioned above. Thus, considering globalization in terms of exchange of commodities requires to take into account at least three components of exchanges: social characteristics, terms of exchanges, and geographical distance (Eggertsson 1990, Shastitko 1998). The first one concerns the degree of identity of exchange participants. In this respect there is a continuum from a highly personalized exchange with self-enforceable

---

[4] This corresponds to the description of globalization by Martin Albow (Albow 1996: 88): "...the active dissemination of practices, values, technology and other human products throughout the globe... when global practices... exercise an increasing influence over people's lives...when the globe serves as a focus for, or premise in shaping human activities".

agreements and low explicit transaction costs to impersonal exchanges usually requiring a third party to enforce contracts. The terms of exchange range from instant exchanges without any asymmetry (temporal, informational etc.) in the fulfillment of commitments (as in case of unrealistic Walrasian auctions[5]) to long-term, complex agreements with a significant time asymmetry in the contracting actions of the participants. Finally, the geographical dimension is critical for definition of the space boundaries of commodity markets and allows us to identify the region within which buyers might purchase and producers (traders) might sell their goods.

Historically, a variety of aspects of globalization are closely related to the development of world trade in the 16th to the 19th century and even earlier (long-distance trade). With respect to Russia, it is a very important to point out that the process of globalization and numerous reverse tendencies in the Russian economy might be explained by referring to positive transaction costs and to the dependence of economic performance on the choice or "as if choice" of institutional arrangements.[6]

In the neoclassical research tradition, the only factor usually considered for the definition of geographical boundaries of commodity market is the transportation cost. However, there are instances in economic history when the development of transportation technology and, correspondingly, the decrease of pure transportation costs was accompanied by the localization of markets (North 1978).

The use of unified, harmonized rules of the game (embodied in such international conventions as, for example, Paris Convention of 1883 on industrial property enforcement, Rome Treaty of 1957 containing clauses on competition protection etc.) has a very important feature: network externalities. The more people use one and the same procedures in the same situation, the simpler (ceteris paribus) co-ordination problems can be resolved, the less transaction costs occurs per transaction. But to guarantee the successful fulfillment of international transactions it is necessary to provide cost-effective enforcement procedures, creating credible commitments for game participants.

2. Market failures and barriers to entry/ performance

There are important factors of market failures: increasing return to scale, externalities, public goods, information asymmetries, and finally transaction costs. The consequence of market failures is the deviation of production volumes

---

[5] For a review of the assumptions of the Walrasian general equilibrium model, see North 1990.
[6] Institutional arrangements might be considered as a contractual relation or governance structure between economic entities that defines the way in which they cooperate and/or compete (Williamson 1996: 378).

from socially efficient levels. In some cases it is possible to talk about so-called closed markets for the reason of prohibitively high transaction costs.

Frequently state regulation is suggested as a remedy of negative consequences of market failures. There are price regulation, taxation, court procedures, licensing etc. as particular examples of regulation instruments to improve economic performance. In some cases state regulation literally creates markets of goods and services. To what extent does state intervention stimulate profit-making behavior instead of rent-seeking and rent-extorting behavior? This question is important because the assumption of "benevolent government" as it was used in macroeconomic modelling for long period of time was plainly unrealistic. It is obvious from the standpoint of the economics of regulation where the problem of "state capture" is one of the most important. The theory of "state capture" has been elaborated in the 70s of 20th century by economists of the Chicago school (Stigler 1971, Posner 1974, Peltzman 1976).

The last point is especially important in explanation of administrative barriers in Russia at the turn of the millenium. Each good and service comprises in fact a complex set of useful attributes for the consumer. This is the fundamental idea of the New Theory of Consumption (Lancaster 1966). This approach was very fruitful not only as such but also from the perspective of production cost theory development (North/ Wallis 1994: 612). Useful attributes mentioned above may be physical or transactional in nature. For example, the size of the apartments, the height of ceilings, the location of the flat in the house and the location of the house on the street are important physical dimensions of the good influencing the value for the consumer or buyer. However, rights from the list of Svetozar Pejovich, Arthur Honore or other classifications of rights contribute to the value of the apartment. Ceteris paribus possession of the right to change physical parameters of the flat or to sell it contribute to the total value.

At the same time it is costly for consumer to obtain and evaluate information on these goods and services, particularly, on experience and credence goods. Experience goods (unlike search goods) have a quality which is relatively easily measurable ex-post, after the purchase and after consumption has begun, while the quality of credence goods is not easily measurable even after consumption. Thus, the problem of adverse selection arises, and the scope of the market shrinks. One of the institutional remedies is market signals. Some of them are produced by the state regulations – licensing, certification, the state registration of enterprises, confirmation of goods identity, inspections. Ideally, it might provide for an expansion of market transactions in different directions (social, temporal, geographic). These kinds of regulations are implemented in developed countries, too. Does it mean that there is nothing specific about transition in Russian economy? The answer to this question has to take into account that the scope and the pattern of these practices do matter. We shall consider briefly some ways of regulation as a means of creating administrative barriers. The figures below provide the basis for conclusions even without a sophisticated quantitative analysis.

Registration of legal entities. This procedures covers all kinds of business where legal entities are created.[7] It means the following: to have legally enforceable rights to run a business it is necessary to receive permission based on compliance with the anything but trivial procedure of preparing packages of documents.

The total cost of registration in Moscow is about 12.000 Rbl. (more than US-$ 400) or about 100 minimum wage rates (in 2000). In regions this figure varies from 2.000 to 10.000 Rbl. There are two possibilities to pass registration: with payment for the service of inter-mediation to specialized firms and without it. This is not unique for the contemporary Russian economy. Empirical studies on other emergent market economies show the same phenomenon, for example in Chile and Brazil (Stone/ Levy/ Paredes 1996).

For comparison, the regulated fee for registration was not higher than 10 minimum wage rates (about US-$ 40). Even keeping in mind the differences between real and official rates for registration, the actual sum would not be so high if entrepreneurs could get rid of other regulations.[8]

Certification. Only 4% of the goods are covered by obligatory certification in the European Community. At the same time in Russia this indicator reaches 80%! Are we dealing with a singularly efficient system of certification? According to official data of the Russian agency on standardization (Gosstandart), only 2% of the applications for certification of goods are not approved. However, more than 30% of goods are subsequently disqualified from the sphere of trade. Currently, the introduction of certification of particular goods and services does not require statistics of accidents like in the European Community. According to minimum estimates of turnover (direct expenditures of producers for certification[9]) in this sphere rent extortion amounts to US-$ 150-200 millions per year[10] at the end of the century.

Licensing. Before 2000, more than 500 kinds of businesses has been certified according to federal and regional rules comparing with 30-90 in different countries of the European Community. In fact, the number of licensed businesses is significantly higher in Russia. An average procedure of license application requires visits of eight agencies, the elaboration of more than 20

---

[7] For some kinds of businesses it is not necessary to pass this procedure.
[8] Recently, the procedure of registration has been changed on the basis of principle "one window". It was expected to create a more friendly environment for new firms (especially small and medium size firms). But experience shows that it is not the end of the story.
[9] Intrafirm transaction costs are not counted.
[10] http://www.inp.ru

documents, expenses around 15.000 Rbl. (more than US-$ 500), and 270 hours of work. Turnover reaches the equivalent of US-$ 100 Million. The problem is to work out operational definitions of types of businesses for licensing.

Inspections. Preliminary controls are complemented by subsequent controls by various institutions: police, licensing agency, antimonopoly agency, sanitary, certifying, tax agencies, tax police and trade inspection, fire inspection, price inspection etc. According to the results of a field study in 2000 among 600 small and medium enterprises, licenses were checked by the agencies just mentioned more than 35 times on the average. At the same time certificates were checked more than 120 times. It costs not only time but money, too.

Taking into account the points mentioned above it is necessary to remember another kind of failure – the state failure. There is a logic to the multiplication of administrative barriers. There are about 55 controlling organizations on the federal level as mentioned in the new Administrative Code which became valid after July 1st, 2002. Each of them elaborates its own regulations frequently contradicting each other and federal laws. Failures in coordination are expressed in the duplication of functions. It means different inspectors have one and the same object of control.

According to recent estimates of Russian researchers, the weight of "administrative barriers" in the total turnover of retail trade was about 188 billion Rbl (more than 6,5 Billion US-$) or 10% of the total turnover in retail trade (Auzan/ Kryuchkova 2001: 77). The administrative barriers obviously lead to extra-legal activities described in detail by Hernando de Soto in his famous book "The Other Path" (De Soto 1995).

3. Features of the enforcement system contributing to the persistence of administrative barriers

As it was pointed out in section 1, enforcement is part and parcel of the institutional framework of resources allocation. Enforcement mechanisms transform rules as simple prescriptions of allowed or/and prohibited behavior to constraints influencing choices of economic agents. In other words, enforcement mechanisms create cost for rule violators.[11] At the same time the description of the general features of enforcement mechanisms is not sufficient to understand tendencies in many emerging market economies, including Russia.

There are costs and benefits for enforcement implementation. The distribution of these costs and benefits are crucial circumstances for the explanation of the incentives of economic agents and the outcomes of transactions. Rule enforcement is carried out by agents with own economic interests under

---

[11] For more details on the general questions related to rules enforcement see Barzel 2000, Cooter 1996, Ménard 2000, Shastitko 2002.

asymmetry of information. Additionally, the capacity of enforcement is constrained by the scale of the enforcing agencies. The ways in which violations of rules are identified, the technology of sanctions imposition as well as the efficiency of coordinating different enforcing organizations are important factors for the general efficiency of enforcement mechanism .

There are particular features of the sanctions system providing fertile ground for rent extortion and expansion of extra-legal activities:

1. There are no fixed and/ or clearly defined amounts of payments for each violation. As such it would be not problem. However, the way in which a fair amount is determined is not transparent to outsiders. It means the enforcing agency or agent and the violator have the space for bargaining. The result is that the violator pays less than he would have to, and the enforcing agent gets overpaid. This factor provides fertile ground for corruption.[12] Some studies classify this form of corruption as administrative corruption. From this point of view, administrative barriers and corruption under asymmetry of information might be considered as close correlates.

2. The rate of temptation. On the one hand the salary of civil servants is very low relative to corresponding levels in the private sector. On the other hand, civil servants have power which might be used in different ways. Under the veil of information asymmetry in creates powerful incentives for abuse.

3. Specific features of rules enforcement are related to the problem of the informalization of rules (Radaev 2001). This tendency is conditioned by contradictions in formal rules which might be used to regulate one and the same situation in different ways as well as by an excessive harshness of prohibitions and restrictions which create incentives for the privatization of benefits originating from the enforcement of established rules.

4. Some controlling organizations are financed partially and directly from fines. There are a lot of decrees and other rules establishing extra-budget sources for the funding of state organizations. The problem would be even worse if there was not a collusion among all controlling agencies (Grigoriev/ Kosarev 2000). If it is not the case, the problem of free access[13] (problem of commons) arises (Eggertsson 1990): alleviation of the base for taxation and rent extortion. Collusion in this case means a set of rules constraining the behavior of controlling agencies representatives. This logic is quite akin to

---

[12] There are at least two opportunities for corrupt transactions from the perspective of payment. The economic agent pays no fine, and pays the enforcing agent only part of the official fee. The second one is payment of an additional fee for the service reglemented by the law (Shleifer/ Vishny 1993: 600-604).

[13] The problem of free access is related to exploitation of scarce resources without any property rights. There are two main consequences: over-exploitation and exhaustion of resources in free access.

the consequences of Olson's roving bandit activity. The prosperity of these actors does not result from the development of production technology but from the development of rent-extortion technology. One of the key elements of this technology is producing regulations, instructions etc.

5.   Another aspect is the fact that enforcers generally are not held responsible for the abuse of their rights and the discriminate application of rules. The reason for this is that there is little chance that they are caught and punished for their acts. The results of enforcing activities cannot easily observed by principals as actors whose interests are influenced by agents. This causes problems of stimulating contracts design.

All of these factors create additional transaction costs for newcomers on different commodity and service markets. The experience of the last decade shows the sustainability of administrative barriers. It is conditioned by the following factors:

*   *First*, by the free-rider problem. Each servant involved in the process of licensing, certifications, inspection etc is interested in diminishing the burden of the administrative barriers as a whole. It is quite rational for him because abolishing excessive barriers for legal economic activity creates conditions for fair competition and incentives for innovations and consequently, for economic development. At the same time he/ she will suffer from the removal of a particular barrier as a source of rent. As a rule, in the first case this agent is a member of the latent interest group, while in the second case he is a member of a small group. The advantage of a small group is the presence of selective incentives to overcome the free-rider problem.

*   *Second*, the learning effect. Ongoing processes of rent-extortion create a more or less certain state of affairs for all players. The removal of barriers in one area creates the risk that new barriers are created in another. The recent experience of barriers removing as a part of institutional reforms shows that the control over the process of de-bureaucratization is limited because special interest groups have sufficient experience in adapting to all sort of political campaigns.

4. The political economy of de-bureaucratization

This part contains ideas on de-bureaucratization and conditions of effective de-bureaucratization based on considerations of desirability, feasibility and credibility. The general directions reforms should take are more or less clear: simplifying and abolishing excessive registration and control procedures, increasing transparency of regulation for the general public, creation of conditions for the development of self-regulation as a substitute and simultaneously creating complementary mechanisms to government regulation.[14] However, knowing the remedy does not necessarily mean that it will be applied.

There are three aspect of reform which are useful to mention (Shirley 1995: 234-235): desirability, feasibility and credibility. With regard to the first aspect, there are two important conditions that desirable reforms will be translated into actual reforms: the creation of pro-reform coalition and/ or an economic crises.

Recognizing the desirability to reform economic policy is a necessary but not a sufficient condition for the successful implementation of institutional changes. Obviously, there are complementary conditions of incentives on the side of rule-makers and enforcers like support on the side of potential beneficiaries of the reform and lowering the resistance of the main losers. There is the perspective that the rent flow from natural resource extraction and export (especially oil and natural gas) will be exhausted in future. The longer the decision-making horizon, the more likely will the rulers understand the necessity to diversify sources of income for the budget to secure stability and maximize support of voters in the future.

To overcome the problem of administrative barriers proliferation opportunities for institutional design and institutional innovations have to be available within the framework of the new "social contract" which in turn has to emerge from the understanding of key actors that administrative barriers have far-reaching negative consequences not only for the economy, but also for their own legitimacy. As a step in this direction, a package of new federal laws has been elaborated in 2000.[15] At the same time it is not appropriate to consider this contract as based on offers, explicit promises and (external) enforcement procedures.

However, at the moment there are no guarantees for the sustainability of the deregulation process (in the sense that excessive regulations will be abolished) and for the integration of the Russian economy in the world economy not only as a exporter of raw materials and capital but also of a more diversified set of goods and commodities. This is one of the key problems in agenda of economic policy reform in Russia.

There are two aspects to be considered for a new institutional environment for business: (1) the design of laws; (2) the design and enforcement of compensatory contracts. In the following, we concentrate on the second point.

To analyze perspectives of institutional reforms in a positive way it is necessary to understand expected consequences of institutional changes in form of rules

---

[14] In more details see Kryuchkova 2001, 2002 (forthcoming).
[15] Some information on this can be found under this address: www.economy.gov.ru/program/soderzanie.html.

and especially mechanisms of enforcement. De-bureaucratization of the economy means an increase of transparency in rules and enforcement mechanisms, simplification of rules and procedures for profit-oriented entrepreneurs. At the same time it means an increase of the costs of rent-seeking and rent-oriented behavior. Obviously, we have to expect resistance to changes in case compensation mechanisms for the loosing parties are lacking.

According to an empirical classification of compensations we may identify five kinds (Edwards/ Lederman 1998): direct and indirect compensations, cross and excluding compensations, and political compensations. These compensations mean not only direct payment in pecuniary form or in kind, but also changes in economic policy, support of some privileges or status of losers. The main point in this classification are the instruments of compensation, although it would be more appropriate to consider opportunities for institutional changes on the basis of *compensatory contracts* (Shastitko 2002a). There are the following important dimensions of compensatory contracts: (a) determination of the compensation amount[16], (b) elaboration of payments mechanism[17], (c) ex-post control (including violators identification procedures), (d) implementation of sanctions.

A satisfactory quality of compensatory contracts can be attributed to the credibility of the commitments for the loosing parties to be compensated in future. In fact, the key problem is the enforcement of compensatory schemes. Even if institutional changes meet Kaldor-Hicks criterion taking into account opportunities for compensation and the transaction cost of compensatory contract enforcement, there are still problems with the fact that reforms change the bargaining power of the losing actors in the future. The expected redistribution of bargaining as a consequence of reforms may cause additional complications if key actors calculate their costs and benefits under the new system.

---

[16] For this case it is necessary to estimate losses for a particular group along with other dimensions: number of members, degree of homogeneity, stability.
[17] Contract performance as a matter of real time. Thus, it is important to identify the sequence of actions, the form of payment, sources and time (if necessary to define) of payment.

References

Albow, Martin 1996: The Global Age, Cambridge Polity Press.

Auzan, Alexander/ Kryuchkova, Polina 2001: Administrativnie bariyeri v ekonomike: zadachi deblokirovaniya. In: Voprosi ekonomiki, No. 5.

Barzel, Yoram 1989: Economic Analysis of Property Rights. New York, Cambridge University Press.

Barzel, Yoram 2000: The state and the diversity of third-party enforcers. In:Menard, Claude (ed.): Institutions, Contracts and Organizations: perspectives from new institutional economics, Edward Elgar, pp. 211-233.

Bromley, Daniel 1989: Economic Interests and Institutions. The conceptual foundations of public policy, New York.

Chhibber A. (et al.) 1997: The State in a Changing World/ World Development Report 1997, Oxford University Press.

Coase Ronald: The nature of the firm, Economica 4 (13-16), November 1937 pp.386-405.

Cooter, Robert 1996: The Rule of State Law and the Rule-of-Law State: Economic Analysis of the Legal Foundations of Development. In: Bruno, Michael/ Pleskovich, Boris (eds.): Annual World Bank Conference on Development Economics, The World Bank, Washington, D.C., pp. 198-221.

Edwards, Steven/ Lederman, David 1998: The Political Economy of Unilateral Trade Liberalization: The Case of Chile. In: Bhagwati J. (ed.): Going Alone: The Case for Relaxed Reciprocity, MIT Press and American Enterprise Institute, Cambridge/ Mass/ Washington, D.C.

Eggertsson,Trainn 1990: Economic behavior and institutions, Cambridge University Press.

De Soto, Hernando 1995: Inoy put'. Nevidimaya revolutsia v tret'yem mire, Moscow, Catallaxy.

Furubotn, Eric/ Richter, Rudolf 1991: The New Institutional Economics: An Assesment. In: Furubotn, E.G./ Richter, R. (eds.) The New Institutional Economics, pp. 1-32.

Grigoriev, Leonid/ Kosarev, Andrei 2000: Problema begstva kapitala. In: Ekonomichesky zhurnal VSE, 4:4, pp. 454-474.

Kapelyushnikov, Rostislav 1990: Ekonomisheskaya teoriya prav sobstvennosty.

Keefer, Philip/ Shirley, Mary 2000: Formal versus informal institutions in economic development. In: Ménard, C. (ed.): Institutions, Contracts and Organizations. Perspectives from New Institutional Economics, Edward Elgar, Cheltenham.

Kryuchkova, Polina 2001: Samoregulirovaniye biznesa kak sposob upravleniya kontractnimi otnosheniyamy. In: Voprosy ekonomiki, No. 6, pp.129-143.

Kryuchkova, Polina 2002: Self-regulation: comparative advantages, forms and conditions of development. In: Shastitko, A.E. (ed.): Three studies on competitive policy, Bureau of economic analysis, Moscow, TEIS.

Lancaster, Kelvin 1966: A New Approach to Consumer Theory. In: Journal of Political Economy 74:2, pp.135-157.

Ménard, Claude 2000: Enforcement procedures and governance structures: what relationship?. In: Ménard, C. (ed.): Institutions, Contracts and Organizations: perspectives from new institutional economics, Edward Elgar/ Cheltenham, pp.234-253.

North, Douglas 1978: Structure and Performance: The Task of Economic History. In: Journal of Economic Literature, Vol. XVI, September, pp.963-978.

North, Douglas 1990: Institutions, Institutional Change and Economic Performance, Cambridge University Press.

North, Douglas/ Wallis, John 1994: Integration Institutional Change in Economic History. A Transaction Cost Approach. In: Journal of Institutional and Theoretical Economics, 150:4, pp. 609-624.

Peltzman, Sam 1976: Toward a More General Theory of Regulation. Journal of Law and Economics, Vol.19, pp.211-240.

Posner, Richard 1974: Theories of Economic Regulation. The Bell Journal of Economics, Vol.5, pp.335-358.

Radaev, Vadim 2001: Deformalizatsiya pravil i ukhod ot nalogov v rossiyskoy khozyaistvennoy deyatelnosty. In: Voprosy ekonomiki, No. 6, pp.60-79.

Shastitko, Andrei 1998: Neoinstitutsionalny podkhod v ekonomicheskom analise. In: Tambovtsev, V. (ed.): Factor transaktsionnih izderzhek v teorii i praktike rossiyskih reform, Moscow, Teis.

Shastitko, Andrei 2002a: Novaya institutsionalnaya ekonomicheskaya teoriya. Moscow, Teis.

Shastitko, Andrei 2002b: Ekonomichesky analyse obespecheniya soblyudeniya pravil. In: Voprosy ekonomiki, No 1.

Shirley, Mary et al. 1995: Bureaucrats in Business. The Economics and Politics of Government Ownership. Oxford University Press.

Shleifer, Andrei/ Vishny, Robert 1993: Corruption. In: The Quarterly Journal of Economics, August, 1993. pp.599-617.

Stigler, George 1971: The Theory of Economic Regulation. The Bell Journal of Economics. Vol.2, pp.3-21.

Stiglitz, Joseph 1998: More Instruments and Broader Goals: Moving Toward the Post-Washington Consensus:
http://www.worldbank.org/html/extdr/extme/js-010798/wider.htm.

Stone, Alan/ Levy, Brian/ Paredes, Ricardo 1996: Public Institutions and Private Transactions: a Comparative Analysis of the Legal and Regulatory Environment for Business Transactions in Brazil and Chile. In: Alston, Lee/ Eggertsson, Trainn/ North Douglas (eds.): Empirical Studies in Institutional Change, Cambridge University Press, pp.95-128.

Wallis, John/ North, Douglas 1987: Measuring the Transaction Sector in the American Economy, 1870-1970. In: Engerman, S. (ed.): Long-term Factors in American Economic Growth, Chicago.

Williamson, Oliver 1996: The Mechanisms of Governance. Oxford University Press.

9

NATALIA ZUBAREVICH

The Socio-Economic Cleavage of "Open" and "Closed" Russian Regions and Resistance to Globalization

Globalization has multiple effects that manifest themselves in politics, the economy, the sphere of information and social relations. Many analysts believe that globalization processes weaken the role of the state and strengthen the supranational and subnational (regional and local) levels of power (Beck 2001, Strange 1998, Sassen 1996, Volodin/ Shirokov 1999), a process which lead to the special term "glocalization" (Robertson 1995) (a mixture of global and local tendencies) in spatial development, the trend especially characteristic of countries of the European Union.

In Russia, however, regionalization (decentralization), in our opinion, was caused by other, internal political reasons and had to do with a systemic crisis that weakened federal authority rather than with globalization. The policy of tough re-centralization pursued in Russia in the past two years has revealed the weakness and even artificiality of Russian regionalization of the 1990s. Municipal bodies of authority and local structures of civil society have so far remained weak. It would therefore be a mistake to view Russian regionalization in the context of European processes: conditions are still lacking for the full-fledged development of subnational structures of authority and society in Russia.

Though manifestations of economic and information globalization are especially evident, their influence can hardly be interpreted unambiguously. The global world is still divided into leaders and outsiders, therefore the advantages and dangers of the global economy are debated especially heatedly in the developing countries and those in the state of transition, such as Russia. The most complete analysis covering the problems of globalization in Russia was made in the international project "Explaining Post-Soviet Patchworks" (Segbers 2001).

In addition to states being involved in globalization processes to a different extent, the impact of globalization can be assessed on a different, regional scale. Being an innovation process, globalization spreads in the form of diffusion and is unable to evenly cover states, especially those that are big and heterogeneous. Strong internal contrasts are most characteristic of "catching up" countries, such as China, Brazil, Mexico and India. Russia, too, has huge internal differences in resource endowment, economic and infrastructure development, and the degree of social modernization. Therefore its regions are involved in the global exchange of information, capital, goods and services to a fairly different extent.

Russia is distinguished by the fact that globalization influenced its regional development against a background of a systemic (socioeconomic and political) crisis of the 1990s. The socioeconomic crisis resulted in a sharp decline in production and living standards, badly worsening the starting conditions for integration in the global economy. The political crisis promoted decentralization, which in turn exacerbated regional polarization. First, the re-distribution of resources for the sake of evening out regional development was reduced to the minimum, with underdeveloped regions sinking into worse poverty. And second, growing independence of regional authorities enabled them to pursue their own policy, thus either creating conditions for or obstructing the inflow of capital, information, goods and services. In our opinion, it is therefore impossible to consider the influence of globalization per se on regional development outside the context of systemic transformations.

The following questions will help us to structure our analysis of the impact of globalization processes on the Russian regions:

- In what form does the impact of globalization manifest itself?

- What is the regional picture of the influence of globalization?

- How does resistance to globalization manifest itself on the regional level?

It is difficult to get exhaustive answers to these questions. The reason is that many indicators, statistical data in particular, are lacking or inadequate, economic trends are unstable and the institutional environment together with the mode of living have been changing rapidly. Many tendencies can nevertheless be assessed on more than merely the qualitative level.

1. Forms of Globalization in Russian Regions

The across-the-border flow of capital (foreign investment), growing economic openness (the scale and role of foreign trade), the spread of global information networks (primarily the Internet), the unification of consumption standards and the development of world cities that influence the entire world economy are usually considered to be the main forms, in which globalization manifests itself. Russia, too, saw those forms of globalization manifest themselves to one extent or another in the 1990s.

1.1. Direct foreign investment

Though the amount of foreign investment in Russia in global terms so far is small - direct foreign investment totaled US-$ 4.3 billion, or US-$ 30 per capita, in 1999 - its distribution inside the country is quite indicative. Between 1995 and 1999 Moscow received more than half (52.6%) of total foreign investment; the Moscow region, which came second, lagged far behind with its 4.2% and was followed by St. Petersburg and Tatarstan, the most developed republic of the Russian Federation, each with 3.8%. The Sakhalin region, in which Western companies engaged in oil extraction on product sharing agreement terms and which thus received 3% of foreign investment, can be singled out from among the resource regions. In per capita investment the Nenets autonomous district, another new oil extracting region, leads with US-$ 7,700; Moscow, a major investment center, comes next with its US-$ 2,600 and is followed by the Sakhalin region with its US-$ 2,200.

The paramount importance of the metropolitan area to foreign investors is explained by the following reasons:

• Investment was made primarily in the tertiary sector (business and hotel services, retail networks, etc.) because demand for them and investment efficiency are highest in the capital.

• Investment grows increasingly in the food industry, which has a short investment period and is concentrated around major consumption centers.

• Faced with the institutional problems of "entering" a difficult and unstable market, foreign investors need alliances with Russian partners, who serve as intermediaries and are likewise concentrated in the capital. Intermediaries are also needed to secure support from the federal bodies of authority and transfer investment deeper inside the country. This strategy of relying on the "metropolitan channel" makes it possible to minimize the costs of entering regional markets.

• The technological backwardness of the manufacturing industry makes it unattractive for foreign investors.

• Barriers raised by major Russian businesses prevented investment in the main oil, gas and other export resources extracting regions (see below *Resistance to Globalization*).

1.2. Foreign Trade

The degree to which Russian regions are involved in world trade can be estimated only approximately in the absence of exact statistics. Some exports are registered at places where companies controlling exporting industrial businesses have their headquarters rather than in the regions where these businesses are situated. Thus, Moscow accounts for 28.9% of Russian exports only because Gazprom and leading oil companies are headquartered there. The Tyumen region accounts for 12.3% and the rest of the top ten regions for another 23.3% of total Russian exports. In general, the top ten subjects of the Russian Federation[1] accounted for two-thirds of national exports in the late 1990s. Per

---

[1] The Russian Federation consists of 89 units.

capita export figures differ vastly from an annual US-$ 2,500 in the Tyumen region to US-$ 2-8 in the underdeveloped republics of Tyva and Adygei (Human Development Report 2000: 107).

At the same time Moscow is in reality the biggest importer (39.4%) and import distributor among the Russian regions. Though St. Petersburg came second with a modest 9.3%, import concentration was on the whole tremendous, with the two federal cities accounting for nearly half the entire national imports in the late 1990s. The top ten regions received 68.4% of Russian imports. Regions with favorable customs regimes, such as the Kaliningrad exclave and the Ingush, Kalmyk and Altai republics, featured prominently among importers. These underdeveloped republics were granted preferences to enable them to boost their tax revenues and thus cut their federal budget subsidies. The experiment, however, met with little success as any preferential treatment invariably bred corruption in Russia and the federal budget received shrinking customs duties. Favorable regimes were abolished in the republics in 1999-2000. Regional differences in per capita imports are just as big as in exports, ranging from an annual US-$ 16 in the Kostroma region to US-$ 1,800 in Moscow.

As far as the direction of trade flows is concerned, by the mid-1990s Russia became divided into the zones of influence of two world centers – European and Asian, with the dividing line going through Eastern Siberia (Vardomsky/ Treyvish 1999: 192). The lopsided division is explained by the different roles played by trade partners: European countries account for over half the Russian foreign trade turnover. Meanwhile, trade with the USA, the third party to the world triad, is not expressly tied to any Russian region.

1.3. Consumption globalization

The impact of this type of globalization can only be considered tentatively as representative surveys of regional consumer behavior are yet to be made in Russia. Though the *Expert* journal and the Monitoring.ru group studied middle class consumer behavior and preferences, their sampling makes it possible to distinguish between only two groups, Moscow and regional consumers in general.

The large-scale importation of cheap goods from third countries (China and Turkey), which made it possible to satisfy the famished Russian consumer, was, in our view, the first channel of "specific" globalization. Shoddy products - cheap copies of world standards – gave an idea of the global market. Food imports, often of low quality and unsafe, played the same role. Consumption experience of this type resulted in persistent distrust of imported food (especially meat) displayed by a significant section of the Russian population.

Imports of famous brands from developed countries came later, giving Russian consumers with higher incomes an idea of global quality consumption standards.

The spread of brands as a middle class consumption norm marked a veritable breakthrough. An *Expert* survey showed that as incomes grow consumer preferences sharply change from cheap markets of Turkish and Chinese goods to retailers offering brands for the middle class. The fast spread of global Benetton network outlets and growing demand for Western cars (especially second-hand) are characteristic examples of the trend, which is so far more evident in the capital than in the regions, but nevertheless should not be underestimated. Acceptance of global standards through the consumption of brands changes the way of life of at least 20% of the Russian population (10 million families) (Gurova 2001), which accounts for over half Russian consumption. This is a huge market, 90% of which is occupied by non-resident manufacturers.

In addition to goods, consumption of services, primarily in the field of recreation and entertainment, has emerged as another channel of globalization. The middle class spends about US-$ 600 per family on recreation, mostly on foreign travel. Growing mobility of the population and first-hand acquaintance with the world recreation industry also promote consumption globalization. Young middle class Muscovites have resumed regular visits to movie-houses, fitted out with state-of-the-art equipment but still too expensive for the mass of the people, as a consumption norm. Foreign movies, for the most part American blockbusters, account for more than 90% of screening in these movie-houses.

Consumption globalization is strictly limited by personal incomes. Average regional income figures are fairly conventional, bearing in mind the fact that even according to official data there is a 1200% - 1300% gap between the incomes of the first (the poorest) and the last (the richest) decile population group and an over 3900% gap according to independent economists. However, even average figures lay bare interregional differences.

Relatively high incomes have been registered in a mere ten to twelve out of the 89 Russian regions. Moscow is in the lead, with major oil and gas extracting regions (autonomous districts of the Tyumen region) following suit. Average per capita money incomes in this group amount to a monthly US-$ 250-350, which is 300%-500% higher than the subsistence level, meanwhile the poor with incomes below the subsistence level account for no more than 20% of the population. Other exporting regions of Siberia (the Krasnoyarsk territory) and European Russia (the Samara, Perm and Belgorod regions, and the Komi Republic) are relatively well off. Incomes registered in St. Petersburg, the city ranked second in the Federation, differ little from the Russian average of US-$ 90. At the other pole are ten to fifteen regions, with average per capita money incomes of a monthly US-$ 30-40 staying below the subsistence level and the poor accounting for 50-70% of the population. These regions have no middle class to speak of, and consumption is unlikely to come close to global standards even in a distant future.

1.4. Information globalization

The diffuse nature of globalization processes is most seen in the spread of the Internet. Until 1998 world web users concentrated in Moscow and St. Petersburg, 1999 saw the full-scale spread of the Internet in major cities with a population of over 1 million people, and from late 1999 Internet connection became widespread in major cities and towns with a population of over 500,000 people. Though inhabitants of cities with a federal status have been estimated to account already for only 20% (Perfilyev 2001: 348) of the total number of Internet users in Russia, the concentration is still very high because the cities with a federal status account for less than 10% of the total Russian population.

The Internet has shown that globalization processes spread unevenly not only among the regions but also among the different types of settlements. Inhabitants of major cities and large towns get involved in information globalization much faster owing to rapid modernization of their mode of living and higher incomes. On the other hand, inhabitants of small and mid-sized towns, together with the rural population have "fallen" out of the global information space, and the gap between major urban centers and the outlying areas keeps growing.

This polarization is even more graphically manifest in the spread of advanced types of communications, especially cellular communications, the large-scale expansion of which has only just begun in regional centers. In December 2001, Moscow residents accounted for 57%, St. Petersburg residents 11% and those of other Russian regions a mere 32% of the 6.7 million subscribers to cellular communications in Russia (J'son & Partners 2001: 3). Global TV channels (CNN and such like) are even less widespread, and the number of their users is small even in the metropolitan areas.

1.5. World cities

Though many authors point to the importance of this phenomenon among globalization processes (Friedmann 1986, Hall 1984, Sassen 1991, Soja 2000, Knox/ Taylor 1995, Marcuse/ van Kempen 2000), in our opinion, it would be premature to consider prospects for the development of world cities in Russia: Moscow has indisputably retained the status of a macro-regional center within the CIS but has yet a long way to go to gain the world city status. The Russian capital lacks the needed concentration of financial resources, the central position in the world communications system and the leading role in decision-making and world economic management.

Attempts by Moscow authorities to speed up the "course of history" and create the environment for global business development nevertheless merit attention. These include the new Moscow-City financial center construction project and the modernization of the municipal transport infrastructure.

2. Types of Regions According to the Nature of Globalization Impact

Under the impact of the systemic crisis and globalization processes Russia split into two unequal parts by the mid-1990s. Approximately a quarter of the regions inhabited by one third of the national population managed to become part of the world market of capital, goods and services, mostly as raw materials periphery of that market. The other regions remained barely exposed to globalization processes and restricted to the domestic market. Without aspiring to give a full picture, we can single out the following distinctive types of regions.

Four types of regions can be classified as "*open*". As was the case with other countries, globalization processes manifested themselves first of all in metropolitan areas, which became postindustrial economic centers. Russia was distinguished by the utmost concentration of the positive results of globalization in its capital. Moscow accounts for one-third of Russian foreign trade, half the entire foreign investment in Russia in the period from 1995 to 1999 and over one-third of national retail trade. Other major cities, such as St. Petersburg, Nizhni Novgorod, Novosibirsk and Samara, have considerably lagged behind in attracting investment and the global exchange of goods and services (Zubarevich 2001).

Export-oriented extracting regions, which became a resource periphery of the world economy, constitute the second type. Unlike the developing countries, however, export productions in the Russian regions are controlled primarily by local companies, which have their headquarters in Moscow. As a result financial flow globalization is inconspicuous at the regional level, foreign investment comes from offshore areas and is more often than not of Russian provenance. The bulk of those engaged in exporting sectors have no production contacts with the outside world and their way of life differs little from that of inner Russia.

Globalization influence is manifested in orientation to Western consumption standards and world trade brands and growing recreation services thanks to higher household incomes. The diffusion of the information and services components of globalization is nevertheless much slower, with the exception of a certain type of political technologies. Western election technologies, including "dirty" ones, are more actively used in regional elections in exporting regions as considerable allocations are made to finance election campaigns, which are conducted by experienced Moscow specialists. According to expert estimates, over US-$ 30 million was spent on the gubernatorial elections in the Tyumen region, and US-$ 10-15 million in the Krasnoyarsk territory.

Several border regions (the Kaliningrad region in the west, the Primorsky territory in the east and the Krasnodar territory in the south), crossed by major foreign trade flows, represent the third type. These regions differ in their economic development and household incomes (though official statistics do not reflect the real situation), but have in common a very high share of shadow or criminal economy. The results are rampant corruption among their higher-ups and the election of governors with close links with the criminal elements.

The Kaliningrad exclave occupies a special place among these regions. The only positive effect of globalization there is the growing mobility of the population, engaged primarily in small-scale border trade, and rising incomes. Most of these incomes, however, are made in the shadow economy (Smorodinskaia 2001). Despite proximity to EU countries, per capita foreign investment in the region is not higher than the mean registered in Russia. Though the expansion of the European Union creates prospects for the development of the Kaliningrad region within the framework of the European Regions program, negative consequences of globalization have so far been more conspicuous: there is a big number of AIDS patients and drug addicts and foreign trade flows are crime-ridden.

Regions with the image of "open" ones constitute the fourth type. Their involvement in the world exchange of capital, goods and services is in reality not very high, but their authorities create a special image in the press and public opinion, projecting the image of an "open" region. This is especially true of the Novgorod region in northwestern Russia, which accommodated several businesses of foreign investors, the fact widely publicized in the media. The Karelia Republic is a somewhat different example of information and managerial openness. Local authorities use to the utmost extent the proximity to Finland and other northern EU member-states (with active aid from these neighbors) in order to step up information exchanges and undertake joint programs in education and environmental protection. Karelia has been receiving numerous grants for social purposes. Economic contacts – attraction of foreign investment and the development of trade and mutual business – have so far been less successful.

Regions with import substituting industries situated primarily in European Russia have remained *relatively closed*. In the past two or three years though, they saw industrial growth and bigger investment, including foreign capital. Old industrial regions have a more favorable geographical situation, developed infrastructure and high degree of urbanization and education, which will enable them to catch up with economic globalization in the future. The fairly fast spread of the Internet in large towns of these regions attests to their globalization potential. The impact of globalization is, however, less reflected in the consumption standards of the overwhelming majority of the local population due to low household incomes.

The underdeveloped republics of the Russian Federation are the most *closed* areas, where globalization processes are least observed, and there is practically no foreign investment or foreign trade. These regions have extremely low household incomes, semi-agrarian economy and patriarchal forms of family and social relations. Their political system rests on patronage and nepotism at every level of government authority. It is only the consumption practice of the elite, which has high incomes from the shadow economy, that attests to the impact of global consumption standards, which more often than not take exotic local forms. Similar consumption patterns are characteristic of the elite of many underdeveloped countries.

There is one more specifically Russian type of a closed region. It is the northern territories, whose raw materials resources found no outlet to the world markets in the 1990s due to low efficiency and high transportation costs. This type is found among the sparsely populated autonomous districts of northeastern Russia (the Chukchi, Koryak, Evenki and Taimyr districts) and the Magadan region. In fact, they are depressed underdeveloped territories, whose economy deteriorated in the 1990s, paying for the inefficient Soviet strategy of large-scale development of areas with extreme climatic conditions.

Big Russian business has late begun to strive for political power in precisely such regions. To win gubernatorial elections in sparsely populated districts requires little funds but brings absolute control over an area with promising export reserves. Newly-elected governors from among the top managers of leading Russian exporting companies in fact turn the region into an appendage of their corporations, act in their interests and potentially may deprive any outside investor of access to local resources.

In general, globalization processes and growing openness of the Russian economy of the 1990s led to two trends of regional development.

One trend is characteristic of developing countries and is manifested in growing regional (economic and social) disproportions between major cities or regions integrated in the global economy and the rest of the country. Compared to the Soviet period, regional contrasts have become more pronounced in Russia: per capita household incomes differ by as much as 1100% and per capita foreign investment hundred times depending on the region.

Under the other trend, which is characteristic of the more developed countries, some of the manufacturing regions have sunk into a depressed state in the face of global competition. Russia went through an especially severe economic recession because of a surplus of military production. The economic situation of old industrial regions of the Center and the Urals deteriorated especially badly as a result.

Thus, major cities and exporting regions benefited most from globalization, while underdeveloped and depressed regions for the most part got more problems.

Economic differences have been accompanied by mounting social contrasts. The metropolitan way of life is undergoing fast modernization owing to information globalization and higher incomes. Meanwhile, the inhabitants of rural areas, small towns and underdeveloped regions have been left out of the global world and are conserving patriarchal values and survival strategies, tying their political preferences with Communist ideas. The experience of the 1990s has nevertheless shown that polarized regional development failed to provoke dangerous political destabilization.

Nevertheless, some social tensions can be observed. For instance, a negative attitude to Muscovites, who are thought to be better off "at the expense of the rest of Russia," has become widespread in the regions. A significant portion of the Russian population has a low opinion of Moscow's new look. The social geographer O. Vendina quotes the following utterance, "Moscow is veering outside the boundaries of real Russia, emerging as a cosmopolitan enclave of sorts, an outpost of modernization, which has broken away from the rest of the nation...." (Vendina 2001: 90).

3. Resistance to globalization

Resistance to globalization on the part of authorities can be found in raising barriers to foreign investment and restricting open information. Public resistance is manifested in the protection of a traditional way of life and an increasingly negative attitude to "Western" products, culture and consumption standards. To one extent or another all of that can be found in the Russian regions.

Resistance to globalization is not necessarily connected with the degree of regional openness. Indeed, in the more open *major cities* resistance is minimal because the benefits of globalization and the inflow of investment in the services are most obvious. Examples of economic globalization are plentiful: Russian mobile communications companies of Moscow and St. Petersburg are being taken over by nonresident businesses, foreign investment in the hotel business and the food industry is on the rise, as well as business services provided by nonresident companies.

Major *export-oriented extracting regions* of Siberia and the Urals have put up extremely strong resistance to the advent of foreign investors and even largest companies, unless they are linked with Russian businesses. The reason is rentseeking behavior characteristic of big Russian business. In the course of privatization businessmen obtained, at an exceedingly low price, assets (already developed oil, gas and metal deposits, operating metallurgical mills and chemical factories) bringing export revenues without considerable investment. To protect their property, Russian businesses operating in exporting regions control, in addition to raw materials extraction, regional authorities and use them to raise institutional barriers to their competitors. For instance, half of the

Tyumen Oil Company board of directors is made up of the governors of the regions, where the company extracts oil, treats it and sells petroleum products.

There is a direct connection between the economic weight of a Russian exporting company, which has "privatized" a certain region, and investment problems faced by Western companies wishing to extract resources in that region. Thus, nonresident companies are either barred from regions controlled by Gazprom, Norilsk Nickel or Russian oil companies or else they operate on minimal quotas, as is the case with small oil extracting joint ventures in the Tyumen region or French Total in the Komi Republic.

Even in new oil extracting regions in the north of European Russia (the Nenets district) Russian companies are gradually squeezing out nonresident competitors, despite the fact that Western oil extracting companies were the first to arrive in that region. Though they lost at the start of regional development, major Russian companies have augmented their financial resources in the past two years owing to high oil prices and begun to use all means, including administrative pressure, to consolidate their hold on the new extracting region. The Sakhalin oil extraction project, which, however, took over five years to be coordinated, is the only example of sizable foreign investment. This success of the Exxon Company is explained by the fact that Russian business lacks advanced machinery for offshore oil extraction and adequate funds to develop deposits situated in the most remote area with embryonic infrastructure.

Russian business and regional authorities connected with it are not alone in displaying rent-seeking behavior: oil-extracting companies of Arab countries and other exporting regions behave in a similar way. Royalty rent was, however, completely abolished in Russia in the 1990s, and it was not until quite recently that investment began in the development of new deposits and exporting regions.

The criminal economy and close informal relations between regional authorities and local business *in border regions* create a highly unfavorable investment environment and formidable institutional barriers. Access to these markets costs too much, while informal agreements are far too unreliable. Such barriers can hardly be viewed as direct resistance to globalization; rather these are systemic problems of a transition society. As a result major foreign investors are absent in the Primorsky territory. In the Krasnodar territory attempts were repeatedly made to deprive the few investors (such as Germany's TIGI-KNAUF construction business) of their property. Every investment project launched in the Kaliningrad region with the support of federal authorities has proved unsuccessful. The Leningrad region at the Russian border is the only example of a more civilized area for foreign investment, where the proximity of St. Petersburg is, however, a factor of no small importance.

Though the *old industrial regions* of Central Russia are more open to investment, their economic potential is still ignored by the world market with the exception of metallurgical, chemical and some types of military products. Local anti-globalism finds expression in protectionist ideology ("protection of local producers"), which has to do with the preponderance of import substituting productions. A survey conducted by the author in the Orel region has shown that protectionist ideology goes hand in hand with a positive attitude to Russian businesses gaining entry to the world market as it promises stable wages and growing employment and serves as a symbol of managerial success.

Resistance is minimal in the *underdeveloped republics* because globalization as it is generally understood is nonexistent: there is next to no investment inflow, the role played by these republics in foreign trade is infinitesimal, and local population mobility is low. Patriarchal society has for the most part retained a traditional way of life and has next to no access to global information networks. Another type of globalization – the extremely fast and destabilizing diffusion of Pan-Islamic ideas through the republics of the North Caucasus – should not be overlooked, however.

In general, the division into "*open*" or "*closed*" regions is far too oversimplified: it is important to take into account the influence of many factors on the development of different forms of globalization. Thus, economic globalization in the "open" exporting regions is confined to the sale of resources and more developed consumption, while institutional barriers stand in the way of foreign investment inflow. Though institutional barriers are less strong in "closed" import substituting regions, investment inflow and trade are held back by the absence of competitive productions and low household incomes. It is only in the largest cities that the impact of globalization manifests itself to the fullest extent.

Individual forms of globalization diffuse from leading city-centers to the periphery at a different speed, which depends on the existing institutional barriers, incomes and degree of modernization of the way of life. Consumption and the development of information networks and the Internet appear to be the most promising globalization channels. They can hardly be blocked by institutional barriers and are facilitated by the high level of education and modern requirements of the population. However, faster progress of these forms of globalization can be forecasted only on condition of stable economic growth, on which both the dynamics of household incomes and the development of regional infrastructure depend.

4. Conclusions

To sum up, we can state that globalization has an extremely controversial effect on regional development. The most important consequences are as follows:

- Polarized spatial development and the division of the country into "rich" and "poor" regions from the point of view of their economic development and household incomes.

- The global market integration of primarily resource regions and those specializing in "dirty" productions from the point of view of environmental protection.

- Growing population mobility (labor, learning and recreation mobility) in leading cities, rich regions (mostly recreation mobility) and border regions (labor mobility among those engaged in shuttle-merchant small business).

- Modern consumption standards in major centers and "rich" exporting regions.

- Greater information openness in leading cities accompanied by stronger socio-cultural phobias in response to globalization.

- Political institutes given a facelift and effective election technologies imitated, while preserving the largely informal institutional environment.

In general, the economic and socio-cultural split of the country into two unequal parts has come as a result of the impact of globalization against the background systemic crisis. Though the borderline between these two parts is vague and shifting, most of Russia remains on the periphery of the global world.

References

Beck, Ulrich 2001: Was ist Globalisierung? Moscow.

Friedmann, John 1986: The World City Hypothesis. In: Development and Change, No. 17, pp. 69-84.

Gurova, Tatyana 2001: Na starte rossiyskoy mechty (At the Start of Russian Dream). In: Expert, 45:305, pp. 42-48

Hall, Pete 1984: The World Cities. 3rd ed., New York, St. Martin's Press.

Human Development Report 2000: Russian Federation: Human Rights Publishers, Moscow, 2001, p. 107.

J'son & Partners Management Consultancy 2001: Obzor rynka sotovoy svyazi v dekabre 2001 goda (Cellular Market Survey in December of 2001), Moscow, p. 3.

Knox, Paul/ Taylor, Peter (eds.): World Cities in a World-System 1995, Cambridge.

Marcuse, Peter/ van Kempen, Ronald (ed.) 2000: Globalizing Cities: a new spatial order?, Oxford.

Perfilyev, Yuriy 2001: Internet v regionah Rossii (Internet in Russian Regions). In: Petrov, Nikolay (ed.): Regiony Rossii v 1999 gody, Moscow Carnegie Endowment Center, Moscow, p. 348.

Robertson, Roland 1995: Globalization. In: Featherstone, Mike (ed.): Global Modernities, London.

Sassen, Saskia 1991: The Global City: New York, London, Tokyo/ Princeton.

Sassen, Saskia 1996: The Spatial Organization of Information Industries: Implications for the Role of the State. In: Mittelman, J. H. (ed.): Globalization: Critical Reflections, Lynne Rienner Publishers, London, pp. 33-52.

Segbers, Klaus (ed.) 2001: Explaining Post-Soviet Patchworks, Volumes 1, 2, 3, Ashgate, Aldershot.

Smorodinskaia, Natalia 2001: Rent-seeking in the Regions: The Politics of Economic Privilege in Kaliningrad. In: Segbers, Klaus (ed.): Explaining Post-Soviet Patchworks, Vol.3: The political economy of regions, regimes and republics. Ashgate, pp.56-82.

Soja, Edward 2000: Postmetropolis: Critical Studies of Cities and Regions, Oxford.

Strange, Susan 1998: The Retreat of the State. In: Cambridge Studies in International Relations, Cambridge University Press.

Vardomsky, Leonid/ Treyvish, Andrey (1999): Problemy ustoychivosty economicheskogo prostranstva Rossii (Problems of Russian Economic Space

Sustainability). In: Vardomsky, Leonid (ed.): Vneshneeconomicheskiye svyasy i regionalnoye razvitiye, Epikon, Moscow, p. 192.

Vendina, Olga 2001: Moskva - obraz goroda, ne pohozhiy na portret (Moscow-the image of the city, not similar to portrate). In: *Politiya,* 3, p. 90.

Volodin, A., Shirokov, G. 1999: Globalizasiya: istoky, tendenzii, perspectivi. (Globalization: sources, tendencies, prospects). In: POLIS, No. pp. 83-93.

Zubarevich, Natalia 2001: Polyarizasia gorodov Rossii kak sledstvie krizisa 90-h godov (Russian Cities' Polarization as a Result of the Crisis of 90th). In: Vestnik Eurasii, No. 1, pp. 5-29.

10

ANDREAS BOECKH

The Painful Transition of a Rentier State: Globalization and Neopopulist Regression in Venezuela

1. Venezuela as a Rentier

There is hardly a country in the world which has had a longer career as a rentier than Venezuela. Since 1925 oil has contributed more than 50% to the export earnings, and ever since 1929, more than 50% of government income has originated from the oil sector. Its peak was reached in 1974 when 85,6% of government revenues were oil rents (Banco Central de Venezuela 1978). In 1934, the Venezuelan government made a crucial decision which set the country irrevocably on the path of a rent-fueled development: It did not devalue its currency parallel to the US-Dollar. This increased rapidly the import capacity of the country, providing the society with cheap dollars which pushed up investment and consumption simultaneously and eliminated the international competitiveness of all other economic sectors except oil. The government was aware of what it was doing: Venezuela at that time was a dirt-poor country without any industries to speak of. Therefore oil could not be used as a cheap source of energy for national industries. Under such circumstances, the only way to participate in the oil wealth was to raise oil rents as much as possible. It made perfect sense to follow a policy of rent-maximization which was exactly what the government did from then on (Baptista/ Mommer 1987: Chapter 1). During World Was II, in 1943, the dependence of the allies upon Venezuelan oil provided the opportunity for the Venezuelan government to extend the right to tax to the foreign oil companies which until then had only been paying royalties. The Venezuelan share of the oil profits jumped from 21% in 1940 to over 50% in 1943 and reached its historical peak in 1974 (94%), that is, shortly before the oil industry was nationalized in 1976 (Table 1).

The dangers of this course of development were seen quite clearly. Without government intervention, Venezuela could not get beyond the production of untradable goods and services. There would be a complete export and revenue dependence on only one product, and the temptation to consume the oil wealth would be paramount. In Venezuela, the issue how to invest the oil income ("to sow the petroleum", as one prominent economist once called it – Uslar Pietri 1984 (original: 1936)) was one of the major topics. The debate followed the line of classical political economy in which, with the exception of Malthus, rent was considered a parasitic income. In this discourse, Venezuelans were depicted as "fat parasites of oil" (Uslar Pietri 1984: 9), as a "society of crooks" living in "Sodom and Gomorra" (Pérez Alfonzo/ Rangel 1976: 269-275, 340).

Table 1: Oil Production and Government Income from the Oil Sector 1930 - 1974

Year	Production (1000 barrels/year)	Government Income (Mio. US-$ at current prices)	Government Share of Total Profits (in %)
1930	135.246	15,3	19
1935	148.516	19,2	18
1940	183.831	31,5	21
1945	326.404	132,9	58
1950	546.766	330,5	51
1960	1.041.675	887,4	68
1970	1.353.420	1.409,1	78
1974	1.086.240	8.567,0	94

Source: Boeckh/ Hörmann 1995.

Of course, the oil rent could not be kept out of consumption just with arguments of morality. A strictly capitalistic use of the oil rent purely for purposes of investment was politically not feasible, particularly not under democratic conditions. That Venezuela turned into a rentier was unavoidable. But Venezuela always was a rentier with a bad conscience. At the end of his life, a former oil minister who was one of the architects of OPEC in 1960, and who always complained that Venezuela was denied the "just price" for its oil, in deep despair called oil "the devil's excrements" (Pérez Alfonzo 1976).

At this point, it is not possible to describe in detail the mutation of the country from an underdeveloped agrarian country to a rentier society (Karl 1997). The result of this transformation certainly was more than "opulent underdevelopment", as a Venezuelan sociologist once claimed (Briceño León 1985). The oil wealth was not just wasted, as political folklore in Venezuela has it: Capital formation and industrial production grew much faster than in industrial societies and most Latin American countries (for details, see Baptista 1985b, Table 2).

Paradoxically, it was the oil rent which turned Venezuela from a mostly precapitalistic into a capitalistic market society of sorts: The result was a hybrid with features of modern capitalism and rentier society which can be described as "rentier capitalism".

Unlike the rentier states in the Middle East, the influx of international rents did not lead to the formation of a state class and a rentier state and did not result in the stabilization of an authoritarian regime. The oil rent helped to consolidate the Venezuelan state which for the first time in its history began to show some administrative presence and effectiveness in all parts of the country. After the death of the long time dictator Juan Vicente Gómez in 1935, this process was accompanied with a gradual, albeit not uninterrupted, transition toward democracy which after 1958 turned into a stable and consolidated democratic regime.[1]

Table 2: Yearly Growth Rate of Capital Stock and Employment in International Comparison (in %)

	Capital Stock	Employment	Capital/ Employment
Canada 1950-1978	5,76	3,18	2,58
France 1950-1978	4,71	1,05	3,66
Germany 1950-1978	6,29	1,60	4,69
Italy 1950-1978	5,08	0,84	4,24
Japan 1950-1978	8,44	1,49	6,95
UK 1950-1978	4,17	1,24	2,93
USA 1950-1978	4,35	2,39	1,96
Venezuela 1945-1982	8,41	3,12	5,29

Source: Baptista 1985a: 129

After 1958, the Venezuelan democracy was based on a very broad political pact, accommodating not only the major political parties with the exception of the Communist party, but also all important social forces: The military, employers, labor unions, peasant unions and the Catholic Church (Karl 1987). The inclusiveness of this democratic pact and its stability were made possible by the oil rent. The democratic regime rarely was forced to set priorities, neither politically nor economically. Social conflicts could be defused by open and hidden subsidies and a very effective political clientelism which incorporated labor unions and peasant leagues into the political system. This type of inclusive and distribution-oriented democracy found widespread support (Baloyra/ Martz 1979, Baloyra 1986). Even the Marxist guerrilla could be re-integrated into the political system at the beginning of the 1970s, mostly by giving the guerrillas government stipends at prestigious foreign universities. Quite a few of the former guerilla fighters held high government positions in later years. Venezuela seemed to live in the best of all economic and political worlds: High growth and rapid industrialization without inflation, rapid modernization without serious social disruptions, a low political and social conflict level which posed no problem for the integration capacities of the regime. While almost all Latin American countries experienced serious authoritarian regressions in the 1960s and 1970, Venezuela developed a stable and functioning two-party-system.

---

[1] The process of transition towards democracy did not run as smooth as this summary description indicates. After a period of gradual political liberalization (1936-1945), the country had its first experience with democracy between 1945-1948, after a coalition of civilian politicians and young officers had overthrown the government of General Medina Angarita. The absolute political hegemony of the party Acción Democrática (AD) during this period led to another military coup in 1948 which resulted in a brutal military dictatorship which was chased out of power by a combined civilian uprising and a military coup in January 1958.

2. Economic Crisis and Political Decay

When the Venezuelan President Carlos Andrés Pérez announced the nationalization of the operations of foreign oil companies in a national ceremony in 1975, Venezuela had reached its peak as a rentier. A year before, oil prices had quadrupled and government revenues had tripled. The mood was one of triumph. The speech was given the title "Toward a Great Venezuela" (Pérez 1975). The nationalization of oil was celebrated as "the second declaration of independence", but it also contained the sentence; "From now on we do not have any more excuses for our failures". Eight years later, and after the oil prices had doubled once more in 1979/1980, the country was unable to pay its debts and had to devalue its currency. Ever since, the economy has been in a downward spin, wiping out the welfare gains of about 50 years, annihilating large parts of the middle classes[2] and raising poverty to unprecedented levels. In the 1990s, the average growth rate was 1,9% (that is below the population growth), and the average inflation rate was 47%. At the end of the 1970s, the investment rate amounted to 30% of the Gross Domestic Product, in 1999 to 5% (Venezuela Analítica Aug. 25, 2000). "Since 1980, Nicaragua, Haiti, and Guyana are the only three Latin American countries that have experienced a worse economic performance than Venezuela" (Naím 2001: 21). How can one explain what many Venezuelans with bitter humor call the "Venezuelan economic miracle", and how did it affect the political system?

First of all, the outbreak of the crisis had nothing to do with falling oil prices, as it is often ascertained. The crisis set in at the very moment when oil prices were at their historical peak. The doubling of the oil prices in 1980 coincided with the beginning of a recession. It became apparent that rising prices were no any longer stimulating economic growth. The internal market was too small to absorb massive new investments, and the exchange rate policy did not provide any chances for export lead growth beyond the oil sector. Ever since, the sole effect rising oil prices has had is to boost government income. From then on, it was possible to translate high oil prices into economic growth only through increased government spending. Government spending itself, however, can do little more than start up a short-lived boom on the demand side. It cannot provide the basis for sustained growth. In other words, the rent-fueled development model had reached its limits. The rent itself had turned into an obstacle to development. This has to be remembered when we later discuss the attempt of the present government to turn the economic tide by means of government spending.

In the early 80s, there was a lot of excess capital in the country which could not be invested profitably in Venezuela. This was the beginning of capital flight which was one of the causes of the debt crisis of 1983 (Boeckh 1988: 644).

---

[2] The middle classes had been the winners in the rent-induced development since the 1950s (Nissen 1983).

Since then, the amount of private Venezuelan capital abroad has been consistently higher than the foreign debt of the country.

However, government and politics also contributed to the economic crisis. The government proved unable to manage the bonanza after 1974. It overextended its already meager administrative capacities with the attempt to lead the "great leap forward" toward a modern industrial society. Countless new government agencies produced little more than administrative chaos,[3] while the classical tasks like maintaining a functioning infrastructure were neglected. Huge sums were squandered, the famous "pharaonic works", that is the big government investment projects, often were oversized and produced constant deficits, and corruption exploded. The government lost control over its own apparatus: Shortly before the bubble burst, government agencies had begun to finance their current expenses (mostly pay raises for their employees) with short term foreign loans. When debt negotiations began after the default, the central government had no idea about the total amount of its foreign debts.

The bonanza of the 70s also corroded the political balance which had existed since 1958 and the political pact which was based upon it. The nationalization of the operations of the international oil firms and of the steel industry and the high oil prices after 1974 turned the government into an economic agent of overwhelming importance. It spelled the end of its subsidiary role in relation to the economic activities of the private sector. The explicitly etatistic approach after 1974, aggressively articulated by the Ministry of Planning, threatened to marginalize the private sector. The political pact of 1958 ceased to exist, at least where the private sector was concerned. When the government tried to negotiate a "social pact" between the private sector and labor unions to manage the distribution crisis after 1983, the private sector refused to participate.

By that time, the ideological mood had changed completely. The devaluation of 1983, though still modest, was generally and correctly understood as the beginning of the end of the oil bonanza. In public opinion, there was no doubt whatsoever who was to blame for the disaster: The government, indeed, had "no more excuses for its failures". It was the crisis of the 1980s which prepared the ground for the neoliberal hegemony in the development discourse and made Venezuela susceptible to liberal adjustment concepts of the IMF. At this moment, Venezuela for the first time in its modern history was confronted with the pinch of capitalistic reality: Competitiveness, the management of scarcity, and the need to set priorities became important issues, at least as far as the political discourse was concerned.

---

[3] In 1958, there were 40 autonomous administrative units outside of the administrative structure of the ministries, in 1984 the estimate stood at 449 (Bigler/ Voiloria V. 1984: 193).

However, the ideological hegemony of neoliberalism was not matched by an economic hegemony of the private sector. The privatization of state enterprises was limited and did not touch the crucial areas of oil and steel. The relative economic weight of the state did not really decrease after the crisis, on the contrary: with every devaluation of the Bolívar the government income exploded in terms of the local currency while those sectors of the society which had not bought Dollars in sufficient amounts were left poorer. Two of the five powerful private conglomerates which seemed to have dominated the private sector in the 1980s disappeared during the 1990s. The discourse on "Venezuela after the oil" (Academia Nacional de Ciencias Económicas 1985, see also the special issue of Número 6/1985) in which alternatives to the rent-based development were discussed, did not have any practical results.

Moreover, the country was completely unprepared for the – albeit timid – policy shift in the mid-eighties and less so for the radical adjustment attempt of the second administration of Carlos Andrés Pérez in 1989. The political structures which had proved appropriate for managing the rent-dependent development model were inadequate for dealing with the crisis. The failure of the "social pact" indicated that the time for corporatistic, pacted solutions was over. The consensus between the major social actors no longer existed, and the political consensus between the major parties also had begun to unravel.

Parallel to the economic discourse there was a political debate revolving around the issue of liberal politics and the transformation of the populist, "omnipotent" state into a state guided by the rules of liberal, pluralist democracy (Granier 1984, 1987, Romero 1987). A government commission also was concerned with the issue of state reform (Comisión Presidencial Para la Reforma del Estado 1988). Some reforms were implemented, such as political decentralization, but the reform impetus died down in the 1990s. The Chávez government does not talk about reforms, but about revolution which, apart from all foggy rhetoric, implies the resurrection of a highly centralized and populist state. The chance to improve the efficiency of the government by way of decentralization and to regain some of the lost legitimacy by offering new level of political participation was wasted.

When the raise of public transportation prices sparked a violent outburst of fury among the poor shanty town dwellers in Caracas in February 1989, surprising all political forces in the country, two things became apparent: First, that the established political parties were out of touch with the social realities of the country and had lost political contact with the poor population, and second, that it would be politically extremely costly to push through a standard IMF-adjustment program which the Pérez government was attempting to do. After two failed military coups in 1992, the first of which was tremendously popular among wide segments of the population, the political establishment panicked and deposed

Carlos Andrés Pérez for alleged corruption.[4] The following elections were won by the former President and founder of the Christian Democratic Party COPEI Rafael Caldera who this time ran on a populist anti-party platform, sidelining both of the dominant parties, including his former party. However, he still tried to work within the established constitutional rules. Scared by the explosive social situation, he tried to use the oil income to fend off any more adjustment measures. Attempts to avoid the inevitable by means of foreign exchange controls and a fixed exchange rate, garnished with populist rhetoric, failed miserably.

When the next election approached, the political system of 1958 was completely discredited. The traditional parties did not even present their own candidates in the end, and their support for promising outsider candidates turned out to be their kiss of death. The 1999 election was won by the leader of the first coup attempt of 1992, Hugo Chavez who, without much concern for constitutional details, immediately set out to create his own constitution.

Presently, the political structures of the country resemble exactly what Guillermo O'Donnell has called "delegative democracy" (O'Donnell 1994). All political power is turned over to the executive for one term, there are no checks and balances, no real accountability of the executive to any other institutions, constitutional and procedural norms are brazenly ignored,[5] parties and other intermediary organizations have lost importance, pluralism has become a bad word. In the classical populist vein, political communication takes place between the president and the masses, with the president doing most of the talking. Compared with earlier political structures, the political system has lost complexity and certainly has experienced a political regression regardless if it is going to mutate to an openly authoritarian system or not. The democratic system of 1958 has crumbled under the impact of the crisis of the rent-based development model.

3. Why did adjustment fail and end in a political regression?

In almost all Latin American countries, governments followed more or less and sooner or later the rules laid down by the "Washington Consensus" and accepted globalization as a fact which they had to adjust to. The macroeconomic adjustment – measured by the decline of inflation – was quite successful. The balance

---

[4] In Venezuela – and in many other Latin American countries, for that matter – it is almost always correct to accuse leading politicians of corruption. To actually do so, therefore, is a matter of political convenience and not a question if somebody is corrupt or not.
[5] The emergency law was forced through Congress in 1999 with the undisguised threat to break the Constitution, military officers were promoted in open violation of the Constitution. The Constitutional Assembly in which the President had an overwhelming majority in fact eliminated the old Constitution before a new one was approved, doing away with the elected Congress as a legislative and controlling body. When the Supreme Court declared this to be unconstitutional, it was threatened into submission.

of the so-called second generation of reforms, comprising tax reforms, state re-forms and the installation of the rule of law which is so dear to neo-institutional economists, is far less convincing, however. In Argentina and Peru, neopopulist style politics were used to dismantle the old populist development coalitions and to eliminate the development model established by classical populism some decades ago. In these countries, neopopulism served as an instrument of adjust-ment to the *economic* rules and requirements of globalization. It did not square with the political demands of a globalized world, however, insofar as in both cases the economic transition was pushed through with authoritarian means. Neopopulism also is detrimental to any type of second generation reform since it reduces the complexity of the political system, leaves the old patterns of infor-mal politics intact (Faust 2000), and certainly does not improve the rule of law.

In the Latin American context of crisis and adjustment, Venezuela is the odd man out, with the exception of Cuba, of course. Neopopulist style politics were used by the previous government and are used by the present one to avoid eco-nomic transformation. As an oil country with ample currency reserves, the coun-try can afford to swim against the current without being punished by the "mar-kets" right away. However, this strategy depends entirely on the oil prices which tend to be very volatile. Therefore, it is not sustainable in the long run. This be-came quite clear when after the fall of the oil price under the level estimated in the budget planning the government run up a tremendous deficit,[6] which forced the government to float the currency. So why was this strategy maintained with such stubbornness?

Market reforms affect the distribution pattern of any society, but particularly in rentier societies, and even more so in countries living off an oil rent which tend to be much higher than other forms of rental income. In Venezuela, the rental income benefited all sectors of society for many decades, basically by three mechanisms of rent distribution.

- The overvaluation of the Bolívar provided the poor segments of society with cheap food and other consumer goods (until the 1980s, 60% of the basic foods were imports) and the private sector with cheap imports of capital goods. The overvaluation was the most important mechanism of rent distri-bution. Therefore the devaluation in February 1983 was correctly considered the beginning of the end of the bonanza. It also explains why governments still try to keep the currency overvalued in spite of the detrimental effects for the competitiveness of all sectors save the oil sector.

- Another important mechanism to distribute the rent was the low tax level which benefited mostly middle and higher income groups and the private

---

[6] The fiscal deficit expected for 2002 was estimated to be around US-$ 8-10 Billions (El Na-cional 2/13/2002).

sector in general. While in comparable countries the tax level was around 20% of the GDP, in Venezuela it was 9% (Boeckh 1988: 649). Falling oil revenues call for higher internal taxes. Ever since the beginning of the crisis, governments in Venezuela have tried to raise taxes and to reform the tax administration. However, as soon as oil revenues go up again, those efforts crumble. An increase of the oil prices by just one dollar per barrel brings much more money into the government treasury than even the most efficient tax reform. It is estimated that 60% of the taxes are evaded, and of all incompetent and corrupt government institutions, the tax office has probably the worst reputation (Boeckh/ Rubiolo 1999).[7]

- The third, least important but highly visible mechanism of rent distribution is government spending and government transfers. The end of plenty means that the conflicts over the structure and beneficiaries of government spending increase immediately. Government spending on food and transportation subsidies came under attack from liberal ideologues, while undertaxation was not mentioned at all even though it costs the government much more than the subsidies.[8]

At least within the formal sector, it can be shown statistically, that the mechanisms of rent distribution benefited all social actors.[9] In terms of income distribution, the income of the middle strata grew faster that of any other class (Nissen 1983). Between 1953 and 1974, the profits after taxes in the modern industry (firms with more than 4 employees) grew in almost perfect correlation with the growth of rental income of the country from 17,7% to 36,1%. In 1953, industry received around 4% of the rent, in 1975 45%. Other social strata benefited, too. Between 1936 and 1974, the real wages of workers and employees grew 1.45 times faster than labor productivity (all figures from Baptista 1980, 1985b). Needless to say that under normal capitalistic conditions, such a result would be impossible.

In other words, in such a society, market reforms spell disaster for almost everybody. If we consider market reforms as part of the globalization process, "resistance to globalization" comes natural in a society in which the oil rent has set the parameters of all economic activities and welfare gains. The private sector had become dependent on rental income to such a degree that some analysts considered its investment behavior as a mere pretense to get access to the rent (Baptista

---

[7] In 2001, it was discovered that quite a few officials of the government tax administration were involved in private extortion schemes, blackmailing businesses for alleged tax evasion (El Nacional.4/28/2001)

[8] In 1985, government subsidies for basic foods and transportation amounted to Bolívares 2,6 Billion, while undertaxation cost the government Bolivares 32 Billion (Mommer 1987: 39).

[9] One can assume that members of the informal sector benefited, too, as a consequence to cheap imports of food and other items of mass consumption. However, for the informal sector, statistics are hard to come by.

1985a, Briceño León 1985: 77, Gutman 1981 for the agrarian sector). Even though the private sector always was dedicated to a liberal market discourse, it panicked when the first and still very timid government attempts at market reforms became visible in the early 1980s (Lopez Contreras 1982/83). Falling real wages and a significant increase of poverty wiped out the welfare gains of the middle and lower classes.[10] Everybody has good reasons to be angry and to look for the villain in that game. In this respect, the situation in Venezuela is different from the one in other Latin American countries. Globalization and market reform in the short run do not produce a few winners and many losers, but only losers and – may be on the long run – some winners. While in other countries market reforms do have some supporters in society and have to overcome opposition of the remaining rent seekers, in Venezuela they would have to overcome the opposition of a society in which everybody was and still is a rent-seeker, and in which the only rational economic behavior had been rent-seeking, given the economic parameters of the country.

It should be repeated at this point that the social deterioration since 1980 is not the result of market reforms which, compared with other Latin American countries, were insignificant. "Savage capitalism", as neoliberal reforms are called in Venezuela and elsewhere in Latin America, has hardly reached the country. Globalization may not be the solution for Venezuela, but it is certainly not at the root of its problems.[11] The social disaster is mainly the result of the failure of rentistic capitalism to provide further impulses for growth and welfare gains (see section 1).

In Venezuela, the political discussion about the roots of the disaster revolve around different topics. The most common explanation points toward corruption. The argument runs like this: Since the country is rich and the population is poor and becomes even poorer, somebody must be stealing what rightfully belongs to the people. Once corruption is eliminated, prosperity will return (for a similar argument, see Naím 2001).[12] And since the political class in Venezuela, indeed, is incredibly and very visibly corrupt, this argument enjoys immediate plausibility. Consequently, the fight against corruption overrides any other political con-

---

[10] The statistics on poverty in Venezuela vary considerably depending on the source and the statistical definition of poverty. But regardless of the source, all statistics point to a tremendous increase of poverty since 1980. Real wages are 70% below the level of 1980 (Naím 2001: 21). The most widely accepted poverty index in Latin America shows an increase of poverty for Venezuela from 22% of the population in 1981 to 34% in 1990 and to 44% in 1999 (CEPAL 2001, 4).
[11] Out of 50 countries, Venezuela ranks only 36th in the Foreign Policy Magazine Globalization Index (quoted by Naím 2001: 25).
[12] For Naím, the basic flaw of the argument lies in the assumption that Venezuela is a rich country. He points out that "in 1974, oil contributed $1,540 per person to the national treasury and represented more than 80% of total government revenue; 20 years later, that figure had dropped to $ 200 per person and accounted for less than 40% of total fiscal revenues"(Naím 2001: 21). With these figures, however, he does not prove that Venezuela is a poor country, but that Venezuela is not as rich as it used to be.

cern and hides the fact that the country lacks everything which is needed for the solution of the poverty problem: an adequate development model, functioning institutions, a style of politics which does not produce waste, and political and economic elites who are not utterly incompetent and corrupt.

Politically, corruption and the loss of prosperity were blamed on the rule of the parties which had held power since the political pact of 1958. "Party rule" and "political pact" became bad words and synonymous for abuse of power, irresponsibility and corruption. With his anti-corruption tirades, the former Colonel Chavez who had failed with his coup attempt in 1992, was able to literally wipe out the traditional parties in the elections of 1999 and 2000, and to transform the political system of the country.

Of course, corruption has not been eliminated in Venezuela. The old beneficiaries have been replaced by new ones. The already disastrous institutional make-up of the country has become worse, and compared to the present government, the previous ones look like models of competence and efficiency. The political regression and the institutional decay certainly provide no solutions for the economic problems, and the distribution-oriented populism is completely dependent on high oil prices, that is on the rent. Nevertheless, the return to a plainly populist rhetoric and distribution patterns did stabilize the political system. The approval of democracy and the satisfaction with the results of democracy have skyrocketed since 1998 (Latinobarómetro 2000). Quite obviously, in the present situation what is needed economically is not compatible with what is politically sustainable. This, of course, spells trouble for the future.

In some parts of the world, particularly in Africa, the disappearance of rents has not resulted in the creation of a sound market economy and a pluralist democracy but in the complete break down of what little state there was. This is not a likely outcome for Venezuela. Nevertheless, one can expect a dramatic increase of political instability regardless of the strategies followed: Since the politics of populist distribution is not economically sustainable in the long run, it will run into trouble. On the other hand, market reforms have caused and will cause immediate political unrest. In any case, for political reasons it is hard to share the optimism of economists that market reforms and the acceptance of globalization as a frame of reference will be the solution. It seems that the country is stuck in a no-win situation. The case of Argentina should be a warning to everybody who expects quick solutions for the economic and political transformation in rentier societies (Boeckh 1980). In Argentina it took about 40 years after the disappearance of the agrarian rent before the society could be forced to accept some market rules and to stop fighting over a rent which had ceased to exist a long time ago. And even then, politics did not adjust the new economic parameters: Governments kept piling up debts for political reasons after the could not print money any more after the Peso was pegged to the US-Dollar. They were unable to control the informal networks of rent-seekers who reappeared in new disguises, and they were not able to put an end to the "predatory federalism" (Faust in this volume) which made fiscal discipline all but impossible. In Venezuela, the process of adjustment to market rules had not even begun yet.

4. Future Perspectives: Is Venezuela the Last or the First Drop Out?

In Latin America, the results of 10 to 15 years of market reforms have been modest at best. The economic development has been extremely volatile. In the 1990s, every country in the region was affected by at least one external shock, and presently many countries are adversely affected by the world recession. Social progress in the context of market reforms has been minimal. The number of persons living in poverty has jumped up in the so called "lost decade" and has been increasing ever since, while the percentage of the poor population has decreased only insignificantly during the 1990s. Survey data in many countries indicate that hope that the economic situation will improve is dwindling, and the satisfaction with the results of democracy is getting dangerously low. The satisfaction with democracy decreased from 37% in 2000 to 25% in 2001 (Latinobarómetro 2001). The expectations which were raised about the long term effects of the market reforms clearly have not been met. The market reforms are not necessarily to be blamed for the poor economic and social results. It is becoming increasingly clear that the poor record of the "second generation of reforms" which include administrative reforms, tax reforms, legal reforms, and the elimination of informal politics has contributed considerably to the external vulnerability of many Latin American countries and to their disappointing economic performance. For the general public, however, this remains purely theoretical.

The question arises if Venezuela is the last drop out from globalization in Latin America or the first one. The present government is quite convinced that its "third" or "fourth" road presents the project of the future in Latin America, combining elements of a Latin American nationalism focused on a deified Simón Bolívar with an anti-pluralistic, anti-liberal, anti-imperialistic, and anti-globalization discourse. The foreign policy of Venezuela obviously is supposed to spread the message among its regional neighbors, and not only their political leadership is being addressed: The relations with Colombian guerrilla groups are dubious at best, and the constant rhetoric of revolution keeps some neighbors worried (Boeckh 2002).

So far, the Venezuelan "model" has found support only in Cuba. The political elites of all other countries are quite aware of the fact that they would court disaster if they were to follow the Venezuelan lead. However, no one can tell how long they can resist the pressure of their population to do something to improve their lot, and to do it fast. If following market rules does not bring any rewards, and if the international crises keep eliminating whatever welfare gains may have been made, the political costs to maintain the new development model may become unsupportable. Other countries, too, may slide into the Venezuelan dilemma that whatever is economically necessary becomes politically unfeasible. This would be the hour for other anti-pluralistic and anti-liberal politicians to consider a populist approach to social problems as a promising road to power.

References

Academia Nacional de Ciencias Económicas (ed.) 1985: El futuro como historia: ¿Hacia la Venezuela postpetrolera?, Caracas.

Baloyra, Enrique A. 1986: Public Opinion and Support for the Regime: 1973-1983. In: Martz, John D./ Myers, David J. (eds.): Venezuela. The Democratic Experience, New York etc., pp. 54-71.

Baloyra, Enrique A./ Martz, John D. 1979: Political attitudes in Venezuela. Societal cleavages and political opinion, Austin etc.

Banco Central de Venezuela 1978: La economía venezolana en los últimos treinta y cinco años, Caracas.

Baptista, Asdrubal 1980: Gasto publico, ingreso petrolero y distribución del ingreso. In: El Trimestre Económico 47:2, pp. 431-464.

Baptista, Asdrubal 1985a: El estado y el petróleo. In: Fundación Universidad Metropolitana (ed.): Apreciación del proceso histórico venezolano, Caracas, pp. 103-137.

Baptista, Asdrubal 1985b: La dinámica de la economía venezolana: una apreciación analítica, Caracas.

Baptista, Asdrubal/ Mommer, Bernhard 1987: El petrolero en el pensamiento económico venezolano. Un ensayo, Caracas.

Bigler, Gene E./ Voiloria, Enrique V. 1984: State Enterprise and the Decentralized Public Administration. In: Martz, John D./ Myers, David J. (eds.): Venezuela. The Democratic Experience, New York etc., pp. 183-217.

Boeckh, Andreas 1980: Grundrente und Staat: Argentinien und Venezuela im 19. und 20. Jahrhundert. In: Hanisch, Rolf/ Tetzlaff, Rainer (eds): Historische Konstitutionsbedingungen des Staates in Entwicklungsländern, Frankfurt, pp. 47-98.

Boeckh, Andreas 1988: Die Schuldenkrise und die Krise des bürokratischen Entwicklungsstaates in Venezuela. In: Politische Vierteljahresschrift 29:4, pp. 636-655.

Boeckh, Andreas/ Hörmann, Marion 1995: Venezuela. In: Nohlen, Dieter/ Nuscheler, Franz (eds.): Handbuch der Dritten Welt, vol. 2, Bonn, pp. 516-543.

Boeckh, Andreas/ Rubiolo, Monica 1999: Finanzkrisen, Steuerblockaden und Finanzreform in Lateinamerika. In: Peripherie 73/74, pp. 53-76.

Boeckh, Andreas 2002: Die Außenpolitik Venezuelas. In: Calcagnotto, Gilberto/ Nolte, Detlef (eds.): Südamerika zwischen US-amerikanischer Hegemonie und brasilianischem Führungsanspruch. Konkurrenz und Kongruenz der Integrationsprozesse in den Amerikas, Frankfurt/M., pp. 212-225.

Briceño León, Roberto 1985: Los efectos del petróleo y la Venezuela post-petrolera. In: Academía Nacional de Ciencias Económicas (ed.): El futuro como historia: ¿Hacia la Venezuela post-petrolera?, Caracas, pp. 25-37.

CEPAL 2001: Panorama Social de América Latina 2000-2001, Santiago.

Comisión Presidencial para la Reforma del Estado 1988: La reforma del estado. Proyecto de reforma integral del estado, Caracas.

Faust, Jörg 2000: Informelle Politik und ökonomische Krisen in jungen Demokratien. In: Aus Politik und Zeitgeschichte B21/2000, pp. 3-9.

Granier, Marcel 1984: La generación de relevo vs. el estado omnipotente, Caracas.

Granier, Marcel (ed.) 1987: Más y mejor democracia, Caracas.

Gutman, Garciela 1981: Renta petrolera y agricultura en Venezuela. In: Flichman, Guillermo et al. (ed.): Renta del suelo y economía internacional, Amsterdam, pp. 207-231.

Karl, Terry Lynn 1987: Petroleum and Political Pacts: The Transition to Democracy in Venezuela, 1958. In: Latin American Research Review 22:1, pp. 63-94.

Karl, Terry Lynn 1997. The Paradox of Plenty. Oil-booms and Petro-States, Berkley etc.

Latinobarómetro 2000:
http://www.latinobarometro.org/00Graf3.htm

Latinobarómetro 2001:
http://www.latinobarometro.org/ano2001/graficos/grafico2.htm

Lopez Contreras, Manuel 1982/83: La crisis y el imperativo de la protección. In: Venezuela metalúrgica y minera 14:53 (Dec.-Febr.), pp. 13-16.

Mommer, Bernhard 1987: La distribución de la renta petrolera. El desarrollo del capitalismo rentístico venezolano, Caracas.

Naím, Moises 2001: The Real Story Behind Venezuela's Woes. In: Journal of Democracy 12:2, pp. 17-31.

Nissen, Hans-Peter (ed.) 1983: La distribución del ingreso en Venezuela, Caracas.

O'Donnell, Guillermo 1994: Delegative Democracy. In: Journal of Democracy 5:1, pp. 55-69.

Pérez, Carlos Andrés 1975: Einem großen Venezuela entgegen, Caracas.

Pérez Alfonzo, Juan Pablo 1976: Hundiéndonos en el excremento del diablo, Caracas.

Pérez Alfonzo, Juan Pablo/ Rangel Domingo Alberto 1976: El desastre, Valencia.

Romero, Anibal 1987: La miseria del populismo. Mitos y realidades del populismo en Venezuela, Caracas.

Uslar Pietri, Arturo 1984: Venezuela en el petróleo, Caracas.

11

JÖRG FAUST

Brazil: Resisting Globalization through Federalism?

1. Introduction

Governments often choose strategies of economic liberalization to integrate the country's economy into a globalizing world economy, hoping to augment its competitive advantages and to create productivity-oriented development. Integrating an economy into a globalizing world economy of free trade and free finance confronts policy-makers with the task of implementing adjustment programs with substantial redistribution effects. The resulting conflicts among potential winners and losers of economic reform will even tend to increase if the country faces fundamental political change, such as democratization. Since democratization is about shifting property rights away from a former autocratic coalition, those who are negatively affected by democratization will try to influence the reform process in order to keep their economic privileges. While those conflicts about the course of economic liberalization and democratization are of relevance in all countries, domestic institutions tend to influence the way of how such conflicts are disputed and settled. In such a context, recent research (Verdier 1999, Garmann et al. 2001, Wibbels 2001) has highlighted the importance of federal arrangements in times of globalization and democratization as intermediary variables between conflicts over distribution and macroeconomic outcome.

In general, two advantages are associated with fiscal decentralization. First, the dispersion of political power is an important instrument of constraining the central government. In liberal theory, besides the horizontal accountability at the federal level, vertical decentralization is another mean to achieve power dispersion. Second, fiscal decentralization is often thought to have a positive impact on the efficient allocation of resources and higher legitimization of state entities. The expectation is that state entities closer to the problems of the citizens will deal with those problems more efficiently, increasing the relation between the provision of public goods and state spending. Furthermore, taxpayers are involved more closely in governmental spending, which enables them to articulate their needs more effectively. The normative connotations evolving around fiscal federalism therefore contend that "each public good and service should be provided by the jurisdiction that would most fully internalize its benefits and costs" (Garman et al. 2001: 205).

However, those normative goals are not easy to achieve. Politics is often about shifting property rights from the weak and uninformed to the strongly organized and well informed. Empirical evidence suggests that fiscal decentralization as other forms of institutional reforms offer many opportunities for rent seeking and the misallocation of public resources.[1]

Especially, if fundamental economic and political changes parallel the reorganization of federal arrangements, improved veto-power of subnational entities can create severe collective action problems. In many countries of the southern hemisphere such fundamental changes consist of the parallel processes of economic liberalization and democratization. As economic liberalization like democratization mirror redistribution processes, potential losers of such transformation will tend to organize opposition in order to sustain their privileges. Therefore, fiscal decentralization within a federal framework tends to be influenced by actors who want to preserve rents threatened by the parallel process of economic opening and political democratization. As the findings of this case study suggest, in times of democratization, effective resistance to the global trend of economic liberalization through federal arrangements puts macroeconomic stability at risk. This, because the conflicts over distribution in the course of democratization might affect the relationship between national and subnational governments, hereby creating difficulties to adopt sound macroeconomic policies, which successfully cope with the challenges of market-friendly regulation.

To highlight the relevance of the above made assumption about the problematic influence of federal arrangements on macroeconomic policy during times of economic and political reform, the following arguments focus on the case of Brazil. Since the establishment of a federal constitution at the end of the nineteenth century, Brazil's political structure has been oscillating between attempts of centralization and decentralization.[2] Because of the political transition process of the 1980s, federal arrangements were fostered to constrain the power of the central government (Serra/ Rodrigues 1999: 5-6). Especially the 1988 constitution has given regional and local state entities more autonomy. Yet, this process of decentralization was only one of the major changes. The transition from autocracy to democratic rule was also accompanied by mounting pressures to liberalize the Brazilian economy. Brazilian policy-makers like many of their Latin American colleagues, were seeking to adopt the Brazilian development model to a globalizing world economy. However, the macroeconomic results of these reform attempts have been disappointing in general. Even the policy switch in the mid-nineties towards a new currency regime, the Plano Real, was not a viable solution to overcome the problem of fiscal imbalances. By binding the Brazilian currency in a "crawling-peg-system" to the US-$ and starting a process of capital account liberalization, the macroeconomic strategy aimed at reducing

---

[1] See for example Burki/ Perry/ Dillinger 1999, Wibbels 2000, Garmann et al. 2001.
[2] Created in 1891, the Brazilian Federation was characterised by a relatively weak central culminated in the "Estado Novo" under Getulio Vargas in 1937. Democratization in 1946 pushed decentralization again until 1964, when the military came in command and started a process of re-centralization (Serra/ Rodrigues 1999: 5-6).

inflation and augmenting growth via capital inflows. Yet, with the devaluation of the Real in February 1999, Brazil joined many other emerging markets facing financial embarrassment. Again, in 2002, this time under a regime of a floating currency, Brazil faced severe debt problems. This in spite of the fact, that international organizations like the IMF or the World Bank have been praising the federal government for its sound macroeconomic approach.

While much analysis has put the blame for recent financial crisis in emerging markets on increasing international capital volatility resulting from worldwide financial liberalization, my argument concentrates on domestic institutions.

First, I will try to demonstrate that the causes of the Brazilian inability to cope with the macroeconomic challenges of economic globalization are rooted in the discrepancy between macroeconomic policy and federal arrangements. In the late 1980s and in the 1990s, fiscal decentralization á brasileira enabled states to shift their debt to the federal level, forcing the federal government to act like a lender of last resort. Therefore, Brazilian decentralization led to the over-consumption of common pooled resources – the federal budget -, which were inadequately regulated. Consequently, the institutional arrangement of fiscal federalism in Brazil was highly counter-productive to the macroeconomic strategy of the Plano Real and financial liberalization. In the post 1999 period, the federal government made increasing efforts to restrict excessive subnational borrowing. Yet, structural pressures on the state budget remained, as neither the system of pension funds nor the responsibilities of subnational entities could be changed substantially.

Second, I propose, that ill-defined fiscal decentralization and the resulting macroeconomic vulnerability can be traced back to the conflicts over distribution arising from the parallel process of democratization and economic liberalization. Fiscal decentralization enabled local and regional interests to prevail over federal interests, sustaining those arenas of Brazilian politics which traditionally are highly contaminated with rent-seeking mechanisms. The persistence of these mechanisms led to a conflict with macroeconomic policies aiming at stabilizing the political system by creating low inflation growth through the influx of external capital.

In order to support my assumptions, first, I shall demonstrate the problematic characteristics of fiscal federalism in Brazil (see Table 1 at the end of this text). Second, I shall try to explain how fiscal decentralization increased collective action problems in the Brazilian reform process leading to macroeconomic instability (see Table 2 at the end of this text). Third, I shall present evidence that the institutions of fiscal federalism in Brazil were embedded in the conflicts Brazil: 'Resisting Globalization through Federalism?' over distribution arising from the process of democratization.

2. Fiscal Federalism, Economic Liberalization and Democratization in Brazil

2.1 Predatory Federalism in Brazil

While the transition from autocracy to democracy in Brazil began with the elections of governors in 1982, it was formally concluded only in 1988 with the establishment of a new constitution. The new constitution had a strong impact on fiscal decentralization and the distribution of public resources to subnational governments. It included explicit rules about the distribution of revenues between different levels of governments. States were assigned a Value Added Tax (VAT) of which 25% had to be distributed to the municipalities.[3] The Brazilian transfer system included several types of transfers from the federal government to the states and municipalities, the most important being the transfer of 21,5 % from its most important taxes[4] to lower levels of government. The lion share of these 21,5% went to the less developed and less populated regions in the North, Northeast and Center-West regions, while the most developed and most populated regions of the South and Southeast relied only modestly on federal transfers. In 1998 for example, through the federal transfer system, the southern region would only receive 18% of the IT and IPT collected in the region. Fiscal federalism did not only decentralize fiscal policy at the vertical level. It also meant a redistribution of revenues between the states (Serra/ Rodrigues 1999: 10).

While the constitution explicitly regulated revenue distribution between different levels of government, expenditure responsibilities were not clearly defined (Serra/ Rodrigues 1999: 15). Consequently, decentralization of expenditure had to rest on ad hoc bargaining between federal government and federal legislators, hereby weakening the federal government to restrict expenditures of lower levels of government (Burki/ Perry/ Dillinger 1999: 43). States and municipalities expanded their expenditures, especially in public works and personal payrolls. The latter's impact on fiscal budgets were due to an excessive pension system, established in the 1988 constitution (Selcher 1999: 39). Additionally, the weak position of the federal government set incentives for states to engage in a race to the bottom.

Until 1998, the attempts of federal governments to reform federal arrangements had only limited success because the Brazilian electoral system and party organization set incentives to direct politics to the subnational level, hereby ob-

---

[3] States can also raise taxes on automobiles and property while municipalities are assigned taxes on urban property, a tax on services, and a real estate transaction tax (Dillinger/ Webb 1999: 8)

[4] The income tax (IT) and the industrial products tax (IPT).

structing the achievement of sound macroeconomic policies.[5] Regarding the electoral system, Brazil can be characterized as a "demo-constraining" system in which the upper and lower chambers are worldwide among the most disproportionate. The reason for this judgement has been the overrepresentation of certain states in the senate and the chamber of deputies. The less developed regions were over represented, especially at the cost of São Paulo, the most developed state of the federation. Consequently, representatives of states depending on transfer payments succeeded in building informal coalitions aiming at maintaining the status quo rather than at reforms of fiscal decentralization. As Selcher (1999: 32) notes, "northeastern national deputies and senators are strategically positioned on the key congressional committees, especially those dealing with fiscal and tax matters and infrastructural concerns, and on the joint budget committee of the two houses."

This discrepancy between population, wealth and representation is especially obvious in the senate. Each state sends three senators to the upper chamber of congress. The result has been, that the states of the two less developed regions, who represent only 35,6 % of the Population have 59,2% of the seats in the senate. As the senate has veto-power on constitutional amendments, which have passed the chamber of deputies, the overrepresentation of poor and less populated states makes reform on fiscal decentralization even more difficult. Moreover, the senate is responsible for constraining excessive borrowing by the states, as the upper chamber can define ceilings for state debt, an instrument that the upper chamber did not use properly during the 1990s. Furthermore, the position of the central government was weakened by the fact, that until 1998 the President was restricted to a one time term of four years, whereas senators were elected for eight years giving them an additional bargaining advantage over the federal government.

In general, however, even in such a situation, a federal government could introduce reforms, if parties were primarily oriented towards national goals. Yet, the Brazilian party system is traditionally characterized by a high degree of fragmentation and the parties' weak programmatic coherence. With the exception of the Workers' Party (PT) this tradition was not reversed during the 1990s. Local and regional matters influenced the behavior of congressional members much stronger than party affiliation (Mainwaring 1999). One strong incentive for such behavior is to be found in the electoral system of open lists. Because of open lists, congressional candidates employ personal campaign strategies and get

---

[5] The Cardoso government faced several defeats in congress when trying to reduce spending on oversized public service. As the constitution of 1988 prohibited to dismiss redundant civil servants as well as to reduce salaries in nominal terms and additionally guaranteed civil servants a pension equal to their exit salary, payrolls became an increasing problem during the nineties (Dillinger/ Webb 1999: 9). Only from 1998 onwards the federal government could push through some fiscal reforms.

involved in conflicts with party fellows. Candidates pursue personal strategies that often conflict with the strategies of the party leaders. Additionally, the nomination control of candidates for the federal legislative is located at the subnational level. Subnational party conventions nominate candidates for congressional senate elections. Party leaders do not control the candidates' list, making it more difficult to punish those who adopt locally or regionally oriented strategies rather than national ones (Garman et al. 2001: 214). Furthermore, governors had great influence over legislators, so that alliances between governors and legislators across party lines are common and congress members are generally more loyal toward the governor of their home state than toward their party leaders (Ames 2001).

In summary, a set of institutional incentives led to the uncomfortable lender-of-last-resort-situation of the federal government in Brazil and triggered a fiscal war between the states of the federation. Transfers from the federal government were often based on ad hoc bargaining. The situation of the government was further weakened by the fact that it had difficulties in disciplining excessive state spending. Electoral rules drove the parliament toward local and regional issues, party discipline was low and the misrepresentation in congress lead to constellations, in which those states which profited most from the status quo gained veto positions.

2.2 Trends toward Free Trade and Free Finance in Brazil

Since the first democratic government of President Sarney, the Brazilian economy faced the legacy of an unsustainable development strategy oriented towards import substitution. Excessive state intervention had led to increasing fiscal imbalances and mounting international indebtedness. On the one hand, the increasingly ineffective economic policy during the seventies could only be financed with external resources. On the other hand, the Brazilian state debt, embedded in a globalizing financial world, made the Brazilian economy extremely vulnerable to external shocks, such as the rise of international interests rates and the Mexican Crisis in the early eighties (Schirm 1999: 144). This vulnerability of Brazil's economy resulting from its interdependence then turned into a decade of disappointing adjustment programs, due to the fragmentation of Brazil's political system.

Still, the first democratic government of President Sarney (1985-1990) tried to solve the crisis without economic liberalization, in blatant contradiction with its letters of intent signed with the IMF. Instead of pursuing structural reforms, the government attempted to reduce inflation by means of heterodox price and wage controls in combination with changing monetary policies. However, because the government was split, business was fragmented into sector and regional factions and unions were not united, economic policy faced severe collective action problems (Schneider/ Maxfield 1997). After some initial success, inflation skyrocketed once again in 1987 and the fiscal imbalances led to a government moratorium, suspending international debt related payments. Because of mounting international pressure and the inability of the Brazilian government to finance excessive state intervention, the second democratic government under president Collor (1990-92) opted for economic reforms. It started the process of trade liberalization and privatization but refrained from capital account liberalization. Intensified attempts of the federal government to "globalize" Brazilian economic policy shifted the burden of painful adjustment onto subnational governments. As neither business and unions nor a highly fragmented and polarized party system were able to overcome collective action problems at the national level, the arrangements of federalism provided political actors with powerful instruments to reject the costs of economic adjustment. The constitutional design of federalism enabled states to counterbalance the pressures of trade liberalization and diminishing financial resources through aggressive borrowing.

Already in 1989, the federal government had to take over much of the external debts of the states. In 1993, the federal government took over state debt, in this occasion owed to federal institutions. Again in 1994, the swapping of state bonds for federal bonds represented another form of federal bailout. Finally, a fiscal crisis at the subnational level during 1995-96 resulted from the fact, that the federal government could not convince the senate to exert control over the growth of state debt. The "repeated cycle of the federal government refinancing state debt, had the perverse incentive effects" that states expected the federal government to bailout subnational debt (Burki/ Perry/ Dillinger 1999: 43). The perception of the federal government as a lender-of-last-resort motivated states to engage into a race to the bottom. In the so-called "fiscal war", states started to compete heavily to attract domestic and foreign investment. By offering potential investors tax exemptions on their most important tax, the Tax on Circulation of Merchandise and Services (ICM), the fiscal situation of subnational governments became even more problematic (Varsano 1997). States continued using their own state banks to gain better access to resources, hereby driving those banks into financial difficulties.[6] Even though the most developed states took advantage over the less developed ones during the "fiscal war", they paid a high price. Four of the richest states - São Paulo, Rio de Janeiro, Minas Gerais, and Rio Grande do Sul - were among those with the highest debt.

This destabilizing resistance of subnational actors to bear the major part of economic adjustment also helps to explain, why the initially successful Plano Real, finally failed. Rather, the currency crisis of 1999 introduced Brazil to the club of

---

[6] The banking crisis made federal intervention necessary, which in the early nineties started to privatise those banks or put them under the supervision of the Central Bank. However, the debt remained at subnational or at the federal level.

emerging markets that did not succeed in defending their exchange rate regimes against increasing capital volatility.[7]

The macroeconomic stabilization attempt of the 1994 Plano Real was rooted in the unsuccessful attempts of controlling inflation mentioned above. In 1993/94, the government introduced a new currency pegged to the US-$ and pursued a restrictive monetary policy. As planned, the initial impact of the Plano Real was a substantial decrease in inflation, an increase in real salaries and an increase of GDP. The exchange rate regime became the central instrument in Brazilian macroeconomic policy, since it was the guarantee for price stability. Additionally, besides further trade liberalization, the financial sector also was liberalized. However, the regulation regarding portfolio investment took a much slower pace than in other Latin American countries like Mexico or Argentina. The government only slightly removed capital controls. For example, legislation did not allow residents to open deposits in foreign currency in order to prevent a dollarization process as in Argentina. Private portfolio capital was mainly concentrated in the São Paulo Stock Exchange. Yet, public bonds could be indexed to a foreign currency and credits could be indexed to the exchange rate (Penido de Freitas/ Magalhães 2000: 56). Additionally, in the course of the Mexican Crisis and confronted with a banking crisis, especially at the subnational level, the federal government in 1995 passed legislation which substantially relaxed the entry barriers for foreign direct investment in the financial sector.

Partially opening the capital account and achieving monetary stability through the introduction of a crawling peg caused a large inflow of foreign capital, leading to an exchange rate appreciation and the deterioration of the trade balance. In 1995, the government reacted to the Mexican Crisis and its regional implications by temporarily devaluating the Real. After the solution of the Mexican Crisis it was able to return to the crawling peg. Nevertheless, while the government was successful in defending its exchange rate policy against the financial turmoil coming from the Peso Crisis, it had significantly more problems in establishing a sound fiscal policy against subnational pressures and traditional business suffering from increasing international competition.

In the period that preceded the Plano Real, inflation was an important instrument to reduce public debt, subordinating monetary policy to the requirements of fiscal financing (Mendes Pereira 1999). Excessive debts were not new, for neither the federal nor for the subnational governments. Yet, prior to the Plano Real, states were able to shift their debt onto their creditors via inflation. Since 1994 however, with an inflation reducing exchange rate regime at the center of macroeconomic policy, the traditional instrument of fiscal financing was not available anymore. The sharp decrease in inflation made it impossible for all levels of

---

[7] For a closer examination of the Brazilian Currency Crisis see Fritz 2000, Amann 2000.

government to erase debt by high rates of inflation. Especially expenditures for the civil service and the pension funds created a heavy burden on fiscal policy. The 1995-96 fiscal crisis of the states were at least in part the result of the vanishing "inflation tax". While the consequence of former bailouts of the federal government could be eased by inflation, from 1995 onwards, accumulated debt put a heavy burden on the federal budget. The federal government, well aware of those problems, undertook several attempts of fiscal reform but regionally oriented legislators and lower levels of government acted as veto-players. Thus, the federal government faced a dilemma of relying on a pegged exchange rate, while at the same time being unable to avoid increasing debt rates.

The delays in fiscal reforms resulted in growing operational deficits, which made monetary intervention necessary. By increasing interest rates, the government managed to make the necessary borrowing at national and international capital markets (Fritz 2000). While Brazil relied on bank lending to a much smaller extent than in the previous decade, the current account deficit had to be financed by long and short term investment. At a first glance, external public debt rose only moderately, while domestic debt was heavily increasing. But international financial sector firms, which created subsidiaries after the financial liberalization, owned major part of the domestic debt, taking advantage of high interest rates and a pegged exchange rate.

With the Asian and Russian Crisis in 1997 and 1998, international investors increasingly found the exchange rate regime unsustainable and began to withdraw their investments. Desperate attempts of the federal government to defend the exchange rate regime resulted in a loss of international reserves of the Central Bank and in further increasing interest rate spreads. "Thus the government found itself in a vicious circle: to maintain the exchange rate and to finance its deficit it had to borrow at a rising interest rate, which in turn worsened the fiscal situation and, by extension further undermined investor confidence" (Amann 2000: 1811).

After the re-election of president Cardoso in 1998 the federal government tried again to reform the pension system, this time with more success. Additionally, the US, the IMF and the World Bank set up a rescue package, as they became worried about a possible financial collapse comparable to the one in Russia. However, newly elected governors from opposition parties once again tried to force the federal government into a lender of last resort position. Hereby they severely undermined the government's commitment to defend the exchange rate regime. As international capital started to leave the country, the government finally decided in January 1999 to abandon the crawling peg allowing the exchange rate to flow (Amann 2000: 1817).[8]

Even as Brazil avoided a financial collapse as other emerging economies, the 1999 devaluation increased external pressures on political actors to respond to the fiscal imbalances in order to reestablish investors confidence. The reason for this was that the reliance on international investment to sustain low inflation growth had become crucial for the Brazilian economy. The conditionality clauses of international lenders such as the IMF increased the pressures to reform the fiscal structure substantially. These international pressures have strengthened the position of the Cardoso government to implement fiscal reforms since 1999 (World Bank Report 2002). The closure and privatization of state-owned banks diminished the states' possibilities for excessive lending. With regard to the pension system, initial measures to reduce expenditures have been launched in the 1999-2001 period. Yet, they are far from stabilizing the system. The deficits coming from the pension system are still around 80% of the total public sector deficit, while recipients of public pensions only constitute 5% of all pensioners. Furthermore, the Law of Fiscal Responsibility (LRF) has imposed limits on subnational borrowing. The central government hoped to establish incentives for more fiscal responsibility by increasing the personal risks for subnational politicians and by making excessive borrowing disadvantageous for the jurisdictions they serve. However, the effectiveness of LRF will be constrained, as long as the constitutional definition of state and municipal responsibilities remain vague and the prosecution of law-breaking is hampered by lengthy impeachment processes and an already overburdened court system.

2.3 Democratization and Economic Adjustment in Brazil

Linking the previous arguments of federalism and economic reform with the distribution conflicts of democratization leads to several interesting observations. In Brazil, the autocratic coalition of the military regime consisted mainly of the state bureaucracy, public enterprises and those parts of the private sector profiting from the strategy of import substitution. While traditional patronage was connected with employment in the public sector, more modern forms of patronage arising under the strategy of import substitution included public services, work projects, state contracts, state concessions and state investment (Mainwaring 1999: 177). Illiberal rent-seeking mechanisms such as clientelism, patronage and corruption are still mainly found at the subnational level. Especially in the less developed states, where income distribution is even worse than at the overall national level, traditional forms of patronage are endemic. As Sel-

---

[8] Surprisingly the consequences of the devaluation have not been as disastrous as in Mexico, Indonesia, Korea, Thailand, and Russia. A relatively high amount of net reserves and continuously high interest rates reduced incentives for further capital withdrawal. Additionally, as the Brazilian economy was still characterized by a highly diversified and inward-oriented industrial structure, the rise of import prices resulting from the devaluation had not such negative affects as in Mexico and the Asian countries.

cher (1999: 30) notes:"Patronage is a major source of jobs in the three less-developed regions. Public employment, for example, is much more important as a percentage of the total registered workforce-and therefore as a political issue-in the North (39 percent), the Northeast (34 percent), and the Center-West (30 percent) than in the South (20 percent) and the Southeast (18 percent)."

Throughout the last century, the state has been the source of rents, and legislators and subnational governments stood at the center of the informal rent-seeking mechanisms. Political parties with the exception of reformist and leftist parties functioned more as the formal framework of those informal mechanisms than as programmatic organizations oriented toward national goals (Mainwaring 1999: 176). The informal decentralization of power had quasi-feudal characteristics at the regional level but at the same time, the federal level was constrained by regional interests. This made the governors - "the barons of the federation" - the most powerful actors of the political system as they occupied veto-positions toward the center and at the same time headed the subnational political pyramid (Selcher 1999: 37). Therefore, Brazil is not an example of state capture by strong and nationally highly organized interests such as in Korea. Rather, profiteers of illiberal rule were located within an expanding state bureaucracy and within a fragmented business community profiting from the politics of import substitution. "For a long time, Brazil's private sector has suffered from deep organizational fragmentation. The legacies of state corporatism and the disaggregative effect of massive government intervention in the economy account for this history of division" (Weyland 1998: 89).

In contrast to Mexico, internationally oriented big business in Brazil did not have the influence of pressing the state into more fundamental reforms (Schneider 1997). While democratization induced business to increase their political activities, due to its organizational fragmentation it has not been able to set coherent initiatives on the reform agenda. This organizational weakness can be explained by the interest heterogeneity within the private sector, which is in part a result of the fragmented political system itself, as business depended not so much on its political links with the federal level but rather on successful lobbying at the subnational level. Since the political system was at least informally decentralized, in Brazil's vast economy, business could achieve political influence (voice) by the threat of exit at the subnational level. Attempts of uniting the business sectors at the national level produced severe conflicts between regionally centered business associations (Weyland 1998: 90).

This constellation was of importance during the transition process of the eighties, when the conflict over distribution was concerned with the appropriate institutional framework for the forthcoming democracy. The years between the first election in 1984 and the approval of the new constitution of 1988 where characterized by struggles between different interest groups on how to craft the institutional framework of the new democracy. President Sarney, "a clientelistic conservative from the poor northern state of Maranhão" (Mainwaring 1997: 92), who came to power after the unexpected death of the president elected, was more a member of the autocratic coalition than a democratic reformer. As he headed a coalition, including those who were opposed and those who had backed authoritarian rule, reforms were blocked by intra-governmental conflicts. In 1987, "to overcome those problems, Sarney attempted to forge his own supra-party political base and to use his considerable discretionary powers over federal resources to sway state governors and federal legislators to back him" (Mainwaring 1997: 92). Thus, the divided federal government indirectly strengthened the position of subnational interest at the time of constitution building. Together with the president's conservative position, the highly personalized structure of most parties, the orientation toward regional issues and the continuing influence of the military, the constitution-building process enabled regional and local interests to successfully implement the already mentioned veto-positions. In the early nineties, veto-players at state level and in congress were able to block most of the reform attempts of president Collor de Mello, who tried to bypass congress with a neopopulist decree-policy. In 1994 a further "window of opportunity" was closed, as corruption scandals and a highly fragmented party system led to only moderate changes in the revision process of the 1988 constitution (Thibaut 1996: 231-235).

When President Cardoso was elected in 1994, he probably knew about the difficulties his government would face when touching the problematic issue of state reform. Under these circumstances, it is possible to interpret the exchange rate strategy not only as an instrument to lower inflation but as well as a strategy to impose fiscal discipline on subnational governments. As the opposition from congress and state governments grew, it became increasingly clear, that a substantial state reform could not be concluded within one presidential term. Since the constitution prohibited a successive term, Cardoso, from 1996 onwards, tried to persuade congress to accept a constitutional amendment allowing him to run for a second term. This weakened his bargaining position, since he had to form broad coalitions in both chambers (Flynn 1999: 294). At the time, when he was re-elected in 1998, the macroeconomic situation had worsened to a degree that the exchange rate regime could not be defended anymore without risking a major collapse of the Brazilian economy. Since the devaluation of the currency in January 1999, the central government used the increasing international pressure from lenders and investors to push through several measurements aiming to discipline subnational lenders. Yet, as a recent World Bank report (2002: 6) states, in the long run more substantial changes at the subnational level are needed because of low accountability and persistent clientelistic structures.

3. Conclusions and Outlook

Federal governments are interested in good macroeconomic performance in order to get higher tax receipts and - in case of democratic rule - to increase their chances to win elections. In federal systems however, constitutional rights enable states to influence the macroeconomic goals of the federal government. In federal systems "subnational officials respond to different constituencies" (Wibbels 2000: 687), hereby creating conflicts over distribution with the federal government. Therefore "economic adjustments takes on the quality of a public good requiring the individual states to cooperate, but it is more rational for individual provincial politicians to avoid the political costs associated with austerity" (Wibbels 2000: 688).

Political institutions, which constrain actors' choices, play an important role in solving the conflict over distribution. For a sound fiscal policy, institutions therefore should lead to hard budget constraints and regulate the mechanisms of revenue-sharing (Weingast 1995). In Brazil however, political institutions were ill-defined and contributed to the success of subnational attempts to capture the federal budget. Transfers from the federal government were often based on ad hoc bargaining instead of being rooted in legal mechanisms. Increasing transfers from higher levels of government were seldom accompanied by a consistent delegation of functions to lower levels of government. Furthermore, the federal government was not able to set up effective rules aiming at avoiding unsustainable subnational deficits. Finally, electoral rules in Brazil subjected the parliament to subnational interests, weakened overall party discipline and led to unequal representation of interest in both chambers.

This type of predatory federalism was successfully used to shift costs of economic adjustment onto the federal government. As institutional changes toward free trade and free finance often cause a redistribution of economic resources at the expense of local and regionally based producers (Verdier 1999), trade liberalization and financial deregulation posed serious threats to those economic actors, who had long profited from strategies of import substitution. Because of those threats, the federal governments from Collor to Cardoso faced the dilemma of introducing market-friendly reforms while at the same time being unable to restrain subnational entities from excessive borrowing. Therefore, the 1999 currency crisis can be attributed to the dilemma between economic liberalization and predatory federalism, the latter allowing subregional entities to externalize their adjustment costs onto the federal government. Like many other emerging markets, the Cardoso government pegged the local currency to the US-$, privatized state owned firms and began to open the capital account. The expectation connected with the monetary strategy of financial liberalization and a pegged exchange regime was to combine growth by importing capital with lowering inflation rates by "importing" the stability of a foreign currency (Fritz 2000:

259). As a result of initial fiscal cuts at the federal level, inflation quickly diminished and foreign capital, often in the form of short-term portfolio investment, fuelled overall growth. Unfortunately, this strategy was crisis-prone, as the federal government was not able to impose fiscal discipline. "If capital is fully mobile across borders, interest rates are constrained to be the same in all countries and national monetary policy can have no effect on national interest rates" (Frieden 1991: 431). Therefore, when pegging the exchange rate and opening capital accounts it becomes essential that the expansion of domestic money and credit do not undermine the exchange rate regime. If an adjustment of the exchange regime is delayed, as was the case in Brazil, the economy is prone to speculative attacks and massive capital outflow.

The missing link between predatory federalism and destabilizing macroeconomic policies in Brazil is to be found in the process of democratization. As the process of democratization triggers conflicts over distribution between former profiteers of autocratic rule and the excluded part of the population, governments in new democracies are caught in conflicts over distribution between different coalitions, each equipped with substantial bargaining power. While capital owning members of the old autocratic coalition can augment their voice by the threat of exit or by threatening the democratization process itself, the former oppressed masses can mobilize social protest and have the possibility to "punish" the government with their vote.[9] As autocratic rent-seekers were mainly located in the subnational bureaucracies and in inward-oriented state and private firms, democratization further increased the conflict between federalism and economic opening.

In sum, all three components of recent political change in Brazil - democratization, federalism and economic liberalization – are trends towards decentralization. Consequently, all three of them induced conflicts over distribution, increasing the difficulties to establish encompassing coalitions, which are necessary for creating collective goods such as macroeconomic stability and rule-of-law-based democracy. In this context, the institutional arrangements of federalism in Brazil did not help to promote collective action but rather led to a further fragmentation of the political system. Taking together the three aspects that shaped Brazilian recent development – democratization, fiscal decentralization and monetary oriented macroeconomics, Olson's free rider problem became evident. The resistance to the increasing distribution consequences of free trade and free finance through federal arrangements did not diminish the macroeconomic vulnerability of the Brazilian economy.

---

[9] As the work of Mancur Olson (2000) suggests, autocracies are rent-generating regimes, while the institutional arrangements of liberal democracies are oriented toward public competition through inclusive mechanisms of political participation (Dahl 1971).

Yet, the currency crisis of 1999 demonstrated that this kind of resistance to globalization does not seem to be sustainable at the long run. While Brazil is certainly not among the forerunners of economic liberalization, it has made substantial efforts of liberalizing trade and capital flows. This trend toward free trade and free finance constitutes a strong counterweight to the resistance of an "old clientelist" state at the subnational level. The partial integration of the Brazilian economy into global trade and global finance has made it increasingly dependent on international investors' preferences. These dependencies have increased pressures on governments to reform ill-defined fiscal institutions. Therefore, Brazil's collective action problems at the century's turn stem from the conflict's between subnational interests and the increasing pressures induced by the country's path to world market integration.

Tables

Table 1: Fiscal Federalism in Brazil

Table 1.1: Tax revenue and Expenditure

	Tax revenue/ Level of Government		Expenditure/ Level of Government	
	Federal	Subnational	Federal	Subnational
1980-84	74%	26%	73,7% (1975)	26,3% (1975)
1988	43,7%	56,4%	68%	32%
1998	34,2%	65,8%	62%	38%

Source: Serra/ Rodrigues 1999: 9, 23, Garman et al. 2001: 218.

Table 1.2: Public Sector Debt as % of GDP

	1990	1992	1994	1995	1996	1997	1998	1999
Internal Debt	16,5	18,9	20,3	24,5	30,2	30,2	36,6	38,6
Central Bank + fed. gov.	1,6	0,8	6,2	9,6	14,8	16,8	21,6	22,3
Subna-tional	6,4	8,4	8,3	10,1	11,5	12,5	13,7	14,9
Public enterpr.	8,5	9,7	4,9	4,8	4,0	0,9	1,3	1,4
External Debt	20,1	19,2	8,2	5,4	4,0	4,4	6,3	11,0
Central Bank + Federal Gov.	12,4	11,6	6,0	3,4	1,6	2,0	4,3	8,3
Subna-tional	1,0	1,1	0,3	0,3	0,4	0,5	0,7	1,0
Public Enterpr.	6,7	6,5	1,9	1,7	2,0	1,9	1,3	1,7
Total Debt	36,6	38,1	28,5	29,9	34,4	34,6	40,9	49,6

Source: Amman 2000: 1812.

Table 1.3: Economic and political indicators of the major regions in Brazil (1998)

Region	South	Southeast	Center-West	Northeast	North
Number of Federal States	3	4	4	9	7
% National Territory	6,8	10,9	18,9	18,2	45,2
% National Population	14,9	42,6	6,8	28,3	7,3
% of GNP	15,9	59,6	7,1	12,6	4,8
% of Seats in Chamber of Deputies	15,0	34,9	8,0	29,4	12,7
% of Seats in senate	11,1	14,8	14,8	33,3	25,9
Tax Revenues collected from Regions	13,3	65,9	9,6	8,7	2,6
- by Federal Government (%)	12,6	67,4	11,1	6,9	2,0
- by states (%)	15,1	61,0	6,5	13,3	4,1
- by municipalities (%)	13,0	70,9	5,3	8,6	16,1
Total Tax Revenues at dispose	15,7	53,5	6,2	19,5	5,1

Source: Selcher 1999, Serra/ Rodrigues 1999: 24, 25.

Table 2: Macroeconomic Indicators

Billion US-$	1988	1994	1995	1996	1997	1998	1999	2000	2001
Trade Balance	19,2	10,5	-3,4	-5,6	-6,8	-6,6	-1,2	-0,7	2,6
Current Account	4,2	-1,7	-18,0	-23,1	-30,8	-33,6	-24,4	-24,7	-23,2
Net Portfolio Investment	6,65 (1993)	7,28	2,29	6,04	5,3	-1,8	1,5	6,9	0,9
Net FDI	2,6	2,0	3,5	9,5	15,4	22,3	28,6	32,8	22,6
Net Reserves	9,1	38,8	51,8	60,1	52,2	44,6	36,3	32,5	35,9
Gross Foreign Debt	115,1	199	222,8	239,8	253,4	223,8	225,6	216,9	210
Gross foreign debt (% of Exports)	312,7	373,6	382,9	430,6	390	418	382	319	296
Public Debt (%GDP)	-	-	4,9	-5,9	6,1	-8,1	-10	-4,6	-5,8
Exchange rate R$ per US-$	-	0,64	0,92	1,01	1,08	1,16	1,81	1,83	2,33
Inflation (%)	--	2407	68	9,3	7,5	1,7	8,9	9,8	10,4
GDP (%)	-4,3 (1990)	5,9	4,2	2,7	3,6	-0,1	0,8	4,4	1,5
Real Interest Rate	7,1 (1993)	56,4	38,9	23,9	42,0	31,2	19,0	15,8	19

Source: IPEA, Banco Central

References

Amann, Edmund 2000: The Illusion of Stability: The Brazilian Economy under Cardoso. In: World Development 28:10, pp. 1805-1819.

Ames, Barry 2001: The Deadlock of Democracy in Brazil. Ann Arbor, Univerity of Michigan Press.

Burki, Shahid Javed/ Perry, Guillermo E./ Dillinger, William R. 1999: Beyond the Center: Decentralizing the State. World Bank, Washington, DC.

Barrios, Harald/ Röder, Jörg 2000: Entwicklungsfortschritte und Entwicklungsblockaden in Brasilien - Fragen der Regierbarkeit, der Systemeffizienz und der Legitimität. In: Dosch, Jörn/ Faust, Jörg (eds.) 2000: Die ökonomische Dynamik politischer Herrschaft. Das pazifische Asien und Lateinamerika. Opladen, pp. 49-72.

Dahl, Robert 1971: Polyarchy – Participation and Opposition. New Haven and London.

Dillinger, William R./ Webb, Steven B. 1999: Fiscal Management in Federal Democracies: Argentina and Brazil. Worldbank Working Paper 2121, Washington, DC.

Faust, Jörg 2000: Informelle Politik und ökonomische Krisen in jungen Demokratien. Aus Politik und Zeitgeschichte (APUZ) B21:2000, pp. 3-9.

Flynn, Peter 1999: Brazil: the Politics of Crisis. In: Third World Quarterly 20:2, pp. 287-317.

Frieden, Jeffrey 1991: Invested Interests: The Politics of National Economic Policies in a World of Global Finance. In: International Organization 45:4, pp. 425-451.

Fritz, Barbara 2000: Stabilisierung und De-Stabilisierung. Währungskrise als Kehrseits des Modells wechselkursbasierter Entwicklung - der Fall Brasilien. In: Boris, Dieter et al. (ed.): Finanzkrisen im Übergang zum 21. Jahrhundert, Marburg, pp. 253-287.

Garmann, Christopher/ Haggard, Stephan/ Willis, Eliza 2001: Fiscal Decentralization: A Political Theory with Latin American Cases. In: World Politics 53:1, pp. 205-236.

Haggard, Stephan/ Maxfield, Sylvia 1996: The Political Economy of Internationalization in Developing Countries. In: International Organization 50:1, pp. 35-68.

Mainwaring, Scott 1997: Multipartism, Robust Federalism, and Presidentialism in Brazil. In: Mainwaring, Scott/ Shugart, Mathew Soberg (ed.): Presidentialism and Democracy in Latin America. Cambridge University Press, pp. 55-109.

Mainwaring, Scott 1999: Rethinking Party Systems in the Third Wave of Democratisation. The Case of Brazil. Stanford University Press.

Mendes Pereira, Rodrigo 1999: O Ajustamento Cíclico dos Gastos Públicos Federais Brasileiros. IPEA 1999 Instituto de Pesquisa Económica Aplicada, Discussion Paper 632, Brasilia.

Olson, Mancur 2000: Power and Prosperity. Outgrowing Communist and Capitalist Dictatorships. New York.

Penido de Freitas, María C./ Magalhaes Prates, Daniela 2000: La experiencia de apertura financiera en Argentina, Brasil y México. In: Revista de la CEPAL (CEPAL Review) No. 70, pp. 53-69.

Schirm, Stefan 1999: Globale Märkte, nationale Politik und regionale Kooperation in Europa und den Amerikas, Baden-Baden.

Schneider, Ben Ross/ Maxfield, Sylvia 1997: Business, the State, and Economic Performance in Developing Countries. In: Schneider, Ben Ross/ Maxfield, Sylvia (eds.): Business and the State in Developing Countries. Ithaca, Cornell University Press, pp. 3-35.

Selcher, Wayne A. 1999: The Politics of Decentralized Federalism, National Diversification, and Regionalism in Brazil. In: Journal of Interamerican Studies and World Affairs, 40:4, pp. 25-50.

Serra, José/ Rodrigues Afonso, José Roberto 1999: Federalismo Fiscal à Brasileira: Algumas Reflexões. In: Revista do BNDES (Rio de Janeiro) 6:12, pp. 3-30.

Souza, Celina Maria de 1997: Constitutional Engineering in Brazil: The Politics of Federalism and Decentralization. New York.

Thibaut, Bernhard 1996: Präsidentialismus und Demokratie in Lateinamerika. Opladen.

Varsano, Ricardo 1997: A Guerra Fiscal do ICMS: Quem Ganha e Quem Perde. Texto para Discussão 500, Instituto de Pesquisa Económica Aplicada, Rio de Janeiro.

Verdier, Daniel 1999: Domestic Responses to Free Trade and Free Finance in OECD Countries. In: Business & Politics 1:3, pp. 279-317.

Weingast, Barry 1995: The Economic Role of Political Institutions: Market Preserving Federalism. In: Journal of Law, Economics and Organizations 11, pp. 1-31.

Weyland, Kurt 1998: The Brazilian State in the New Democracy. In: Journal of Interamerican Studies and World Affairs 39:4, pp. 63-94.

Wibbels, Erik 2000: Federalism and the Politics of Macroeconomic Policy and Performance. In: American Journal of Political Science, 44:4, pp. 687-702.

World Bank 2002: Brazil: Issues in Fiscal Federalism: World Bank Report No. 22523-BR, Washington.

List of editors and contributors

Dr. Harald Barrios, Assistant Professor, Institute of Political Science, University of Tuebingen, Germany.

PD Dr. Martin Beck, Visiting Associate Professor at Birzeit University, West Bank, Palestine.

Prof. Dr. Andreas Boeckh, Institute of Political Science, University of Tuebingen, Germany.

Dr. Jörg Faust, Assistant Professor, University of Mainz, Germany.

PD Dr. Henner Fürtig, Center of Modern Oriental Studies, Berlin, Germany.

Dr. Sonja Hegasy, Center of Modern Oriental Studies, Berlin, Germany.

Dr. Alena Ledeneva, School of Slavonic and East European Studies, University College London, United Kingdom.

Ivesa Lübben, Cairo University, Egypt; University of Bremen, Germany.

Prof. Dr. Andrey Makarychev, Department of International Relations and Political Science, Nizhny Novgorod Linguistic University, Russia.

Prof. Dr. Klaus Segbers, Institute for East European Research, Free University of Berlin, Germany.

Prof. Dr. Andrey Shastitko, Professor of Economics, Moscow State University, Russia.

Natalia Zubarevich, Department of Geography, Moscow State University, Russia.